Panama

WORLD BIBLIOGRAPHICAL SERIES

General Editors:
Robert G. Neville (Executive Editor)
John J. Horton

Robert A. Myers   Hans H. Wellisch
Ian Wallace   Ralph Lee Woodward, Jr.

John J. Horton is Deputy Librarian of the University of Bradford and was formerly Chairman of its Academic Board of Studies in Social Sciences. He has maintained a longstanding interest in the discipline of area studies and its associated bibliographical problems, with special reference to European Studies. In particular he has published in the field of Icelandic and of Yugoslav studies, including the two relevant volumes in the World Bibliographical Series.

Robert A. Myers is Associate Professor of Anthropology in the Division of Social Sciences and Director of Study Abroad Programs at Alfred University, Alfred, New York. He has studied post-colonial island nations of the Caribbean and has spent two years in Nigeria on a Fulbright Lectureship. His interests include international public health, historical anthropology and developing societies. In addition to *Amerindians of the Lesser Antilles: a bibliography* (1981), *A Resource Guide to Dominica, 1493-1986* (1987) and numerous articles, he has compiled the World Bibliographical Series volumes on *Dominica* (1987), *Nigeria* (1989) and *Ghana* (1991).

Ian Wallace is Professor of German at the University of Bath. A graduate of Oxford in French and German, he also studied in Tübingen, Heidelberg and Lausanne before taking teaching posts at universities in the USA, Scotland and England. He specializes in contemporary German affairs, especially literature and culture, on which he has published numerous articles and books. In 1979 he founded the journal *GDR Monitor*, which he continues to edit under its new title *German Monitor*.

Hans H. Wellisch is Professor emeritus at the College of Library and Information Services, University of Maryland. He was President of the American Society of Indexers and was a member of the International Federation for Documentation. He is the author of numerous articles and several books on indexing and abstracting, and has published *The Conversion of Scripts and Indexing and Abstracting: an International Bibliography*, and *Indexing from A to Z*. He also contributes frequently to *Journal of the American Society for Information Science*, *The Indexer* and other professional journals.

Ralph Lee Woodward, Jr. is Director of Graduate Studies at Tulane University, New Orleans. He is the author of *Central America, a Nation Divided*, 2nd ed. (1985), as well as several monographs and more than seventy scholarly articles on modern Latin America. He has also compiled volumes in the World Bibliographical Series on *Belize* (1980), *El Salvador* (1988), *Guatemala* (Rev. Ed.) (1992) and *Nicaragua* (Rev. Ed.) (1994). Dr. Woodward edited the Central American section of the *Research Guide to Central America and the Caribbean* (1985) and is currently associate editor of Scribner's *Encyclopedia of Latin American History*.

VOLUME 14

Panama

Revised Edition

Eleanor DeSelms Langstaff

Compiler

CLIO PRESS

OXFORD, ENGLAND · SANTA BARBARA, CALIFORNIA
DENVER, COLORADO

British Library Cataloguing in Publication Data

Langstaff, Eleanor DeSelms
Panama. – Rev. Ed. – (World bibliographical series; v. 14)
1. Panama – Bibliography
I. Title
016.9´7287

ISBN 1–85109–251–X

ABC-CLIO Ltd.,
Old Clarendon Ironworks,
35A Great Clarendon Street,
Oxford OX2 6AT, England.

ABC-CLIO Inc.,
130 Cremona Drive,
Santa Barbara,
CA 93117, USA

Designed by Bernard Crossland.
Typeset by ABC-CLIO Ltd., Oxford, England.
Printed and bound in Great Britain by print in black, Midsomer Norton.

THE WORLD BIBLIOGRAPHICAL SERIES

This series, which is principally designed for the English speaker, will eventually cover every country (and some of the world's principal regions and cities), each in a separate volume comprising annotated entries on works dealing with its history, geography, economy and politics; and with its people, their culture, customs, religion and social organization. Attention will also be paid to current living conditions – housing, education, newspapers, clothing, etc. that are all too often ignored in standard bibliographies; and to those particular aspects relevant to individual countries. Each volume seeks to achieve, by use of careful selectivity and critical assessment of the literature, an expression of the country and an appreciation of its nature and national aspirations, to guide the reader towards an understanding of its importance. The keynote of the series is to provide, in a uniform format, an interpretation of each country that will express its culture, its place in the world, and the qualities and background that make it unique. The views expressed in individual volumes, however, are not necessarily those of the publisher.

VOLUMES IN THE SERIES

To Oscar Cooper, who as a child heard the stories of surviving, striving and success, and who, as a youth, participated in the struggle, and now, in his years of wisdom, watches from afar as Panama's saga unfolds.

Contents

Contents

Contents

Introduction

As this bibliography goes to press, Panama is swept by the invigorating new breezes of hope and expectation that energize initiatives whose origins may be a quarter of a century old, but whose 'feel' is newer than new. In part, these changes have been enabled by the new technologies, and in part the changes stem from new political sensibilities. If history has shown mankind capable of beating swords into ploughshares, we now see a canal that, nearly a century ago, had been dug with minimal concern for the people who lived in the land and whose needs carried very little weight. This canal, built for the economic benefit of the United States in competition with France, a fierce commercial competitor if also its oldest political ally, now enters the twenty-first century. It is now an internationally managed concern with regional values and services and a national symbol of autonomy and of equal worth. As Adam Clymer of *The New York Times* wrote on the occasion of the transfer of power from the United States to Panama, Panama as a place is doomed to own what others covet. As the twentieth century was for it an American century, today it has entered a post-imperial, post-colonial phase, but still remains an enviable piece of real estate.

This bibliography has been enhanced by the new technologies because it is easier for authors to publish in this time of cold type and hot Internet connections. In small countries where print runs of the latest novel rarely exceed a thousand copies, publishing has now become economically viable for a broader group. Moreover, global democratization tends more and more to establish a political climate that is open to minimizing censorship and giving a voice to people from more sectors of society. This revision of *Panama* is a case in point. There are more women's voices, more black voices speaking to us, enticing us to read them even within the staid confines of a bibliographical citation. Much of the new material in English described here reflects both a diversity and a commonality not found in earlier publications. Studies that are concerned with the exotic and the quaint were usual in the nineteenth century and the first seventy-five years of the twentieth, but have now nearly vanished. Instead, what is appearing in the international press concerning Panama is more about global issues, such as preserving the environment and making the transition from an extractive and agricultural economy to a high-tech service economy. These changes call for expanded educational needs, and broader considerations of the all parts of the citizenry in terms of both their potential contributions and rising expectations.

Further, searching for material has benefited to an unheard-of extent by being able to investigate electronically the resources of remote libraries. In some cases – not many, but importantly – materials that were not known, and therefore not included in the first version of this bibliography, have now been included, although in general, most of the material annotated here was published from about 1982 to the present.

Panama lies at the southernmost part of Central America and is formed by a narrow isthmus separating the Atlantic from the Pacific Ocean. To the north it abuts Costa Rica; to the south, a dense forest and swampland separate it from Colombia, of which it once formed a province. The red volcanic soil and luxuriant vegetation contrast with the white beaches and sea-green coastal waters. The tropical climate enables a simple life-style that fulfils basic needs in areas that have maintained the ideal ecological balance, but its cities share in all the pleasures and artificialities that mark modern cities throughout the world.

It is the isthmus that has shaped Panama's destiny. The land-bridge between the seas is short enough to walk; an ideal meeting-point that during the colonial period allowed the great market of Portobello to flourish; that allowed those rushing towards the gold mines of California to move on to the next part of their journey (or conversely, plod back to the eastern states, failures who lacked the Midas touch); and that, ultimately, suggested to Ferdinand de Lesseps that this land was as near as could be found to the flatness of Suez, and just the place for an interoceanic canal.

The terrain ranges from steep, rugged mountains, the highest point of which is the 3,500-foot Volcan de Chiriquí, to the two thousand miles of coastline. Of Panama's natural resources, gold was mined and worked from earliest times. Today, copper and other minerals used in modern manufacturing are extracted and exported, and there is mahogany in the forests.

The people who make up Panama are diverse. The major indigenous groups, especially the Kuna people, have a rich culture that has been much studied by outsiders, many of whom have published the results of their research in English and thus figure largely in these pages. But the population is three-quarters of mixed ancestry, indigenous and European or West Indian. Indigenous peoples *per se* make up about six per cent of the population. Much interesting work has been done in the area of preserving traditional values, and is represented here in the categories of nationalities, the arts, education and linguistics.

The prehistory of Panama has been explored by archaeologists and anthropologists who have done much to recreate the history of the early peoples and to find, preserve and describe the artefacts they have left behind. The Institute of National Culture, aided by UNESCO, has done much to preserve the heritage, and to make that heritage known and appreciated by all Panamanians.

Panama's history is a textbook case of the New World. First – if we disregard the prehistory, which has minimal amounts of surviving written documentation upon which history depends – came the Age of Exploration, with the intermittent visits of Balboa, Columbus and lesser chance voyagers. Next came the colonial epoch during which Panama, tidily mapped into New Granada by the early *conquistadores* for administrative purposes, reported to Spain, a major mercantile power, and became the great trade market that Christopher Ward has described so excitingly in his writings – for which he was able to use newly available resources. This was also the first real experience that Panama had in being a pawn of major powers, when those knightly pirates Drake and Morgan marauded in furtherance of England's foreign policy. The sacking of Panama City in 1671 led to its relocation and rebuilding, so important was it to Spain.

The events of the last years of the seventeenth century and the first decade of the eighteenth included the establishment of a Scottish settlement in Darien under the auspices of Sir William Paterson. This well-designed but unlucky foundation almost immediately failed. Paterson was more fortunate in founding the Bank of England.

The eighteenth century saw a Panama under the sway of Colombia, but still isolated from the capital by a dense jungle that even today defeats the builders of the Inter-American Highway. During this time escaped slaves formed villages and developed a self-hood. The Panama Railroad was built and put to use as each section was put down; it was finally completed in 1855. This project disregarded the needs of the people of Panama, but some found it an outlet for their entrepreneurial talents. Its importance was as an international public way, especially for the Americans crossing from the east coast to California to take part in the Gold Rush. Mercedes Chen Daly's 'The Watermelon Riot' describes one incident in 1856 in which the rushees push the residents of Panama City beyond bearing on an especially hot and idle Sunday. This bibliography references the republished documents relating to this period, which has once more come under scholarly scrutiny.

The nineteenth century in Panama, as in most of the world, was one of engineering feats. In the second half of the 1800s work was begun towards the building of a canal. The French, under the direction of the aged Ferdinand de Lesseps, began the canal, although concessions had been granted to the United States and Belgium as well, and the enterprise was capitalized by an international group of investors. Negotiations were entered into with Colombia of which Panama formed a province, although a restless one that several times attempted independence.

The tensions leading up to the formation of the Republic of Panama in 1903 were exacerbated when Nicaragua was again considered as the site for the interoceanic canal. The War of the Thousand Days marked a point of no return. Panama's first Constitution came into effect in 1905. Much work based on the archives of France, Spain, Colombia, Panama and the United States has been described in this volume. Modern surveys of these events are given in the work of scholars such as Michael Coniff and John Major.

In the biography section, it will be seen that there is a dearth of substantial collective biography along the lines of *Who's Who*, possibly because the ruling classes tend to be related to each other in this small country. As more multinational activities are developed, the need for such a reference tool will no doubt become acute. Women as biographical subjects are featured in this section, as well as large and detailed biographies of key figures such as Generals Omar Torrijos and Manuel Noriega.

Population and nationalities have been much considered in the past decade or so since the previous bibliography appeared. Materials relating to the population include statistical estimates of indigenous peoples from the sixteenth to the twentieth century, national population policy, and population and environment. Studies of specific groups of people have been uneven. The various groups that comprise Panama today are the indigenous peoples, West Indians and other black people, those of European descent and various combinations of these groups. Some Indian groups have been the subjects of study more than others, with the Kuna having the longest history of investigation. More attention is now being paid to other groups, and Chris Gjording has contributed several monographs relating to the interaction of the Guaymí and multinational business. George Westerman has pioneered West Indian studies, and there are several strong scholars currently researching the topic.

Such a diverse population speaks many languages. The books and articles listed here discuss indigenous languages, their vocabularies and grammars, Panamanian Spanish, and the Panamanian Creole which uses words from both West Indian and Spanish sources. In general use today are such West Indian formations as 'madama' to refer to a West Indian woman and 'chombo', a West Indian canal worker. Joel Sherzer has led the way in relating the social implications of language, focusing on Kuna. A section of dictionaries is provided, many of which are specialized in their purpose.

Religious publications mainly describe social problems and possible ways of addressing them, and little has been found of a mainstream theological nature. Eric J. Moeller has, however, produced an interesting study of millenarianism among the Kuna and Stanley Fidanque has written a history of his prominent Jewish family.

Both urban and rural social conditions figure in studies of society, and poverty is the focus of several books and articles. In keeping with global trends, much has been published about women. Besides a national-level plan for development among Panamanian women, writings on social organizations include specific studies about women, not only in terms of child-bearing and child-rearing, but also their rights to hold land and their political activities. The World Bank has encouraged examination of the problems especially relating to rural poverty.

In the health sphere, specific diseases feature, and there is a doctoral thesis discussing the training of health care professionals. As might be expected, the trafficking of drugs is an important topic, but as Laura Vasquez and Barbara Jahanoozi show, drug abuse is very much contrary to the mores of Panamanian society.

From its origins as a republic, Panama was ruled under a constitution, one article of which provided for the right of the United States to use its troops to keep peace. This constitution remained in force until 1941 when a new one – that among other items severely restricted citizenship – was put in force by the president, Arnulfo Arias Madrid. A new constitution in 1946 reverted to that of 1904, with some modern touches such as term limits for the president and universal suffrage. This remained in force until 1968. After the military coup the constitution was changed to regularize the dictatorship of Omar Torrijos for six years, although it continued for many more. The strong central control, however undemocratic, made possible the treaties of 1977. The constitutional reforms of 1983 detailed civil liberties and broadened decision-making opportunities for the Panamanians, a provision that was curtailed under the leadership of Manuel Noriega. The constitution is now amended to provide for the administration of the canal area, and has restored many democractic elements.

The literature of the political science and law section includes factual gatherings from many sources, discussions of specific topics such as political parties, human rights, the extending of political participation, the role of the United States in internal affairs, and a sampling of the laws that have been revised in the light of the new constitution. Global trends, such as the impact of the fall of communism in Eastern Europe on economic and political structures, some emphasis on economic development in the Third World, and the increasing use of information technologies has affected Panama in specific ways. Alaka Wali's study of the Bayano Hydroelectric Project, 1974-90, describes and evaluates one such. New scholarship on racism as it affects foreign relations is also listed.

As might be expected, there have been quantities of material provided about the Canal Treaties of 1977, which in general provided for the transfer of the control of the Panama Canal from the United States to Panama, the removal of US troops and the hand-over of the lands used for US defence. This treaty was agreed to after fourteen years of negotiation. Currently there is a Panama Canal area, that is the land required to administer the Panama Canal. It represents 40 per cent of the land formerly held as Canal Zone property. The rest was returned to Panama and has been in development ever since, often for educational, eco-tourism and national park purposes. A second treaty guarantees the neutrality of the canal into the 21st century, with the United States continuing to play a defence role. This treaty has many nations as signatories as to the neutrality of the canal, but it is also the source of much concern as suggesting a strong continuing – and not entirely welcome – US presence.

The US Military Intervention of 1989 is important in international and national ways. Much of the analytical writing concerns the legality of the action, with documents from the United Nations, the US government and non-governmental organizations, and these are listed here. The problems to be solved by such an invasion were intractable, involving illegal arms shipments and drug trafficking that were seen as being on such a scale as to be a serious regional threat. Suppression of human rights and widespread internal economic corruption were also part of the rationale. For ease in browsing, the many personal accounts and journalistic reports are in a section separate from the more scholarly items. Information technology has changed the manner in which an event like this is covered journalistically, and its proximity to the United States increased public interest and thus the demand for personal accounts.

The economic potential of Panama in a post-industrial world is high. The World Bank has provided in-depth studies, while Andrew Zimbalist and John Weeks put Panama's economy into its political context. The effect of multinational corporations and external economic assistance, principally from the United States, is discussed for its strengths and weaknesses. Karen Tice breaks new ground in her study of the merger of a traditional economy into today's global economy in her *Kuna crafts, gender and the global economy.* Studies of economic development and environmental impact studies are also included.

Under the terms of the 1976-77 Panama Canal Treaties, 7,000 former US military buildings and more than 300,000 acres of prime real estate have been transferred to the Panamanian government which has decided to privatize much of it. The change-over has opened many investment opportunities for the development of banking, tourism, operation of a free trade zone and the establishment of offshore financial centres. Many items in these sections serve as guides to doing business and examinations of the legal and tax obligations and benefits that accrue. Some articles discuss the arrival of new multinational corporations to participate in the energy industry when half of it was privatized in the early 1990s. Extractive industries, the operation of which had been severely restricted in preceding years, have been opened up to new mining ventures.

Issues in agriculture range from the problems associated with traditional farming, including slash-and-burn land clearance, to the problems caused by one-crop agribusiness, which destroys the balance of nature needed to maintain the environment. Also discussed are food production and import policy matters and the relationship of consumer demand to agricultural production. Many items in the geography, flora and fauna, and environment sections of this bibliography relate directly to agriculture or industry.

Human resource management includes new looks at such issues as the lingering impact of slavery, and multiracial work environments. Michael Coniff's *Black labor on a white canal: Panama, 1904-1981* 'traces the history of the West Indian predicament on the isthmus under both American and Panamanian masters' (introduction). Some 100,000 West Indians came to work and live in Panama. Coniff looks at the discrimination the West Indians suffered from the time of their arrival on the isthmus, including the loss of citizenship and forced repatriation for some groups just before the Second World War, under the short-lived Arias Constitution. This topic is also studied by Elizabeth McLean Petras in *Jamaican labor migration: white capital and Black labor, 1850-1930*. Although many scholars have looked at West Indian labour in recent years, *Labor and politics in Panama: the Torrijos year* by Sharon Phillips Collazos broadens the scope. She examines the condition of labour and the labour movement in the 1970s with particular reference to the Labor Act of 1972. A particularly valuable chapter discusses specific costs and benefits of the act. This labour reform was bitterly fought by business interests and considerably weakened, but nonetheless changed society by extending access to economic benefits to a broad sector of the population.

The last twenty years have seen a vast improvement in the availability of statistical data, which are now collected and processed accurately and published promptly, filling a serious lacuna with important planning information. The full range of demographic, economic, agricultural, health and education statistics are now readily accessible.

Environmental topics represented in items include reports produced as an aid to planning environmentally sound use by such entities as the Nature Conservancy, notably its ecological survey of the former US Department of Defense lands in Panama; impact studies on the developing infrastructures of electrical power and road transport; and the oil spills resulting from land transhipment of crude oil across the isthmus. Both mining and agriculture come under study, and the development of the eco-tourism industry features in several items. The massive contribution of the Smithsonian Tropical Research Institute is described in two items.

Introduction

Educational focus has recently been on higher education and the use of the former US military installations for classrooms and laboratories. Other items urge the trial and adoption of innovative ideas such as privatization, distance learning and the reintroduction of native language instruction in the elementary classroom. The writings of some early educators have been republished.

From world press coverage, one might imagine Panama as a country of drug traffickers and political fomenters overrun with foreign troops. In fact, it is a country that is humanistically orientated. There has always been a passionate interest in the arts in general and literature in particular. The literature section attempts to give a good sense of who the writers of note are and about what they are writing. The themes of importance are the impact of the canal, as in the 'novellas canaleras' of Joaquín Belleño, racism, the life of the immigrant West Indians and their children, with special reference to Cubeno's 'chombo' and Frederick's Colón Man. The surveys listed show the many schools represented in the literature of Panama, as avant-garde ideas are taken up by young writers. Renewed interest in women writers has driven the publication of international anthologies in which Panamanian women are represented. As has been previously referred to in a more general way, the ease of publication today has made it possible for many more – and a greater diversity of – voices to be heard. About sixty novels are published annually, no small volume of production for a country with a population of under three million. Recipients of the Miró prizes are effectively guaranteed publication of their novels, essays, plays and collections of verse.

The arts section is very far ranging – from fine arts to popular culture, including traditional materials, to which much attention has been given in recent years. Monica Kupfer discusses contemporary painting from Panama in one item, and the work of Panamanian artist Guillermo Trujillo in another. Panama is represented in entries from the *Latin American Theatre Review.* In 'El teatro en Panamá: Entre problemas, excepciones y esperanzas', Daniel Dominguez provides a ten-year review of theatre in Panama that includes material on the general arts climate of the 1980s, a description of theatres available for the mounting of theatrical programmes, and some of the more noteworthy productions and directors.

Music, musical instruments and dance are discussed in an array of articles. A very informative article is that written by the noted ethnomusicologist at Indiana University, Ronald Smith. In it he describes the state of music in general in Panama. Topics covered include the historical context, musical instruments and ensembles, dance and dance theatre, such as *congos* and *diabolos,* and vocal music, especially the *décima.* Key festivals are described and musical terms peculiar to Panama are defined. Folk music is almost synonymous with the two Panamanian pioneer folklorists, Manuel F. Zárate and Dora Perez de Zárate. The latter figures in a 1990 biography by Maritza Lowinger. An example of Dora Zárate's work is the 1986 *La saga panameña: una tema inquietante* (The Panamanian saga; a disturbing theme), in which she examines the treatment of supernatural creatures and witches and other humans partaking of supernatural powers, usually evil, to be found in Panamanian folklore. Zárate analyses material along the literary-folklore continuum with the elaborated tale, the 'cuento', at one end of the spectrum and direct myth at the other. The method of this study includes long transcriptions of material as told by informants from both city and country and of all ages, from young adult to those of advanced years.

The *mola*, an appliqué embroidery blouse in the traditional dress of Kuna women, is given much attention. Not only are designs discussed, but the sociological aspects are examined. Designs are intricate, original, often commemorating an unusual event and subject to group evaluation for artistic quality. The *mola* serves much as samplers did for an earlier age in Western cultures, as manifesting a woman's ability to contribute to her society.

Printing and the dissemination of ideas by means of the printed word have ever been a concern of government. Voices of dissent are more acceptable in the Panama of the 1990s, so that although Panama figures in several histories of the book in Latin America and in a sociological study in 1984, it is not until 1997 that a study of the alternative press is published in Panama. Much has been written about media treatment of the US invasion of Panama in 1989, and about the impact of popular reaction in Latin America because of the coverage of the military action. In general this material disregards any impact on Panamanians. Again, the availability of a usable information technology together with the relaxation of censorship has enabled ethnic broadcasting. Marta Lucia De Gerdes describes such a programme in 'Media, politics, and artful speech: Kuna radio programs'. The Kuna of San Blas have become dispersed over the past three decades, many to Panama City. One way of keeping in touch has been Kuna-language radio broadcasts aired on local stations, since the Kuna do not have a broadcast facility of their own. The author has produced the first study of the style and content of these broadcasts.

A listing of periodicals published in Panama is given. Many have been erratically published over the years, with the exception of *Lotería*, a high-level general-interest monthly, but they are given here in the expectation that the new vigour and sense of freedom in Panama will enable some to resume publication. Of the reference books, those published in English in the United States and Great Britain predominate, as being useful for researchers using this bibliography. All dictionaries that could be identified are included, although some are more like glossaries, rather than fully fledged dictionaries. Other reference tools include archival guides and document indexes, finding guides to reports issued by such non-governmental agencies

Introduction

and international organizations as the Commission for Human Rights in Latin America.

Acknowledgements

The compiler would like to acknowledge with thanks the unstinting assistance of the many people who helped to identify and make available the materials described in this bibliography. To the Hispanic Division of the Library of Congress, Washington, DC where the project was discussed at length, to my home college, the Bernard M. Baruch College of City University of New York, especially the Anita and William Newman Library, who put many electronic facilities at my service, to the New York Public Library Center for Humanities, the Library for the Performing Arts, and the Science, Industry and Business Library, and to Bobst Library, New York University, for access to and assistance with their rich collections of Latin American materials. Grateful thanks also to the New York Public Library for research space in the Wertheim Study, a facility endowed by the historian Barbara Tuchman in memory of her father, that made it possible to work with a wide variety of print materials in an efficient manner and in ways that put minimal wear and tear on unique items.

The Country and Its People

1 Area handbook for Panama.
Thomas Weil. Washington, DC: US Government Printing Office, 1972. 400p. maps. (Foreign Area Studies of American University).
A comprehensive and objectively written handbook covering all aspects of the Republic of Panama and the Canal Zone, but with emphasis on socio-economic and political matters. A must for any reader in need of a substantial introduction to Panama. Subjects included are the social system, culture and religion, government, agriculture and industry, security and the penal system, trade and transportation.

2 Central America; the crisis and the challenge.
John D. Martz. Chapel Hill, North Carolina: University of North Carolina Press, 1959. 356p. bibliog.
Martz provides a country-by-country study that emphasizes the political situation and economic development of the region. Panama is discussed on pages 264-319, mostly from the viewpoint of the United States' importance to Panama, for good or ill. Useful for historical comparison.

3 Central America inside out: the essential guide to its societies, politics, and economies.
Tom Barry. New York: Grove Weidenfeld, 1991. 501p. bibliog.
For each country the politics, government and social and economic conditions are described and evaluated.

4 Inside Panama.
Tom Barry, John Lindsay-Poland, Marco Gandasegui, Peter Simonson. Albuquerque, New Mexico: Resource Center Press, 1995. 200p.
Barry, who has written widely on Central American matters, here provides an introductory survey of the government and politics, security forces and human rights, economy, society and environment, and US–Panama relations, giving succinct

1

descriptions and naming and describing the organizations that contribute to Panama's society. Statistical tables provide data, while summaries of laws, treaties, foreign aid (mostly US) and the purpose of a variety of organizations in each sphere of activity are nowhere else so accessible and up to date. A useful chronology and selective bibliography of recent publications add to the overall usefulness of this work.

5   Latin America, 1998.
Edited by Robert T. Buckman.   Harpers Ferry, West Virginia: Stryker-Post Publications, 1997. 32nd ed. 232p. (The World Today Series).

A country-by-country treatment of the current status of the Latin American countries including Panama, with emphasis on US policy with reference to each country. Some readers find that the treatment of the topics is very uneven.

6   Letter from Panama.
E. J. Kahn, Jr.   *New Yorker,* vol. 52 (16 August 1976), p. 64-75.

This lucid and well-written account of present-day Panama is based on the author's visit. Many of his observations seem to have been garnered during cocktail parties, but the guests do seem to have been representative of every political persuasion. The author is supportive of the Panamanian government's policy *vis-à-vis* the United States and critical of the effect of the Canal Zone on the country as a whole. Kahn is a widely respected observer and this early essay provides perspective to what has come after.

7   Letter from Panama; 233,000 Acres, Ocean View.
Jon Lee Anderson.   *The New Yorker* (29 November 1999), p. 50-61.

Anderson has written four books, including *Che Guevara: A revolutionary life.* In this article about Panama on the eve of its assuming full control of the Panama Canal, he touches on all the issues facing the country at the brink of the new millennium, sketching in the historical parallels, sources, and colourful detail that make his points telling. The presidential politics from 1968, the role of the military, the plans and hopes for the economic future of most of the ethnic and social groups, the drug-trafficking problem, and the pervasive US–Panamanian relationship are all covered. The article ends with a summary of his interview with the US ambassador to Panama, Simón Ferro, who is quoted as saying 'The United States is not disengaging from Panama. Rather, we are reconfiguring.'

8   Life after Manuel Noriega: Panama's new regime is off to a rough start.
Linda Robinson, Peter Cary.   *U.S. News & World Report,* vol. 109, no. 5 (30 July 1990), p. 29-31.

Experienced reporters for Panama and the region present an overview of conditions in Panama some six months after the invasion.

9   Panama.
David Howarth.   In: *Latin America and the Caribbean, a handbook.* Edited by Claudio Veliz.   London: Anthony Blond, 1968, p. 227-36.

Panama is covered in an overview by Howarth in which he treats history, politics and government, international relations, economy, education and social welfare. Further mention of Panama is made in the general essays on Latin American economics, labour and culture. Information on the Indians of Panama is on page 702.

10 Panama and the Canal in pictures and prose.
Willis J. Abbot. London; New York: Syndicate, 1913. 444p.

Sub-titled 'a complete story of Panama, as well as the history, purpose and promise of its world-famous canal – the most gigantic engineering undertaking since the dawn of time', there is a distinct pleasure to be found in this quaint and out-of-date survey of Panama. It is also one of the first manifestations of mistrust of the developing American colonial life-style because it is both morally weakening to US citizens and harmful to the host country.

11 Panama and the Canal Zone in pictures.
Peter English. New York: Sterling, 1973. 64p.

The chief value of this very brief and general introduction to the country lies in the illustrations, for many of the more meaty books lack illustrations. There are a few over-generalizations, and the author discounts the desire of many Panamanians for more political participation.

12 Panama, a country study.
Federal Research Division, Library of Congress. Washington, DC: US Government Printing Office, 1989. 4th ed. 337p. (Area Handbook Series).

Edited by Sandra W. Meditz and Dennis M. Hanratty, the fourth edition of this item, the earlier title for which is *Area Handbook for Panama*, has the note: 'Research completed December 1987'. It is a comprehensive and objectively written handbook covering all aspects of the Republic of Panama and the Canal Zone of the late 1980s. The emphasis is on socio-economic matters, and it is a must for any reader needing a substantial introduction to Panama. Topics included are the social system, culture and religion, government, agriculture, trade and industry, security, law and the penal system and the infrastructure. There are maps, illustrations and an extensive bibliography, p. 295-311.

13 Panama; it's much more than just a canal.
Hans J. Massaquoi. *Ebony* (July 1978), p. 44-56.

The main thrust of this heavily illustrated article is that Panama has a successful racial mix and that its problems are economic in nature. Special attention is given in this African-American magazine to the blacks resident in the Panama Canal Zone.

Geography and Geology

General

14   The early maps of Panama.
Kit S. Kapp.   North Bend, Ohio: Kapp Publications, 1971. 38p.
maps.

This is an entertaining and stimulating introduction to old Panamanian maps by a cartographer-antiquarian. There are careful descriptions of 125 maps, and 7 are reprinted on plates. A historical chronology from 1501 to 1914, the opening of the Panama Canal, is useful to both specialist and general reader alike.

15   The early Spanish Main.
Carl Ortwin Sauer.   Berkeley, California: University of California
Press; London: Cambridge University Press, 1966. 306p. bibliog.

A geographer's discussion of the developing awareness of the islands and 'tierra firme' discovered by Columbus in 1492 up to about 1570. Details taken from contemporary documents describe the isthmus of Panama (p. 220-37, 247, 289) as it was seen by the first Spanish explorers. The diet, clothing, agricultural activities and organization of the inhabitants as well as flora and fauna are described. Although treated most thoroughly in the pages referred to above, Panama is discussed in nearly every section of the work.

16   Esquema geográfico de Panamá. (Geographical outline of Panama.)
Angel Rubio.   Rio de Janeiro: Instituto Pan-Americano de
Geográfica e Historia, 1961. 87p. maps. bibliog. (Publicão no. 136).

A detailed description of Panama from the geographical point of view. An outline covers both the country as a whole and each region, and many sources for further information are given. The author was professor of geography at the University of Panama.

17 La función geográfica del istmo; estudio jurídico-político. (The geographical function of the isthmus; a juridical-political study.)
Victor F. Goytía. Panama City: Casa Editorial La Moderna, 1947. 247p.

A collection of essays most of which centre on the theme that Panama's geographical position has affected a good deal of its history – and will affect its future. Some documentation is provided regarding the use of Panamanian areas by the United States for defence purposes, supporting a long essay discussing the threat US military bases posed for Panama.

18 Homenaje a la patria: Latin American national atlases.
Robert B. Kent. *Latin American Research Review*, vol. 30, no. 1 (Winter 1995), p. 256-66.

Six national atlases published in the last few years are here characterized in detail and compared with each other. The Panamanian atlas of 1988 described here is the third edition (see item no. 36). Thematic maps include imports and exports, and land use; statistical data from the censuses are also included.

19 Panama – in pictures.
Minneapolis: Lerner Publications, 1996. Rev. and updated ed. 64p. (Visual Geography Series).

We have here a visual introduction to the geography, history, government, people, economy, and culture of the Republic of Panama and the Panama Canal.

20 La ruta de Balboa y el descubrimiento del Oceano Pacífico.
(Balboa's route and the discovery of the Pacific Ocean.)
Angel Rubio. Mexico City: Instituto Pan-Americano de Geográfica e Historia, 1965. 133p. bibliog. (Publicación no. 289).

Rubio (1901-62) was professor of geography at the University of Panama and enjoyed an international reputation for his geographical publications. The bulk of the book is a diary of the retracing of Balboa's route across the isthmus, undertaken in 1954 by the Expedición de Leopoldo de Belgica al Darien. Appendix I is a bibliography in chronological order (1830-1955) of selected works about Balboa, for the most part in Spanish.

Regional

21   The Caribbean as Columbus saw it.
Samuel Eliot Morison, Mauricio Obregon.   Boston, Massachusetts:
Little, Brown, 1964. 252p.

An expedition was undertaken by the authors to record in photographs the lands that
Columbus mentioned in his logs and journals. Morison, long a Columbus scholar and
naval historian, generally assigns traditional names to places. The aerial photographs are
so void of modern indications – buildings, roads and the like – that one has the impression
of seeing the new land with the eyes of Columbus. Panama, with Colombia, is described
on pages 192-220.

22   Geography of Latin America; a regional analysis.
Kempton E.Webb.   Englewood Cliffs, New Jersey: Prentice-Hall,
1972. 126p. maps. (Foundations of the World Regional Geography).

Webb gives a brief introduction to the geography of Latin America. Panama is discussed
on page 116 in summary form and is covered in the chapters dealing with such aspects of
regional geography as population, economy, and climate.

**23   Historical atlas of Latin America; political, geographic, economic,
cultural.**
A. Curtis Wilgus.   New York: Cooper Square, 1969. rev. ed. 365p.
maps.

The detailed table of contents serves as the index to this work. Maps show boundaries,
ethnological background, revolutions and revolutionary movements and the like. Maps of
Panama are on page 241 and 299.

24   Latin America, a geographical survey.
Harry Robinson.   New York: Praeger, 1967. 499p. maps. bibliog.

Panama is discussed principally on pages 154-78 from the usual geographical aspects,
including physical features, natural resources, population, political and economic
characteristics.

Special features

25   The Chagres, river of westward passage.
John E. Minter.   New York: Rinehart, 1948. 418p.

For centuries uncounted the Chagres has been the highway of Panama. Its role in recorded
history dates from the early 16th century. This book discusses the river from the 16th
century to the building of the Panama Canal, and is frequently cited in contemporary
writings about Panama.

26 Chiriquí.

Ernesto J. Castillero Reyes.   Panama City: Published by the Author, 1968. 130p.

Chiriquí, a province rich in timber, coffee, sugar, rice and other food crops, is the major agricultural area of the country. In this monograph by one of Panama's leading writers, himself a native of Chiriquí, both the early years of exploration and the most modern activities are described. Some historical documents regarding Chiriquí are also reprinted in the appendix.

27 Ecological implications of changes in drought patterns: shifts in forest composition in Panama.

Richard Condit.   *Climatic Change*, vol. 39, nos. 2-3 (July 1998), p. 413-27.

A researcher at the Smithsonian Tropical Research Institute reports on changing and increasing dry periods. He finds that while more rain in these areas would not have a major impact, longer dry seasons will.

28 Excursión a la costa de San Blas en Panamá. (A visit to the San Blas coast in Panama.)

Belisario Porras.   Madrid: Imprenta del Patronato de Huerfanos de Intendencia e Intervención Militares, 1916. 14p.

One of the priorities of Belisario Porras (1856-1942) as president of Panama was to bring the Indians of the San Blas coast into the mainstream of a modern Panama. This essay discusses his impressions during a visit in 1915.

29 The forbidden land, reconnaissance of upper Bayano River, R.P., in 1936.

Fred McKim, edited by S. Henry Wassen.   In: *Comparative Ethnological Studies,* vol. 15.   Göteborg, Sweden: Etnografiska Museet, 1947, p. 115-85. map.

Following a three-day discussion among the Cuna as to its wisdom, the author was granted permission to explore the upper Bayano River. The account of his visit is in diary form, illustrated by photographs and a map.

30 The geochemistry of young volcanism throughout western Panama and southeastern Costa Rica; an overview.

M. J. Defant, T. E. Jackson, M. S. Drummond, J. Z. De Boer, H. Bellon, M. D. Feigenson, R. C. Maury, R. H. Stewart.   *Journal of the Geological Society,* vol. 149, no. 4 (July 1992), p. 569-81.

This is a scientific study of the volcanic action in western Panama, an ongoing phenomenon, as is true in much of Central America.

31   Notes on the Chiriquí, Lagoon district and adjacent regions of
       Panama.
       Burton Leroy Gordon.   Berkeley, California: Department of
       Geography, University of California, 1961. 28p. maps.
Notes from anthropological field research which emphasize the geographical aspects of
studies of the Terraba (or Naso) Indians of the Rio Teribe. Other notes describe the shell
mounds to be found along the Caribbean coastline.

32   A Panama forest and shore: natural history and Amerindian
       culture in Bocas del Toro.
       Burton L. Gordon.   Pacific Grove, California: Boxwood Press, 1982.
       178p.
The author examines the impact of agribusiness – notably cattle-raising and commercial
banana production – on the ecology of Bocas del Toro Province. He is particularly
concerned with deforestation, and models of land use that will slow the process. He sees
the traditional land use to be a combination of agriculture, aboriculture and the nurture of
wildlife, and argues for its restoration as a way of maintaining the ecology. Useful
appendixes give both vernacular and scientific names for plants and animals.

33   Rio Bayano; un ensayo geográfico e histórico sobre la región de
       mañana. (Rio Bayano: a geographical and historical essay of the
       region of tomorrow.)
       José Manuel Reverte.   Panama City: Ediciones del Ministerio de
       Educación, 1961. 445p. maps. bibliog.
A solid treatise on the geography and pre-Columbian history of the Rio Bayano area
which comprises the eastern part of Panama. Maps of early voyages and plans of villages
and towns make a valuable addition, as does the comprehensive bibliography of
geographical works on Panama.

Maps, atlases and gazetteers

34   An analysis of air photo and radar imagery of Barro Colorado
       Island, Panama.
       J. N. Rinker.   Fort Belvoir, Virginia: US Army Corps of Engineers,
       Engineer Topographic Laboratories, 1989. 53p. maps.
This publication comprises aerial photographs and radar images of Barro Colorado
Island, Panama.

35 **Atlas de Panamá.** (Atlas of Panama.)
Panama City: Comisión de Atlas de Panamá, 1975. unpaginated.
71 plates of maps.

The atlas is an up-to-date collection of over seventy maps showing political, economic, and geographical aspects. Natural resources, population distribution, agriculture, fishing, tourism, and historic and archaeological sites are shown in colour. Aerial photographs provide the city maps for Panama, Balboa, Colón and other larger towns.

36 **Atlas nacional de la Republica de Panamá.** (National atlas of the Republic of Panama.)
Panama City: Instituto Geográfico Militar Tommy Guardia, 1988.
3rd ed. 222p.

Printed in full colour, this collection of maps, text and data gives a schematic view of Panama. Population, infrastructures, regions, land resources are some of the topics covered. Maps of the major cities, electoral activity and health and social conditions are also graphically portrayed with accompanying text.

37 **Gazetteer of Panama names approved by the United States Board on Geographic Names.**
Washington, DC: Defense Mapping Agency, 1990. 3rd ed. 509p.
maps.

This current edition contains entries for places and geographical features in Panama and the Canal Zone. Both standard names and variants are given. Historical names, such as Aspinwall, are cross-referenced to current names.

38 **Land and waters of the Panama Canal Treaty.**
United States. Central Intelligence Agency. Washington, DC:
Central Intelligence Agency, 1987. Scale 1:250,000 (W 80005–
W 79025/N 9025–N 8050). 1 map: col.; on sheet 27 x 34 cm.

The political features map is colour coded for such items as canal operating areas, defence sites, civil administrative areas, and navigational sections of the waters and waterways used by the canal. These features figure in the acts implementing the Treaty of 1977.

39 **Panama.**
United States. Central Intelligence Agency. Washington, DC: The
Agency, 1981. 1 map: col.; 24 x 54 cm., on sheet 50 x 59 cm. Scale
1:1,500,000; Lambert conformal conic projection, standard parallels
70N and 90N (W 830–W 770/N 100–N 70).

The work includes distance map, comparative area map, ancillary map of 'Panama Canal area', graph showing 'Ethnic composition', and 4 subject maps of 'Population', 'Ethnic groups', 'Vegetation', and 'Economic activity'.

**40   Panama and the Canal Zone, official standard names approved
by the United States Board on Geographic Names.**
Washington, DC: US Army Topographic Command. 1969. 323p.

'This gazetteer contains about 19,000 entries for places and features in Panama and the
Canal Zone.' Both standard names and variants are given. Historical names, such as
Aspinwall, are cross-referenced to current names, but no dates of name changes are
indicated.

41   A pictorial map of the Panama Canal.
Washington, DC: Panama Canal Commission, 1997. 1 view: col.;
37 x 71 cm.

An official publication that includes inset of world map showing 'Major trade routes',
panoramic view in lower margin, and inset enlarged views of the canal.

Geology

**42   Closure of the Isthmus of Panama: the near-shore marine record
of Costa Rica and western Panama.**
Anthony G. Coates, Jeremy B. C. Jackson. Laurel S. Collins, Thomas
M. Cronin, Harry J. Dowsett, Laurel M. Bybell, Peter Jung, Jorge A.
Obando.   *The Geological Society of America Bulletin*, vol. 104,
no. 7 (July 1992), p. 814-28.

When the isthmus finally closed about three and a half million years ago, the closure
created two separate oceanographic regions. Data, maps and charts depict this
development.

**43   Pliocene carbonates and related facies flanking the Gulf of
California, Baja California, Mexico.**
Edited by Markes E. Johnson, Jorge Ledesma-Vazquez.   Boulder,
Colorado: Geological Society of America, 1997. 171p. maps.
(Geological Society of America Special Papers, 318).

In 'Bryozoan nodules built around andesite clasts from the upper Pliocene of Baja
California: paleoecological implications and closure of the Panama Isthmus', Roger J.
Cuffey and Markes E. Johnson discuss the migration of early fauna from the Atlantic to
the Pacific before the isthmus of Panama finally united the continents (p. 111-17).

Tourism and Travel Guides

44 Adventuring in Central America: Guatemala, Belize, Honduras, El Salvador, Nicaragua, Costa Rica, Panama / David Rains Wallace; in association with the Wildlife Conservation Society, the Caribbean Conservation Corporation, and the Paseo Pantera Project.
David Rains Wallace.   San Francisco: Sierra Club Books, 1995. 445p. maps. (The Sierra Club Adventure Travel Guides).

As part of the Sierra Club adventure travel series, this book looks at the beneficial relationship that can exist between tourism and conservation, with special reference to the importance of the land bridge in the migration of life from one land mass to another. The section on Panama (pages 373-413) begins with the sentence 'Panama is a very unusual country'. It occupies an important place in considering Central America as a land bridge since it is at the southernmost part of this geographical phenomenon. Tours of the national parks, the former Canal Zone and major cities are outlined.

45 Beyond the canal, Panama pristine; traveling among a friendly people, two nature lovers have whole parks to themselves, including one with a view of two oceans.
Michael Finkel.   *The New York Times* (24 January 1999), section 5, pages TR10, TR22.

This enthusiastic account of an off-beat excursion to Volcan Baru National Park and western Panama includes sightseeing and bus travel. A directory for the use of other travellers is provided with the text.

46   Caribbean ports of call from Puerto Rico to Aruba, including the Panama Canal eastern and southern regions.
Kay Showker.   Old Saybrook, Connecticut: Globe Pequot Press, 1997. 2nd ed. 323p. (Caribbean Ports of Call).

Cruises, cruise ships and shoreline sights for the Caribbean ports of call are succinctly and charmingly described.

47   Getting to know Panama.
Michele Labrut, illustrated by Janis Rankin.   El Dorado, Panama: Focus Publications, 1993. 252p. maps.

Published in Panama, this is the most detailed guidebook examined. It would be essential for a traveller spending some time in Panama or for temporary residents – since as well as tourist activities, housekeeping information is included. A helpful feature are the historical maps that accompany touring itineraries. Trekking, though covered in other works listed here, is nowhere else so fully described and helpful in its practical advice.

48   A guide to the West Indies, Bermuda and Panama.
Frederick A. Ober.   New York: Dodd, Mead, 1913. 533p. map.

The canal was a tourist attraction from the very beginning – long before the first ship made the crossing in August 1914. This guide gave the early tourist all the information he needed to know at the time of the First World War.

49   Let's Go. Budget Guide to Central America.
New York: St. Martin's Press. annual. maps.

Part of the series written by Harvard students and others, this guide assumes that its readers have both a high level of informed curiosity and a fairly empty purse. Although the Panama section is necessarily cursory, it suffices for a short-stay visitor.

50   Lonely Planet Panama.
Scott Doggett.   Oakland, California: Lonely Planet Publications, 1999. 384p. maps.

A fairly full coverage of what is available for tourists visiting Panama; it includes sources of local guides and other aids, as well as listings and brief descriptions of hotels, resorts, restaurants, transportation, beaches and parks. The material on the culture, history, and society are useful for the first-time visitor.

51   Panamá.
Marc Rigole, Claude-Victor Langlois.   Montreal, Canada: UlyssesTravel Publications, 1996. 2nd ed. 207p. maps. (Ulysses Travel Guide).

A detailed guide to travelling in both the cities and the countryside, in which the assumptions made about the readers are that they will be using public transportation in many instances, are environmentally minded and adventurous. The sections dealing with travel in the interior are especially detailed and useful.

52   The Panama guide: a cruising guide to the Isthmus of Panama.
Nancy Schwalbe Zydler, Tom Zydler.   Port Washington, Wisconsin:
Seaworthy Publications, 1997. 332p. maps.

Intended for sailors of small craft, this book makes informative reading for many readers
of travel books. Not only are there 186 small charts and descriptions of anchorages, but
there is also vivid historical and cultural detail. Historians will appreciate the rarely found
detail and the descriptions of the Spanish Main, the Caribbean coastline, which has seen
little change over the centuries.

53   Panama preparing for upswing in tourism.
Robert P. Walzer.   *Hotel & Motel Management*, vol. 208, no. 21
(13 December 1993), p. 3-5.

Tourism has become a priority in the new Panama, with millions spent on new hotels.
This article details the accomplishments and plans for the future of tourism in the country.
Illustrations include new construction.

**54   Panama's ecotourism-plus initiative: the challenge of making
history.**
Hana Ayala, César Tribaldos, Mirei Endara, Ceferino Sanchez,
Ira Rubinoff.   *Cornell Hotel & Restaurant Administration Quarterly*
(October 1998), p. 34-37.

Both public and private sectors have mobilized to draw up an Action Plan for the
Development of the Tourism-Conservation-Research Strategic Alliance for the Republic
of Panama. They plan to increase tourism to heritage and ecological places in the country
without endangering the ecology.

55   Two wheels to Panamá.
William Carroll.   San Marcos, California: Auto Book Press, 1995.
143p.

What better way to see the real Panama than to move around on a motorcycle? The author,
who has written a variety of environmentally conscious guidebooks, describes his
adventures from Mexico to Panama, and provides information for those who would
emulate him.

Travellers' Accounts

56 At the extremity of civilization: a meticulously descriptive diary of an Illinois physician's journey in 1849 along the Oregon Trail to the goldmines and cholera of California, thence in two years to return by boat via Panama.
Lord Israel Shipman Pelton, edited by Necia Dixon Liles, with a foreword by J. S. Holliday. Jefferson, North Carolina: McFarland, 1995. 441p. maps.

A description of a passage across the isthmus of Panama in 1851 by an articulate diarist who manifests strong opinions on every topic and a Dickensian suspicion of all things foreign, but brings his physician's eye to bear on the populace which he notes is clean and does not suffer from overfeeding. Crossing the mountains was the dangerous and fatiguing point of the journey, but conditions on the Atlantic side were comfortably maintained by North American expatriates. Panama appears on pages 347-99.

57 Beggars on stools; report on Latin America.
Peter Schmid. Westport, Connecticut: Greenwood Press 1975. 325p. (Reprinted from the 1956 edition).

A travel book by a German, written in a highly personal style, which focuses on Panama's politics and the need to defend the canal from sabotage and military attack. Panama is discussed on pages 134-45.

58 Crossing the isthmus, an anonymous 1846 account.
Edited by Ruth J Campbell. *Americas*, vol. 28 (May 1976), p. 14-16.

First published anonymously in *Godey's Lady's Book*, this article recounts a typical mode of crossing the isthmus to change from ships sailing along the Atlantic coast to those that sailed on the Pacific Ocean: that of mule team conveying baggage and passengers. What was soon to become a four-hour rail journey was then a three-day trip, at best uncomfortable, at worst dangerous because of flood-stage rivers and jungle animals.

59   Cuna.
Joanne M. Kelly.   South Brunswick, New York: A. S. Barnes;
London: Thomas Yoseloff, 1966. 440p.

A travel narrative that makes the experience immediate to the reader. The narrative is rich
in detail, nearly a diary in form. It ends with the author's unwilling participation in the
Balboa riots of 1964, thus providing the reader with not only an eyewitness account, but
also a trope of the causes of the riot in the brutal, even ritualistic, killing of her parrot.

60   The hundred days.
Russell Braddon.   London: Collins, 1974. 222p. maps.

The Darien Gap, 200 miles of nearly impenetrable jungle, divides the InterAmerican
Highway (formerly the Pan-American Highway) and up to the present prevents the
link-up of Alaska to Tierra del Fuego. In 1972 a British expedition, with the co-operation
of the Colombian and Panamanian governments, managed to fight its way through *El
Tapón*, 'the stopper', as the local Indians call it. An exciting book which captures the
atmosphere of the Panamanian wetlands.

61   Hunting for gold; reminiscences of personal experiences and research in the early days of the Pacific coast from Alaska to Panama.
William Downie.   Palo Alto, California: American West Publishing
Co., 1971. 403p.

Panama is treated on pages 303-14 of this reprint of the 1893 edition. Writing in the
waning days of the 19th century, Downie regrets the failure of the French canal project,
which he felt would have opened the country to development. Downie went to Panama as
a metallurgist in a team chiefly devoted to rifling Indian burial mounds, but his comments
on the country show him to be more a scientist than a plunderer.

62   In Balboa's bootsteps.
Franz Lidz.   *Sports Illustrated*, vol. 87, no. 12 (22 September 1997),
p. 6-10.

A modern adventurer retraces Balboa's traverse of the isthmus of Panama. Evocative
photographs enhance the account.

63   In quest of El Dorado.
Stephen Graham.   New York: Appleton, 1923. 334p.

A personal and rather dramatic account of one man's retracing of Columbus's footsteps
until, at last, alone, the author climbed a peak in Darien. The Panama account is only a
part of the adventures here recounted.

64   The long road south to the end of the Pan American Highway.
Mel Ross, Ethel Ross.   Vancouver, Canada: Mitchell Press, 1968.
168p. map.

This is an account of a journey by half-ton truck/camper from Calgary, Canada, to Tierra
del Fuego. The authors stayed in Panama, which is described on pages 75-81, while

arranging the sea passage necessary to bypass the Darien jungle. The Rosses describe their adventure without political commentary.

65 A new voyage and description of the isthmus of America.
Lionel Wafer. Cleveland, Ohio: Burrows Brothers, 1903. Reprinted, New York: B. Franklin, 1970. 208p. maps.

Wafer's voyages, first published in 1699, are frequently reprinted in both England and the United States. This edition includes explanatory notes and an 1891 map for comparison with the map in the 1699 edition. Wafer, who was both a surgeon and a pirate, crossed the isthmus from north to south taking several months to do so, during which time he observed in detail the flora and fauna and Indian life, especially medical lore. Publication of the 1699 edition coincided with the demise of the Scottish colony at Caledonia Bay.

66 Panamexico.
Carveth Wells. New York: McBride, 1937. 343p. map.

This is an observant and lively account of a voyage from Panama to Mexico by automobile and trailer, made by an American family in the mid-1930s. The InterAmerican Highway was a far cry from what it is today and the trip was fraught with adventure. A good description of Panama in the period between the wars.

67 Ports of the sun.
Eleanor Early. Boston, Massachusetts: Houghton Mifflin, 1937. 316p. maps.

This travel book of the Caribbean has a long section on Panama and the canal which had long been a major tourist attraction. The work is of interest to nostalgia buffs, but it is also representative of the attitudes of travellers from the United States just prior to the promulgation of the Good Neighbor policy of the United States government of the late 1930s.

68 Operación Panamá por la ruta de los descubridores. (Operation Panama over the route of the explorers.)
José M. Reverte. Madrid: EDAF, 1977. 288p.

A travel book which recounts the author's travels across the isthmus of Panama along the routes of the Spanish and other early explorers whose story he recounts along with his own. Vivid descriptions of modern Indian life in Panama and the flora and fauna make a good introduction to the interior of the country.

69 Roughing it in the San Blas Islands.
J. V. Tinnin. Panama City: Panama-American Publishing Co., 1940. 135p. map.

Based on a diary written some years before publication in this form, this is a traveller's account of life among the San Blas. The author seems to be unaware of the anthropological research that had been done in this area, but describes what he sees and compares his new impressions with what he has previously experienced. He mentions the impact of Anna Coope and Chief Nele, who figure largely in the history of the region.

70 Sailing south.
Philip Sanford Marden. Boston, Massachusetts: Houghton Mifflin, 1921. 225p.

A tourist, this time travelling by yacht, explores the coasts of several countries bordering on the Caribbean. The first part of the book is a pleasant description of his adventures in Panama.

71 San Blas: millenary land of the Cunas.
Rubén Darío Carles, translated by Edward F. O. Connell.
Panama City: La Estrella de Panama, [196-?]. 24p.

The travel pamphlet written by a one of Panama's leading authors stands in contrast to the essay by Belisario Porras written more or less half a century earlier, in its awareness of the culture of the Cuna. There are short treatments of the Tule uprising and of the ill-starred Scottish settlement founded by William Patterson in the eighteenth century.

72 Unknown tribes, uncharted seas.
M. Richmond Brown. London: Duckworth, 1924. 268p.

This is a travel book in the grand tradition of between the wars. Lady Richmond Brown helped to finance a scientific expedition to Central America headed by Michael Hedges and was invited to join it. Much of the book deals with the expedition to study the Cuna Indians (referred to here by the earlier form of their name, Chucunaque). Lady Richmond Brown describes her experiences and provides highly individualistic interpretations of what she sees.

73 Woman in the wilderness.
Winifred L. James. New York: Doran, 1916. 290p.

Letters written by an Englishwoman married to an American businessman in the Republic of Panama – a somewhat unusual situation since so many Americans worked in the zone. The author gives, as well as a description of daily life as an expatriate in Panama, an eyewitness account of the passage of the first ship through the canal. A well-written book for entertaining reading.

Flora and Fauna

General

74 The ecology of a tropical forest: seasonal rhythms and long-term changes.
Edited by Egbert G. Leigh, Jr., A. Stanley Rand, Donald M. Windsor. Washington, DC: Smithsonian Institution Press, 1996. 2nd ed. 503p.

A comprehensive survey of the forest ecology of Barro Colorado Island, an island that was formed in 1914 when the Chagres River was dammed to form Gatún Lake and that has provided since then an isolated ecology that has been much studied. This work examines the physical setting, the biotic setting, seasonal rhythms in plants, frugivores, insects of tree crowns and their predators, and litter arthropods and their predators. Long-term changes are discussed in a concluding chapter. An appendix lists the research carried on at the Smithsonian Tropical Research Institute from 1980 to 1994.

75 The forests of Panama.
May Larsen, Henry Larsen. London: Harrap, 1964. 136p.

A brief overview of modern-day Panama is followed by a more detailed geographical description emphasizing the tropical forests and their flora and fauna. This work, for the non-specialist, is a translation of *Bois de Panama* (Neuchâtel, Switzerland: A La Baconnière, 1962).

76 The jungle whispers.
Kenneth W. Vinton. New York: Pageant Press, 1956. 221p.

A personal account by a naturalist of his life in Panama during the Second World War when he embarked on an extensive training programme to introduce the military, overwhelmingly American, to the jungle and to basic survival techniques. Long at home with the more dangerous of the flora and fauna of the jungle, Vinton for the most part uses anecdotes to make his point that the jungle is not necessarily threatening to man.

Flora

77 An analysis of late secondary succession in species-rich tropical forest.
Dennis H. Knight. In: *Tropical ecological systems: trends in terrestrial and aquatic research.* Edited by Frank B. Golley, Ernesto Medina. New York; Heidelberg, Germany; Berlin: Springer-Verlag, 1975, p. 53-59.

Barro Colorado Island in Gatún Lake has been virtually undisturbed by man for half a century. Knight studied patterns of growth and developed a method of analysing tropical growth that has been used successfully elsewhere.

78 The botany and natural history of Panama/ Botánica e historia natural de Panamá.
Edited by William G. D'Arcy, Mireya D. Correa A. Saint Louis, Missouri: Missouri Botanical Garden, 1985. 455p. bibliog. (Monographs in Systematic Botany from the Missouri Botanical Garden, vol. 10).

A collection of papers, some in English and some in Spanish, organized in broad subject areas: plant groups, animals groups, plants and geography, plant study techniques, habitats, plants that affect man, indigenous peoples and the biota, modern man and the biota. D'Arcy is also author of *Flora of Panama: checklist and index* (1987), which forms two volumes of the *Monographs in systematic botany* from the Missouri Botanical Garden, vols. 17-18.

79 Elemental and hydrologic budgets of the Panamanian tropical moist forest.
J. T. McGinnis (et al.). *Bioscience,* vol. 19 (August 1969), p. 697-700.

The movement and storage of water in the tropical moist forest of Darien was studied by the authors as part of the Sea-Level Canal Feasibility Project.

80 Impact of leaf-cutting ants on vegetation development at Barro Colombo Island.
Bruce Haines. In: *Tropical ecological systems: trends in terrestrial and aquatic research.* Edited by Frank B. Golley, Ernesto Medina. New York; Heidelberg, Germany; Berlin: Springer-Verlag, 1975, p. 99-111.

Leaf-cutting ants build up refuse hills which decompose, adding nutrients to the soil. The study was done to determine what kinds of nutrients are added to the soil in this manner and how these accumulations affect the environment.

81 Orchids of Panama: a facsimile reprint of the Orchidaceae, flora of Panama, with A checklist of the orchids of Panama as known today.
Louis O. Williams, Paul H. Allen, Robert L. Dressler.   St. Louis, Missouri: Missouri Botanical Garden, 1980. 1 vol. (various pagings). (Monographs in Systematic Botany from the Missouri Botanical Garden, vol. 4).

The classic text of the orchids of Panama dating from the 1940s has botanic descriptions and careful drawings of representative orchids. Appended to this reprint is the Dressler checklist which adds missing orchids, which, as Dressler says were not accessible to the original compiler. 'The Orchidaceae, flora of Panama, was published in four parts in the *Annals of the Missouri Botanical Garden*, appearing in 1946 and 1949.'

82 The structure of tropical forests in Panama and Colombia.
Frank B. Golley.   *Bioscience,* vol. 19 (August 1969), p. 693-96.

Four forest types are described by the authors: tropical moist, premontaine wet, gallery and mangrove. Roughly three-quarters of the Panamanian area studied is of the first type.

83 Traveling across the treetops: a crane's-eye-view of Panama's forest canopy yields biological surprises.
William H. Allen.   *BioScience*, vol. 46, no. 11 (December 1996), p. 796-99.

The canopy of forests is an important subject of research at the Smithsonian Tropical Research Institute (STRI) in Panama. It is this layer which exchanges heat, oxygen, water vapour and carbon dioxide between the atmosphere and living things on the ground. Various types of construction equipment enable this research in ways never before possible. The author, William H. Allen, is a science writer for the *St. Louis Post-Dispatch* and a 1996-1997 Knight Science Journalism Fellow at the Massachusetts Institute of Technology.

84 Tropical forest ecology: a view from Barro Colorado Island.
Egbert Giles Leigh.   New York; Oxford: Oxford University Press, 1999. 245p.

Leigh provides a description of the forest ecology of Panama, with special reference to that found on Barro Colorado Island in Gatún Lake.

85 The vegetation of Panama, a review.
Duncan M. Porter.   In: *Vegetation and vegetational history of northern Latin America*.   Edited by Alan Graham.   Amsterdam; London; New York: Elsevier, 1973, p. 167-201.

Topics covered include climate, soils, man and his influence on vegetation, Darien forest types, and plant communities.

86 **The vegetation of San José Island, Republic of Panama.**
C. O. Erlanson. Washington, DC: Smithsonian Institution, 1947.
12p. (Smithsonian Miscellaneous Collection, vol. 106, no. 2).

An agricultural specialist describes the vegetation of a Panamanian island almost undisturbed in the years prior to the Second World War. Of special interest to ecologists is the impact of two years of limited, confined, military use. Weeds brought in with grass seed or on the clothing of personnel quickly took root and spread, changing the nature of the vegetation.

87 **The view from the top.**
Alun Anderson. *Nature*, vol. 347, no. 6288 (6 September1990), p. 5.

A short article that shows how a construction crane can be used to study the tree canopy. The research described took place in Panama City's large Metropolitan Nature Park.

Fauna

88 **Additional forms of birds from Colombia and Panama.**
Alexander Wetmore. Washington, DC: Smithsonian Institution,
1951. 11p. (Smithsonian Miscellaneous Collection, vol. 117, no. 2).

This addition to the following item, describes common as well as little-known birds of the region. The author uses standard ornithological details, and documents the sighting of birds. There are, however, no photographs or drawings.

89 **The birds of the Republic of Panama.**
Alexander Wetmore. Washington, DC: Smithsonian Institution,
1968. 3 vols.

This work was published in three parts, including the two entries above and below. Part 1: Tinamidae (tinamous) to Rynchopidae (skimmers); Part 2: Columbidae (pigeons) to Picidae (woodpeckers); Part 3: Passeriformes: Dendrocoloptidae (woodcreepers) to Oxyruncidae (sharp-bills).

90 **The birds of San José and Pedro Gonzalez Islands, Republic of Panama.**
Alexander Wetmore. Washington, DC: Smithsonian Institution,
1947. 60p. (Smithsonian Miscellaneous Collection, vol. 106, no. 1).

A brief history of bird study in Panama is given in the introduction, while the bulk of the space is allotted to careful descriptions and classification of birds, including some species more familiar in temperate zones: shearwaters, petrels, boobies, terns, kites and vultures.

91 Ecological effects of a major oil spill on Panamanian coastal marine communities.
J. B. C. Jackson, J. D. Cubit, B. D. Keller, V. Batista, K. Burns,
H. M. Caffey, R. L. Caldwell, S. D. Garrity, C. D. Getter,
C. Gonzalez, H. M. Guzman, K. W. Kaufmann, A. H. Knap,
S. C. Levings, M. J. Marshall, R. Steger, R. C. Thompson, E. Weil.
Science, vol. 243, no. 4887 (6 January 1989), p. 37-44.

Panama has trans-shipped oil for decades, with potential oil spills always a possibility. This article report on the ecological effects of one large oil spill. With the research and publication resulting from the last major oil spill, much comparative material is available on the effect on the habitats of wildlife. Detailed commentary on the impact on mangrove swamps, the coastline and coves is given, with some discussion of areas affected on an ongoing basis by mosquito control and human encroachment.

92 Ectoparasites of Panama.
Edited by Rupert L. Wenzel, Vernon J. Tipton.   Chicago: Field
Museum of Natural History, 1966. 861p.

Some dozen contributors identified, located and described various parasites known in Panama. Of chief interest to the non-specialist are the last three chapters. 'Some relationships between mammal hosts and their ectoparasites' (p. 666-72), 'Mice, landbridges, and Latin American faunal interchange' (p. 725-52), and 'Checklist of mammals of Panama' (p. 753-96). Descriptions of the mammals and their locales are given in the last chapter cited, but the popular names of mammals are not used.

93 Finding birds in Panama.
E. P. Edwards.   Sweetbriar, Virginia: E. P. Edwards, 1971. 2nd ed.
95p.

This brief memoir is also a finding guide to the birds of the isthmus of Panama.

94 A guide to the birds of Panama: with Costa Rica, Nicaragua, and Honduras.
Robert S. Ridgely, John A. Gwynne, Jr.   Princeton, New Jersey:
Princeton University Press, 1989. 2nd ed. 534p. bibliog.

Panama has an abundant, varied and attractive bird life. Detailed standard descriptions of known species are accompanied by 96 plates of coloured scientific drawings. The chapter 'Finding Birds in Panama', provides practical advice and descriptions of the most favourable sites for good bird sightings.

95 Gut thinking.
Peter Radetsky.   *Discover*, vol. 16, no. 5 (May 1995), p. 76-82.

Using non-technical words, the implications of the feeding patterns of the spider and howler monkeys on Barro Colorado, as studied by anthropologist Katherine Milton, are developed in the narrative and then summarized.

96 The jungle bees and wasps of Barro Colorado Island (with notes on other insects).

Phil Rau. Kirkwood, Missouri: Published by the Author, 1933. 324p.

If any reader thinks that concern for the environment is new, this study dating from the early thirties may change his mind. The author writes sensitively of the ecology of Barro Colorado, of its stingless bees and paper-making wasps. There are shorter notes on some spiders, beetles and butterflies.

97 Mammals of the neotropics.

John Frederick Eisenberg. Chicago: University of Chicago Press, 1989. 2 vols.

Volume 1 discusses the northern neotropics: Panama, Colombia, Venezuela, Guyana, Suriname, French Guiana, while Volume 2 covers the Southern Cone: Chile, Argentina, Uruguay, Paraguay.

98 Mammals of San José Island, Bay of Panama.

Remmington Kellog. Washington, DC: Smithsonian Institution, 1946. 4p. (Smithsonian Miscellaneous Collection, vol. 106, no. 61).

Several unusual species of bat, rat, anteater and deer are described from field observation.

99 Mass mortality and population declines of anurans at an upland site in Western Panama.

Karen R. Lips. *Conservation Biology*, vol. 13 (February 1999), p. 117-26.

Frogs and other amphibians are indicators of general environmental health. This study examines the causes of the fungal infection in anurans in Western Panama.

100 Nest predation and differential insular extinction among selected forest birds of central Panama.

Kathryn E. Sieving. *Ecology*, vol. 73, no. 6 (December 1992), p. 2310-29.

The researcher addresses the question of what impact predators of nests have on the survival of some forest birds in central Panama. The research technique is elaborated and conclusions drawn about long-term adaptation to assure survival of nestlings.

101 Nights – and days – of the iguana.

Jeffrey P. Cohn. *Americas* (English Edition), vol. 39 (July-August 1987), p. 34-39.

Protein deficiency is endemic in the tropics. The author describes a project in Soberania National Park to raise iguanas in captivity. The iguana is considered a delicacy and would help resolve the nutrition problem. The researchers learned that iguanas must be raised in captivity from eggs in order to breed.

102 The non-marine mollusks of San José Island, with notes on those of Pedro Gonzalez Island, Pearl Island, Panama.
J. P. E. Morrison. Washington, DC: Smithsonian Institution, 1946. 49p. (Smithsonian Miscellaneous Collection, vol. 106, no. 5).

In this detailed and scientific description of non-marine molluscs, thirty-six species are illustrated in the plates and identified.

103 Production, energy pathways and community diversity in forest birds.
James R. Karr. In: *Tropical ecological systems: trends in terrestrial and aquatic research.* Edited by Frank B. Golley, Ernesto Medina. New York; Heidelberg, Germany; Berlin: Springer-Verlag, 1975, p. 161-76.

A comparative study of birds in the tropical forests of Panama and Liberia and in the temperate forest on Puercos Island, Illinois. It investigates the question 'Why are there more species of birds in tropical than in temperate zones?' The greater abundance of foodstuffs is one answer, suggests Karr, as well as the greater living space the tropical forests offer.

104 Resource use by five sympatric parrotfishes in the San Blas Archipelago, Panama.
S. T. McAfee, S. G. Morgan. *Marine Biology,* vol. 125, no. 3 (July 1996), p. 427-58.

The authors present a scientific study of patterns of fish development in the San Blas Archipelago and their movement through the corals as they grow.

105 Seasonal abundance of migrant birds and food resources in Panamanian mangrove forests.
Gaetan Lefebvre, Brigitte Poulin. *Wilson Bulletin,* vol. 108, no. 4 (December 1996), p. 748-60.

Basic science of migrant birds and their dependence on the present-day ecology of Panama's mangrove swamps is presented here. This research is vital for preservation of the flora and fauna of the hemisphere.

106 Site guides – Costa Rica and Panama: the best birding locations.
Dennis W. Rogers. San José, Costa Rica: Cinclus, 1996. 183p. maps.

An extensive coverage of the most rewarding birdwatching sites in Costa Rica and Panama with lists of species seen in the regions. Checklists are provided for each of the selected areas.

107   Survival rates of Puerto Rican birds: are islands really that different?
John Faaborg, Wayne J. Arendt.   *The Auk*, vol. 112, no. 2 (April 1995), p. 503-07.

Panama birds are used for this comparison study of tropical and temperate zone birds. Focus is on breeding patterns in dry forest environments and species. The study suggests that the generalization that if birds have high survival rates they will have small clutches of eggs does not hold true for the tropics in general.

108   A travel and site guide to birds of Costa Rica: with side trips to Panama and Nicaragua.
A. D. Sekerak.   Edmonton, Canada: LonePine, 1996. 256p. maps.

Although most of this book is devoted to Costa Rica, useful indications of birding sites for Panama are also given. Sites are detailed in chart form. It was co-published by Ediciones Naturaleza, Costa Rica.

109   Turtles collected by the Smithsonian Biological Survey of the Panama Canal Zone.
Karl Patterson Schmidt.   Washington, DC: Smithsonian Institution, 1946. 6p. (Smithsonian Miscellaneous Collection, vol. 106, no. 8).

This is a brief survey of what is known about turtles in Panama and a description of some of the eight land and freshwater turtle species observed there.

110   Where eagles dare: climb to the top of the Panama rain forest.
Ron Magill.   *Wildlife Conservation*, vol. 101, no. 1 (January-February 1998), p. 42-48.

This account of finding and electronically tagging harpy eagles includes details of the capture of both adult and baby eagles, and explains how transmitters are attached to them for further research. The setting is Chagres National Park.

Prehistory and Archaeology

Prehistory

111 A 14 300-yr paleoecological profile of a lowland tropical lake in Panama.
Mark B. Bush, Dolores R. Piperno, Paul A. Colinvaux, Paulo E. De Oliveira, Lawrence A. Krissek, Michael C. Miller, William E. Rowe. *Ecological Monographs*. vol. 65, no. 2 (June 1992), p. 251-65.
This is a detailed analysis of the changes in lowland vegetation in prehistoric times.

112 Adaptive radiation in prehistoric Panama.
Olga F. Linares, Anthony J. Ranere.   Cambridge, Massachusetts: Peabody Museum, Harvard University, 1980. 530p. (Peabody Museum Monograph, no. 5).
The authors present a comparative study of how man adapts himself to his environment. The areas of comparison in this long study are Bocas del Toro on the Atlantic side of Panama and Chiriquí province on the Pacific side. The authors aimed 'to investigate the evolution of agricultural villages from a preceramic hunting-gathering base and then to document the expansion out of the highlands to the coast'. A careful, useful tool.

113 Adaptive strategies in western Panama.
Olga F. Linares.   *World Archaeology*, vol. 8 (February 1977), p. 304-19. map. bibliog.
Two ancient peoples of Bocas and Chiriquí were compared to see how and why they moved their habitations and changed their farming areas.

114 Ancient Panama; chiefs in search of power.
Mary W. Helms. Austin, Texas; London: University of Texas Press, 1979. 228p. maps. (Texas Panamerican Series).
A noted scholar studies the chiefdoms of Panama as they existed just prior to the European discovery of lower Central America. Analogies are made with similar tribal power structures in other geographical areas. The author focuses on the information exchange between powerful Colombian groups and their non-neighbouring Panamanian groups. She concludes that political applications of information were more important than any other application. Records available for this study were those kept by the early Spaniards who controlled the countryside through the chiefs (much in the manner of Lord Lugard in Africa). Topics covered include fields of influence, symbolism and power, ideology and exchange, with special attention to Colombian modes of exercising power over a relatively long distance.

115 Aproximación a la obra de Reina Torres de Arauz. (A sense of the work of Reina Torres de Arauz.)
Panama City: Instituto Nacional de Cultura, 1983. 450p. bibliog.
A commemorative volume that includes essays on the work of Dr Arauz from a spectrum of Panama's intellectuals. Dr Arauz, as professor of anthropology and director of the National Cultural Institute, played a vital role in the dissemination of popular culture in its deepest sense, and in the preservation of the national heritage. There is a very comprehensive bibliography of her publications and a detailed curriculum vitae.

116 The Central American republics.
Franklin D. Parker. London: Oxford University Press, 1964. 348p. map.
The Republic of Panama is not discussed in this book, but its early chapters, 'Birth of an isthmus', 'Remains of antiquity', and 'The indigenous population' are useful for a general understanding of the prehistory period of Panama within the context of Central America as a whole.

117 Colombia.
Gerardo Reichel-Dolmatoff. London: Thames & Hudson, 1965. 231p. maps. bibliog. (Ancient Peoples and Places).
In this comprehensive discussion of the prehistory of Colombia, the isthmus of Panama is given extensive treatment. The introduction provides a survey of early explorers and archaeologists. Other topics covered include geography and climate, economic activities and social organization.

118 Competition, power and succession to office in pre-Columbian Panama.
Mary W. Helms. In: *Frontier adaptations in lower Central America.* Edited by Mary W. Helms, Franklin O. Loveland. Philadelphia: Institute for the Study of Human Issues, 1976, p. 25-36. bibliog.

Women on occasion succeeded their fathers among the élite of pre-Columbian Panama; however, they did not exercise public power. This study assesses available evidence and concludes that major modifications of this factor occurred after the Conquest.

119 Cultural chronology of the Gulf of Chiriquí, Panama.
Olga F. Linares. Washington, DC: Smithsonian Institution, 1968. 119p. maps.

Although this monograph is intended for the specialist, the long introduction offers the general reader a clear description of the geography of Chiriquí and a history of archaeological exploration in the area. The bulk of the monograph details work done on specific sites.

120 Ecology and the arts in ancient Panama; on the development of social rank and symbolism in the central provinces.
Olga F. Linares. Washington, DC: Dumbarton Oaks, Trustees for Harvard University, 1977. 86p. maps. bibliog. (Studies in Pre-Columbian Art and Archaeology, 17).

This carefully illustrated monograph gives a new interpretation to what is usually called 'Coclé art'. The author discusses the effect of the environment, notably the rich alluvial lands along the coast, on the aesthetic development of the peoples of the pre-Columbian period, the spread of certain art forms into neighbouring areas, and related subjects. Clear drawings as well as photographs of the ceramic designs add considerably to the study, as does the survey of earlier work done in the field.

121 Guardians of the life stream: shamans, art and power in prehispanic central Panama.
Armand J. Labbe, with a foreword by Peter Keller, illustrations by Joseph Kramer, edited by Aleida Rodriguez. Santa Ana, California: Cultural Arts Press, The Bowers Museum of Cultural Art; distributed by the University of Washington Press, 1995. 168p.

The author argues that the pre-Columbian art of Panama ranks high for its aesthetic expression and provides a reference text for the art of Central Panama. Thoroughly illustrated, the material is organized around the history, neotropical and new-world shamanism, and a discussion of the dualism of the shamanic cosmos as represented by the art. A chronology places each art form and a glossary defines key terms in the text. The list of photographs includes a standard art description of each item and its location.

122 **Natá prehispánico.** (Natá [Coclé, Panama] before the coming of the Spaniards.)
Reina Torres de Arauz. Panama City: Instituto Nacional de Cultura, 1992. 2nd ed. 155p. bibliog.

The first part of the work establishes the nature and extent of indigenous culture of the people of Natá before the coming of the Spanish conquistadors. The second part describes the partial destruction of that culture with the arrival of the Europeans. The text is enriched by a glossary of specialized terms, black-and white photographs of artefacts and fauna, and modern Spanish versions of relevant historical documents.

123 **The preceramic age of Panama: the view from the interior.**
Anthony J. Ranere. In: *Puerto Rican Symposium on Archaeology, 1, Santurce, P.R., 1976. Proceedings.* San Juan: Fundación Arqueológica de Puerto Rico, 1976, p. 103-39. bibliog.

Little research has been done in the interior of Panama compared to that done on the coasts. Ranere analyses the evidence of both pre- and post-agricultural societies in tropical forests.

124 **Prehistoric agriculture in tropical highlands.**
Olga F. Linares, Payson D. Sheets, E. Jane Rosenthal. *Science* (USA), vol. 187 (17 January 1975), p. 137-45.

The effect of agriculture on social patterns in prehistoric Panama is described in this article, with emphasis on the differences before and after the introduction of corn (maize).

125 **Prehistoric human adaptations to the seasonally dry forests of Panama.**
Richard Cooke, Anthony J. Ranere. *World Archaeology*, vol. 24, no. 1 (June 1992), p. 114-35.

The question the authors pose is what evidence exists today to show that prehistoric man inhabited tropical forests. Based on the Pacific watershed of western Panama, Cooke and Ranere conclude that there is evidence of continuous habitation from about 11,000 BP, that the population increased and some vegetal domestication occurred.

126 **Reinterpreting prehistory of Central America.**
Edited by Mark Miller Graham. Niwot, Colorado: University Press of Colorado, 1993. 336p.

Papers presented at a conference held at the Denver Museum of Natural History, 1-4 November 1990 include Richard Cooke's 'Cosmological chromatics: colour-related symbolism in the ceramic art of ancient Panama', Peter S. Brigg's 'Animal icons and Pre-Columbian society: the Felidae with special reference to Panama', as well as several regional studies. All papers make use of the major revisions in interpreting the development of Central American culture.

127 Wealth and hierarchy in the Intermediate Area: a symposium at Dumbarton Oaks, 10th and 11th October 1987.
Edited by Frederick W. Lange. Washington, DC: Dumbarton Oaks Research Library and Collection, 1992. 463p. maps.

This collection of papers dealing with the antiquities of the Central American area includes several discussions of prehistoric Panama. It is invaluable for contextualizing the several Panamanian anthropology and related studies. A useful bibliography is provided.

Archaeology

128 Ancient American pottery.
G. H. S. Bushnell, Adrian Digby. London: Faber & Faber, 1955. 51p. bibliog.

In this profusely illustrated work with over seventy plates, the most famous examples of Panamanian pottery are discussed and illustrated on pages 25-27.

129 Ancient arts of the Americas.
G. H. S. Bushnell. New York: Praeger; London: Thames & Hudson, 1965. 287p.

The sixth chapter deals with Central America, with illustrations showing metalwork, especially gold, which developed in this area before it developed in Mexico, and stone carvings and polychrome pottery. Some of the artefacts illustrated are housed at Cambridge University.

130 Archaeological investigations in the Parita and Santa Maria zones of Panama.
John Ladd. Washington, DC: US Government Printing Office, 1964. 291p. maps.

Ladd's detailed survey of Panama's archaeology is illustrated by drawings and plates of pottery, with precise technical descriptions of the sites on which they were discovered.

131 Archaeology of southern Veraguas.
Samuel K. Lothrop. New York: Kraus, 1979. 116p.

Originally published as no. 3, vol. 9 of the *Memoirs* of the Peabody Museum of Archaeology and Ethnology, Harvard University, this reprint is a heavily illustrated monograph that covers the chronology of sites in Veraguas province and their stone artefacts, pottery, and metalwork including jewellery. The illustrations are mostly drawings and black-and-white photographs of items at the Peabody Museum.

132 **Archéologie du sud de la péninsule d'Azuero, Panama.**
(Archaeology of the southern Azuero peninsula, Panama.)
A. Inchon. Lille, France: Service de reproduction des thèses,
Université de Lille III, 1974. 507p. bibliog.
This thorough overview of archaeology in the Azuero area of Panama is written by a
member of the Research Institute in Panama.

133 **Archeology and pre-Columbian art in Panama.**
Philip L. Dade. *Ethnos,* vol. 37 (1972), p. 148-67. bibliog.
Dade counters S. K. Lothrop's theory of the spread of Coclé culture throughout most of
Panama with his own more limited theory in which there was more exchange among
aboriginal groups, rather than dominance from Coclé. Ceramics are used as the basis of
his proof.

134 **Central American and West Indian archeology.**
Thomas A. Joyce. New York: Benjamin Blom, 1971. 270p. maps.
An introduction for the general reader to the archaeology of Nicaragua, Costa Rica,
Panama and the West Indies, which, because it includes so much contiguous territory,
must be comparative. Panama is extensively treated on pages 90-152. The author, who
also wrote about the archaeology of South America and Mexico, describes pottery,
religious artefacts and the like. An early work in modern archaeology, this was reprinted
from the 1916 London edition.

135 **Coclé; an archaeological study of central Panama.**
Samuel K. Lothrop. New York: Kraus, 1979. 2 vols.
We have here the unabridged text and illustrations, first published in 1942, from which
selections were made for *Pre-Columbian designs from Panama* (q.v.).

136 **History of Latin American archaeology.**
Edited by Augusto Oyuela-Caycedo. Aldershot, England;
Brookfield, Vermont: Avebury, 1994. 212p. bibliog. (Worldwide
Archaeology Series, 15).
The book is divided into two parts. The first part, Archaeology and State, looks in general
at national interests in archaeological research. The sole Panamanian contribution is by
Carlos M. Fitzgerald: 'Panama: Archaeology, archaeologists and recent developments'
(p. 90-103). The author describes both the governmental and private archaeology
activities, considering the needs for both specialist and generalist archaeologists, and
concludes that since most Central American countries cannot support advanced training
in archaeology, a regional school would be useful. A bibliography of much of the work
of Panamanian scholars mentioned in the paper is appended.

137 Nuevo análisis de carbono-14 para Panamá, al este de Chiriquí: una actualización de los cambios culturales prehistóricos.
(New carbon-14 analysis of Panama east of Chiriquí; a realization of prehistoric cultural exchange.)
Richard G. Cooke. La Antigua (Panama), vol. 5 (May 1976), p. 88-117. map. bibliog.

Cooke's summary of carbon-14 dating of Panamanian archaeological sites gives thirty-nine new dates which are used as the basis of a discussion of changes in cultural patterns in the area east of Chiriquí.

138 Paths to Central American prehistory.
Edited by Frederick W. Lange. Niwot, Colorado: University Press of Colorado, 1996. 379p. maps.

A symposium in honour of archaeologist Wolfgang Haberland which gives a detailed overview of the work of archaeologists and art historians in Panama and lower Central America from the earliest times. It ends with an analysis of knowledge gaps.

139 Pre-Columbian designs from Panama.
Samuel Kirkland Lothrop. New York: Dover, 1976. 108p.

The editors selected nearly 600 illustrations of Coclé pottery from two of the author's publications: Coclé, an archaeological study of central Panama (see item no. 135), and Pottery of the Sitio Conte and other archaeological sites first published in 1942 as part of the Memoirs of the Peabody Museum of Archaeology and Ethnology, Harvard University. Coclé pottery is known for its striking geometric and abstract patterns and animal shapes.

140 River of Gold: precolumbian treasures from Sitio Conte.
Edited by Pamela Hearne, Robert J. Sharer. Philadelphia: University Museum, University of Pennsylvania, 1992. 132p. maps.

The Sitio Conte archaeological site was not known for centuries either to those who lived in Panama or to those who visited it. Then, in 1927 when the Río Grande de Coclé flooded, it changed its channel and revealed a pre-Columbian burial ground. Early excavations discovered architectural remnants and pottery, but in March 1940 the important gold artefacts that form the subject of this exhibition catalogue were found. Included in this collection, now at the University of Pennsylvania, are the gold arm and ankle cuffs and other regalia worn by paramount chiefs, animal effigy pendants, and the like. Other finds, arrow heads and ceramics are included. This exhibition catalogue was prepared for the travelling exhibition mounted in 1992.

141 **Simposium nacional de antropologia, arqueología y etnehistoria de Panamá 11, Panamá, 1971. Actas.** (National Symposium on Anthropology, Archaeology and Ethnohistory of Panama 11, Panama, 1971. Proceedings.)
Panama City: University of Panama. Centro de Investigaciones Antropológicas, Instituto Nacional de Cultura y Deportes, Dirección del Patrimonio Histórico, 1972. 515p. bibliog.

Topics covered in the papers making up this collection about archaeological research in Panama include reports on activities in Chiriquí, Bocas del Toro, Valle de Tonosí, Lake Madden, Sona, Coclé, Chepo, Gatún and Darien – often a summary of several years of fieldwork. Several articles deal with the carbon-dating techniques employed and their results.

142 **Síntesis de arqueología.** (Archaeological synthesis.)
Gladys Casimir de Bruizuela. Panama City: Editorial Universitaria, 1973. 221p. bibliog.

This work covers Panamanian archaeological sites by region, preceded by essays on the geography, economy, technology and social structure. It is well illustrated by time charts showing the development of different groups of inhabitants as manifested in their artefacts.

143 **A study of Chiriquian antiquities.**
George Grant MacCurdy. New Haven, Connecticut: Yale University Press, 1911. Reprinted, Melwood, New York: Kraus, 1976. 249p. map. (Memoirs of the Connecticut Academy of Arts and Sciences, vol. 3).

Basing his remarks on the collection owned by Yale University, the author (who at the time of writing was curator of Yale's Anthropological Museum) discusses and meticulously describes artefacts, mostly ceramics, from western Panama. Nearly 400 drawings illustrate the text and there are black-and-white photographs.

History

General

144 Central America, a nation divided.
Ralph Lee Woodward, Jr.   New York: Oxford University Press,
1976. 344p. bibliog. (Latin American Histories).

A general history of Central America from 1501 to the present, which has as its thesis that a truly viable nation could be formed from the presently existing Central American countries. It is of use to the student of Panama for showing the context in which that country has developed. There is a political chronology table and 'A selective guide to the literature on Central America'.

145 Les grandes heures de l'histoire de Panama. (The greatest hours in Panamanian history.)
Guy Vattier.   Paris: Productions de Paris, 1965. 217p.

These are the key episodes in Panamanian history from the French point of view. The author explains the transfer of the Nouvelle Compagnie, charged with building the canal, to American control as part of American policy to build an American canal 'sur territoire américain'.

146 Historia de Centroamérica. (History of Central America.)
Ernesto Chinchilla Aguilar.   Guatemala City: Editorial José de
Pineda Ibarra, 1975. 3 vols.

The first volume is devoted to pre-Columbian times, the second to the colonial period and the last to modern times. The author is a Guatemalan and emphasizes that country's history, but the work is useful for an overview of Central American history and provides a context for Panama.

147 **Historia de Panamá.** (History of Panama.)
Enrique Jose Arce, Ernesto J. Castillero Reyes. Rosario, Argentina:
Published by the Author, 1949. 4th ed. 173p.
Originally published under the title *Guía histórica de Panamá* (Historical guide to
Panama) in 1942, this work covers from the earliest days to 1942. The last part is a
description of governmental activities only.

148 **La isla que se transformó en ciudad; historia de un siglo de la
ciudad de Colón.** (The island which changed into a city; history of a
century of the city of Colón.)
Ernesto J. Castillero Reyes. Panama City: Published by the Author,
1967. 270p.
A history of the most populous and economically important city on the Atlantic side of
Panama. It covers more than the century of the title and is one of the more substantial
works written to commemorate the centenary of the founding of Colón as a modern city.

149 **Middle America: a culture history of heartland and frontiers.**
Mary W. Helms. Englewood Cliffs, New Jersey: Prentice-Hall,
1975. 367p. maps. bibliog.
In this introduction to Middle America's anthropology from an historical point of view,
there are three parts: the evolution of pre-Columbian civilization, the Viceroyalty of New
Spain, and the challenge of nation-building. The work incorporates recent research and is
well documented. Of special interest for Panama are the chapters 'The banana – and
coffee – republics' and 'Reform and reaction in Central America'.

150 **Panama.**
Ashley Carter. New York: Fawcett, 1978. 380p. (Gold Medal
Books).
A fictionalized and spirited retelling of the story of Panama during the time of the
building of the Panama Canal, by a well-known author of popular novels.

151 **Panama.**
Eric Zencey. New York: Farrar, Straus & Giroux, 1995. 375p.
These fictional accounts of John Hay and Henry Adams during the period of the collapse
of the first Panama Canal Company include some of the legal action that led to the
conviction of Ferdinand de Lesseps. Hay later authored the two treaties relating to the
canal, one denying international control of the canal, and the other acquiring the zone, two
treaties that would shape all subsequent events in US–Panamanian dealings.

152 **Panama, 400 years of dreams and cruelty.**
David Howarth. London: Collins, 1966. 285p. map. bibliog.
The author relates the significant episodes in Panamanian history from 1502 to 1966. The
story of the short-lived Scottish settlement on Caledonia Bay is told, a story which has
been brought into recent prominence by the 1978 marine archaeological expedition to
raise the *Olive Branch*, one of the settlement's supply ships. No new information is given

here; rather the purpose is to convey existing knowledge to a general reader in an entertaining manner. The US edition bears the title *The golden isthmus*.

153 Panama of today.
Alpheus H. Verrill. New York: Dodd, Mead, 1927. 314p.

Verrill lived in Panama during the French attempt to build the canal and for many years afterwards. Although many American and European residents of Panama contributed their memoirs to the written record of Panama's history, Verrill was a student of aboriginal societies in both North and South America and thus has a more informed viewpoint than many of his contemporaries.

154 Panama story.
Jean Niemeier. Portland, Oregon: Metropolitan Press, Binford, 1968. 303p. bibliog.

This volume consists of extracts, chiefly from the *Panama Star and Herald* and *La Estrella de Panamá*, an English- and Spanish-edition newspaper, with a connecting text. It covers the years 1850-1966 and has many explanatory notes.

Age of exploration

155 Bottles from Parita, Panama.
Philip L. Dade. *Archaeology,* vol. 25 (January 1972), p. 35-47. map.

This is a copiously illustrated article on bottles excavated in Parita in 1966 and 1967. Carbon-14 dating techniques suggest that the bottles, whose design and uses are discussed, were buried at some time between 1400 and 1500.

156 Christopher Columbus.
John Stewart Collis. London: MacDonald & Jane's, 1976; New York: Stein & Day, 1977. 208p. maps. bibliog.

On his fourth and last voyage of exploration Columbus discovered Panama, and, as Collis points out in this book, was impatient to continue on his voyage. At this point Columbus considered himself to be in the Strait of Malacca and thus nearly in sight of his goal. This work, with its maps of the world as known today and as known in the time of Columbus, emphasizes the geographical aspects of exploration. Although never letting the reader forget Columbus's misunderstanding of his great contribution to the world, Collis shows him as a great man in his own way. The fourth voyage is treated in the chapter 'The last voyage'.

157 Colección de los viages y descubrimientos que hicieron por mar los espanoles desde fines del siglo XV: con varios documentos ineditos concernientes a la historia de la marina castellana y de los establecimientos españoles en Indias / coordinada y illustrada por don Martin Fernandez de Navarrete. (Collection of the voyages and discoveries made by sea by Spaniards since the end of the 15th century: with various unedited documents concerning the history of Castillan navigation and the Spanish foundations in the Indies, arranged and illustrated by don Martin de Navarrete.)
Martin Fernandez de Navarrete. Madrid: Imprenta real, 1825-37. 5 vols. maps.

Early in the 19th century, Don Martin selected from several archival resources in Spain documents relating to the great Spanish explorations of the Age of Discovery. Four of the five volumes include material relating to the New World, while the fifth concerns Indonesia. Of special interest are the materials in the third volume, which concerns coastal exploration of Panama on the Atlantic side. The documents include journals – Columbus's journals form volume 1 and part of volume 2 – and letters, many from the king and queen authorizing the voyages and detailing the conditions to be met. The copy in the New York Public Library Center for Humanities bears the bookplate of George Bancroft (1800-91), diplomat and historian. His 10-volume *History of the United States* was published between 1834 and 1874, and may have benefited from this documentary collection.

158 De orbe nova; the eight decades of Peter Martyr D'Anghiera.
Peter Martyr D'Anghiera, translated and introduced by Frances A. MacNutt. New York: Putnam, 1912. 2 vols.

This work was translated from its Latin original by Frances A. MacNutt who also provides the long introduction. First published in 1530, *De orbe nova* is an example of some of the earliest documentation of the exploration of the New World.

159 The European discovery of America; the southern voyages, A.D. 1492-1616.
Samuel Eliot Morison. New York: Oxford University Press, 1974. 2 vols. bibliog.

The first volume of this lively, authoritative work contains a discussion of Columbus's fourth voyage and an account of Balboa's discovery of the Pacific Ocean. The Columbus account (p. 236-70) includes a bibliography of sources. Balboa and the Pacific are covered on pages 200-06.

160 El hombre y la sierra en Panamá, siglo XVI, según las primeras fuentes. (Man and land in 16th-century Panama according to original sources.)
Elsa Mercado Sousa. Madrid: University of Madrid, Seminario de Estudias Americanistas, 1959. 460p. maps.

This detailed description of Panama in the 16th century is based on original documents. Topics include not only activities of the major explorers such as Balboa, but also explorations by lesser-known figures such as Rodrigo de Colemares. An appendix gives a list and explanation of Panamanian words in use in the Spanish documents of the period. Spanish archives were the main source of materials.

161 The life and voyages of Christopher Columbus.
Washington Irving. Madison, Wisconsin: University of Wisconsin Press, 1970. 3 vols. (Collected Works of Washington Irving, vols. 5-7).

Irving was stimulated by the publication in 1826 of documents relating to the discovery of the New World and he set out to write a full account of the voyages of discovery. The fourth voyage is covered in Book XV, in the third volume of the work.

162 The lost treasure of Sir Francis Drake.
John Thrower. Powerstock, England: Published by the Author, 1996. 66p. maps.

In this treasure-hunting item Thrower discusses the history of Nombre de Dios and Sir Francis Drake.

163 New voyage and description of the Isthmus of America. Los viajes de Lionel Wafer al Istmo del Darién: (cuatro meses entre las indios). (The voyages of Lionel Wafer to the Isthmus of Darien: [four months among the Indians].)
Lionel Wafer, introduced and translated by Vicente Restrepo, illustrated by Mario Velez. Medellín, Colombia: Ediciones Gráficas, 1990. 3rd ed. 129p. (Colección Biblioteca popular de Uraba, vol. 3).

This modern translation and edition is for the general reader. Wafer's voyages, first published in 1699, are frequently reprinted in both England and the United States. This entry is a South American translation into Spanish. Wafer, who was both a surgeon and a pirate, crossed the isthmus from north to south taking several months to do so, during which time he observed in detail the flora and fauna and Indian life, especially medical lore.

164 The travels of Pedro de Cieza de León, A.D. 1532-50.
Pedro de Cieza de León, introduction by Charles Markham. New York: Burt Franklin, 1977. 438p. maps.

This is the first part of the author's *Chronicles of Peru,* first published in Seville. Cieza de León (1519-60) became a part of the Spanish exploration of the New World at the age of fourteen. He gives a brief account of Panama in the 16th century since he felt that Panama offered the key to understanding Latin America. A lengthy introduction is provided by Charles Markham. The work was previously published in 1865 as volume 33 of the *Hakluyt Society Proceedings.*

Colonial period

165 220 años del período colonial en Panamá. (220 years of the colonial period in Panama.)
Rubén Darío Carles. Panama City: Published by the Author, 1949. 165p. maps.
Panama City is the focal point for a history of the colonial period, 1519-1821.

166 El asalto a la ciudad de Panamá. (The attack on Panama City.)
Ernesto J. Castillero Reyes. *Lotería,* no. 222-23 (August-September 1974), p. 39-49.
The author gives a brief account of the sack of Panama City (1671) from a Panamanian point of view.

167 The buccaneers in the West Indies in the XVII century.
C. H. Haring. Hamden, Connecticut: Archon Books, 1966. 298p. bibliog.
This early 20th-century work, now reprinted from the 1910 edition, has an excellent discussion of the sources for pirate history. Panama, which both sheltered and suffered pirates, is discussed on pages 120-99. Vivid accounts of such events as the sack of Panama City, which marked the apex of buccaneer activity on the isthmus, make exciting reading.

168 The buccaneers of America.
A. O. Exquemelin, translated by Alexis Brown. London: Folio Society, 1972. 194p.
A beautiful and well-designed edition of a work which first appeared in the 17th century and has excited armchair travellers ever since. This translation was originally published in a Penguin edition in 1969. Andrew Lang edited an edition in the late 19th century and his essay on Exquemelin appears in his *Essays in little.*

169 La ciudad de Panamá en el siglo XVIII, propriedad urbane y proprietarios del intramuro en 1756. (Panama City in the 18th century; urban property and property owners in 1756.)
Omar Jaén Suárez. *Estudios Sociales Centroamericanos,* vol. 5 (September-December 1976), p. 33-49.
This is the first part of a two-part series (see also the following item). It discusses sources of data, architecture and city planning, houses and furnishings.

170 La ciudad de Panamá en el siglo XVIII, propriedad urbane y proprietarios del intramuro en 1756. Parte II. (Panama City in the 18th century; urban property and property owners in 1756. Part II.) Omar Jaén Suárez. *Estudios Sociales Centroamericanos*, vol. 5 (January-April 1977), p. 9-22.

This second article describes the property owners and the social and economic environment of Panama City in the second half of the 18th century.

171 Founding of the Darien Colony.

Richard Cavendish. *History Today* (November 1998), p. 48-57.

An exciting retelling of the founding of the Scottish settlement in 17th-century Panama, a land that was a far cry from their native Scotland. Panama was a trading centre (see Christopher Ward, item nos. 172, 174) and William Paterson, an astute financier, was well aware of it, but he was unaware of the rigours of a hot and humid climate. Cavendish links this attempted settlement to the international politics of the time, and places the event in history.

172 Historical writing on colonial Panama.

Christopher Ward. *Hispanic American Historical Review*, vol. 69, no. 4 (November 1989), p. 691-722.

In his critical and annotated bibliography and discussion of the historiography of colonial Panama, Ward has the gift of making his period of history come alive.

173 A history of William Paterson and the Darien Company.

James S. Barbour. Edinburgh; London: Blackwood, 1908. 284p. bibliog.

Paterson (1658-1719) founded the Bank of England in his later years. His association with Panama began when he established the Darien Company in Scotland to compete with the East India Company of England. This work discusses many of the financial aspects of floating a company of this nature, the Caledonia Bay settlement (1698-1700), and the like.

174 Imperial Panama: commerce and conflict in isthmian America, 1550-1800.

Christopher Ward. Albuquerque, New Mexico: University of New Mexico Press, 1993. 272p. maps.

Ward argues for the importance of Panama as a trading centre critical to the continued prosperity of the Spanish Empire. In a vivid account of Portobelo and its annual trade fair, the author brings to life the heady days of political and economic growth of the Panamanian colonies and the region as a whole. Underlying the account is carefully documented scholarship and full references; some contemporary documents are given in full in translation.

175 **Llanto de Panamá a la muerte de Don Enrique Enríquez.**
(Panama laments the death of Don Enrique Enríquez.)
Edited by Antonio Serrano de Haro.   Panama City: Editorial
Universitaria, Universitad de Panamá; Madrid: Ediciones Cultura
Hispánica, Instituto de Cooperación Iberoamericana, 1984. 241p.

Don Enrique Enríquez (1600-38) was an early colonial official, whose death occasioned
this collection of tributes, first published in 1642. This edition is furnished with an
extensive introduction that includes biographies of the contributors as well as one of
Enríquez. It is illustrated by prints, portraits and maps.

176 **Narrative of the proceedings of Pedrarias Dávila in the province
of Tierra Firme or Castilla del Oro, and of the discovery of the
South Sea and the coasts of Peru and Nicaragua.**
Pascual de Andagoya, introduced by Clements R. Markham.
New York: Burt Franklin, 1970. 88p.

Pedrarias was governor of Panama from 1519 to 1526, succeeding Balboa whom he
accused of treason and executed. This work was first published in 1912 as volume 24 of
the *Hakluyt Society Works.*

177 **Old Panama and Castilla del Oro.**
Charles Anderson.   Washington, DC: Sudwath, 1911. 559p. maps.

A detailed history of the discovery, conquest, and settlement of Panama by the Spanish
from the voyages of Columbus to the sack of Panama City by the English pirates and the
foundation and failure of the Scottish settlement at Darien. Anderson dedicated his
leisurely study to the builders of the Panama Canal who were still at work when it was
published. Anderson was a doctor with the Isthmian Commission. Early maps add
interest.

178 **Panama is burning.**
P. S. Lindsay.   New York: Farrar, 1932. 346p.

A fictionalized account of Sir Henry Morgan's march across the isthmus to capture and
sack old Panama City. The historical details are accurate and vividly depicted. This is a
painless way to acquire history.

179 **Pioneers in tropical America.**
Harry Johnston.   London: Blackie, 1914. 320p. (Pioneers of the
British Empire).

Johnston, who made his name and fame exploring Central and East Africa (Fort Johnston
in Malawi was named after him), wrote a series of books of historical adventure. The
pioneers of the British Empire in this case were Henry Morgan, Lionel Wafer and
company and their adventures are described on pages 183-212. The insight of the former
explorer adds much verisimilitude.

180 La plaza fortificada de Panamá. (Panama's fortress.)
Juan M. Zapatero. *Ibero-Amerikanisches Archiv,* vol. 2 (1976),
p. 227-56. maps.

A military historian analyses the development of Panama's fortifications from 1586 to
1818.

181 La política internacional y la piratería en el siglo XVIII.
(International politics and piracy in the 18th century.)
John Parry. *Razón y Fábula,* vol. 35 (1974), p. 60-73.

A noted historian of the sea discusses Spanish and British governmental policy and piracy
on the Spanish Main.

182 Portobelo, a bridge between two oceans.
José Serra-Vega. *UNESCO Courier* (October 1993), p. 45-49.

Today Portobelo is a UNESCO World Heritage Site, but during its heyday it saw bags of
gold piled high in the square during its annual hemispheric trade fair. The romantic ruins
of Fort San Lorenzo, shown in colourful photographs, suggest this past glory which was
blighted by disease and pirate depredations.

**183 The sack of Panama: Sir Henry Morgan's adventures on the
Spanish Main.**
Peter Earle. New York: Viking Press, 1982. 304p. bibliog.

In his entertaining account of a picaresque piece of history – but one based on sound
research – the author has made fuller use of the colonial archives in Seville, the Archivo
General de Indias, than earlier accounts. Although not reversing the usual conclusions
about Morgan's life and works, Earle does reinforce this nearly final use by the English
crown of pirates to further foreign policy, especially the containment of Spain in the New
World. A clear map and reproductions of contemporary engravings of the battles,
fortifications and geographical features that figure in the account enrich the text.

184 The Spanish Main, focus of envy 1492-1700.
Philip Ainsworth Means. New York: Gordian Press, 1965. 278p.
bibliog.

Panama was valuable to marauding pirates, sometimes as many as 400 strong, both for
loot and as a staging area. This book, reprinted from the 1931 edition, discusses the
political policies of various countries towards the Spanish sphere of influence in the New
World, which officially or unofficially, enabled the privateers to control the area as they
wished. The author also treats of the Scottish settlement at Caledonia Bay, giving his
opinion that as this group also dealt in contraband, it therefore should be considered a part
of the privateers. Panama is discussed especially on pages 202-31.

185 **Tercer centenario del Palacio de las Garzas.** (The third centenary of the Palace of the Garzas.)
Ernesto J. Castillero Reyes. *Lotería,* no. 205 (January 1973), p. 1-12.

An illustrated history of Panama's presidential palace from its construction in the 17th century for the colonial governor, through its other uses, to its present role as the official residence of the president. Both the building and its art objects are described and placed in the historical context.

186 **Tertulia española: paginas panameñas de anteayer.** (A Spanish gathering: Panamanian pages from yesteryear.)
Antonio Serrano de Haro. Panama City: Editorial Universitaria, 1986. 207p. (Serie Ciencias Sociales. Sección Crónicas y Monográfias).

Historical sketches and excerpts from documents are arranged in two parts. The first part has sketches, short articles designed to give an impression and sense of the historical past. The second part contains excerpts from a manuscript, the original of which is now in the National Library in Madrid, by Juan Francisco de Paramo y Cepeda. Paramo was the Comisario of the Office of the Inquisition in Panama in 1697 and while there, and perhaps later, produced a long heroic poem telling of the conquest of Panama. Of historic rather than literary value, extended excerpts are given in the Spanish of the seventeenth century.

187 **Testamento y sociedad en el Istmo de Panamá: siglos XVIII y XIX.** (Wills and society on the Isthmus of Panama: 18th and 19th centuries.)
Alfredo Figueroa Navarro. Panama City: Imprenta Roysa, 1991. 207p.

This publication commemorates the fifth centenary of the discovery of America by discussing the historical evidence of wills. It includes bibliographical references (p. 205-07), illustrations and maps.

Colombian period

188 **1903; biográfia de una república.** (1903; biography of a republic.)
Victor F. Goytía. Panama City: Published by the Author, 1953. 408p. bibliog.

Divided into three parts, this long, detailed work treats first the tensions and events that led up to Panama's secession from Colombia in 1903. The second part, 1904-40, details the history of the events of the early years of the republic and later. The third part, 1941-46, describes the increasing frustrations of the Panamanians as they struggled to develop an economy and a government which would assure peace and prosperity in the future.

189 **Bayano. Precurso de la libertad de los esclavos.** (Bayano. Precursor of the slaves' liberation.)
Armando Fortune. *Lotería,* no. 234 (August 1975), p. 1-14.
A historian describes a nineteenth-century village of freed and escaped slaves, with emphasis on the mixed tribal nature of the community thus created.

190 **Before the five frontiers: Panama from 1821-1903.**
Alex Pérez-Venero. New York: AMS Press, 1978. 199p. bibliog. (Reprinted from the 1949 edition).
Covers the Colombian experience, discussing the initial independence from Spain, affiliation with Colombia, the impact of the Panama Railroad and the gold rush in California, and finally the formation of the republic in 1903.

191 **Colombia and the United States, 1765-1934.**
E. Taylor Parks. New York: Greenwood Press, 1970. 554p. (Reprinted from the 1935 edition).
A noted historian of diplomacy analyses the relations existing between Colombia and the United States. A long section is devoted to the events preceding the 1903 secession of the isthmus of Panama.

192 **El Congreso de Panamá y la unidad latinamericana.**
(The Congress of Panama and Latin American unity.)
Pedro Ortega Díaz. Caracas: Editorial San José, 1976. 109p.
A short study of the 1826 Congress of Panama and its contribution to Latin American unity, written by a leading proponent of Communism.

193 **Del Congreso de Panamá a la Conferencia de Caracas.** (From the Congress of Panama to the Caracas Conference.)
Jesús M. Yepes. Caracas: Govierno de Venezuela, 1976. 467p. bibliog.
A study of the international congresses which affected Panama, beginning with the Congress of Panama in 1826, and extending to the Caracas Conference of 1954. Many documents relating to these conferences are reprinted as appendixes to the sections.

194 **El desarme de la Policía Nacional en 1916.** (The disarming of the National Police in 1916.)
Carlos Iván Zúñiga Guardia. Panama City: Ediciones Cartillas Patrióticas, 1973. 31p. (Colección Cartillas Patrióticas).
The United States government asked the Republic of Panama to disarm police because of frequent and violent clashes between them and the US military in 1915-16. The police were disarmed after long and bitter debate in the National Assembly. The essay discusses this event which has echoes in modern Panama's political sensibilities.

195 **Documentos para la historia diplomática de Colombia,**
1820-1830. (Documents concerning the diplomatic history of
Colombia, 1820-30.)
German Cavelier. Bogotá: Editorial Kelly, 1976. 2 vols.

Covering the period of Gran Colombia, including its then province Panama, this
compilation provides the documents for the Panama Congress and other Latin American
international materials.

196 **Episodios del siglo XX en Panamá.** (Episodes in Panamanian 20th-
century history.)
Victor F. Goytía. Barcelona, Spain: Editorial Linosa, 1975. 2 vols.

Active in Panamanian politics for several decades, Goytía focuses on the 1931 coup in
which he engaged. Many letters and other unpublished materials have been included. As
in other works by the same author, the work is essentially family history.

197 **Escritos de José Dolores Moscote.** (Writings of José Dolores
Moscote.)
Lotería, no. 278-79 (April-May 1979). whole issue.

José Moscote (1879-1956) is commemorated on the centenary of his birth by a selection
of his writings that are for the most part on political issues and the development of
Panama. This issue is part of a series of articles in *Lotería* commemorating writers and
statesmen who were born in 1879.

198 **Formación de la conciencia americana; tres momentos claves:**
Walker el filibustero y el Destino Manifesto; la agresión
europea y la guerra de secesión; Panamá y América 1903.
(The formation of the American conscience; three key moments:
Walker, the filibuster and the declaration of Manifest Destiny;
European aggression and the Panamanian war of secession; Panama
and America, 1903.)
Hebe Clementi. Buenos Aires: Editorial La Pleyade, 1972. 196p.

Three episodes in which either the United States or a European nation violated Latin
American sovereignty. The creation of the Panama Canal Zone is discussed on pages
165-90. The author's thesis is that each of these violations served to create in Latin
Americans a stronger self-awareness.

199 **El hispanoamericanismo en la independencia panameña de 1821.**
(Hispano-Americanism in the Panamanian independence of 1821.)
Ricaurte Soler. *Lotería,* no. 190 (December 1971), p. 1-13.

An examination, by a neo-Marxist writer, of early regionalism and its impact on the
political climate of Panama in 1821.

200 Historia documental del Canal de Panamá. (Documentary history of the Panama Canal.)
Diogenes A. Arosemena G. Panama City: Instituto Nacional de Cultura, 1997. 2nd ed. 3 vols.

This three-volume collection of basic documents includes in volume 1: Spanish-language translations of US documents relating to Panama, such as Henry Clay's instructions (1826), the commercial treaty with Colombia (1846) and documents relating to the recognition of the secession of Panama from Colombia. Volume two contains documents relating to the Panama Canal from 1903 to 1955, showing the movement of US interest in Panama from the canal as a commercial enterprise to Panama's value as a defence outpost. Volume three comprises treaties and other official documents relating to the ownership of the Panama Canal.

201 The human tradition in Latin America: the nineteenth century.
Edited by Judith Ewell, William H. Beezley. Wilmington, Delaware: SR Books, 1989. 305p. (Latin American Silhouettes).

Unlike the 20th-century part of this series (see item no. 202), the only thing of note here is a contribution to the discussion of which route to choose to move from the Atlantic to the Pacific Ocean. There is a short biography of W. R. Grace, founder of a shipping company that made extensive use of the canal, although Grace himself had lobbied for a Nicaraguan one (p. 189-203).

202 The human tradition in Latin America: the twentieth century.
Edited by William H. Beezley, Judith Ewell. Wilmington, Delaware: Scholarly Resources, 1987. 311p.

Michael Coniff contributes a biography of George Westerman (p. 141-50) to this anthology of historical biographies of persons who contributed to Latin American life during this century. Westerman, a West Indian who has lived in Panama all his life, rising to ambassador to the United Nations from 1956 to 1960, is respected as a stateman and read as a journalist.

203 Incidents of travel in Central America, Chiapas and Yucatán.
John Lloyd Stephens. New York: Harper & Brothers, 1848. 2 vols. map.

Stephens, a builder of the Panama Railroad, studied the prospect of the Nicaraguan route for a canal and wrote in detail of his findings in this work. It reappeared more recently when Century Hutchinson brought out an edition in one volume in 1988.

204 Panama; a personal record of forty-six years, 1861-1907.
William Smith. Colón, Panama: The Star and Herald Company, 1907. 143p.

One man's experience of an important period of history. Some of the author's conclusions and interpretations may not have withstood the test of time, but the descriptions remain useful.

205 Panama, su independencia de España, su incorporación a la Gran Colombia, su separación de Colombia, el canal interoceánico. (Panama: its independence from Spain, its incorporation into Colombia, its separation from Colombia, the inter-oceanic canal.)
Luis Martínez Delgado.   Bogotá: Ediciones Lerner, 1972. 318p.
Much of this book is a reprinting of material taken from *La historia extensa de Colombia* (The detailed history of Colombia). It covers early history to the independence of Panama from Colombia, from essentially a Colombian point of view. The long second part is a collection of documents, not always readily available, which relate to the building of the canal.

206 Panameños en la gesta libertaria de España, 1821-1824: Francisco Gómez Miro, José Antonio Miro, Tomas Herrera, José Domingo de Espinar. (Panamanians in the independence movement, 1821-24: Francisco Gomez Miro, José Antonio Miro, Tomas Herrera, José Domingo de Espinar.)
Rubén Darío Carles.   *Lotería*, no. 236 (October 1975), p. 35-47; no. 237 (November-December 1975), p. 83-91.
A two-part essay discussing the role of lesser patriots in achieving independence from Spain.

207 El siglo XIX en Panamá, escenarios abruptos. (The 19th century in Panama; brief scenes.)
Victor F. Goytía.   Barcelona, Spain: Editorial Linosa, 1975. 351p.
Based on family documents and reminiscences, this work is important for insights into the 1863 constitutional crisis in which the Goytía family played a signifcant role. The subtitle is more indicative of the form, since the book is not a developed history but essentially an account of an interesting family.

208 Simposium conmemorativo del 150 aniversario de la independencia de Panamá de España, Panamá, 1971. (Symposium commemorating the 150th anniversary of Panama's independence from Spain, Panama, 1971.)
Panama City: Instituto Nacional de Cultura y Deportes, Dirección del Patrimonio Histórico, 1973. 55p.
A collection of papers developing the idea that it can be proved that Panama's desire for independence long predates the United States' interest in the isthmus.

209 The United States and the Republic of Panama.
William D. McCain.   Durham, North Carolina: Duke University Press, 1937. 278p. maps.
A scholarly study, dating from before the Second World War, of the relations between the United States and Panama in which the role of the more powerful partner is carefully and

critically scrutinized. This interesting work reflects the increasing attention to Latin America that characterized American foreign policy in the late 1930s.

210 The Watermelon Riot: cultural encounters in Panama City, April 15, 1856.
Mercedes Chen Daley. *Hispanic American Historical Review*, vol. 70, no. 1 (February 1990), p. 85-111.

Hordes of Americans moved from the eastern parts of the United States to the gold-fields of California by way of the isthmus of Panama. Daley recounts a riot and its aftermath in this examination of the inter-cultural conflicts under which Latin American–United States relations developed.

Republic

211 Colombia en la reparación imperialista: 1870-1914. (Colombia and imperialistic reparations: 1870-1914.)
Alvaro Tirado Mejía. Medellín, Colombia: Ediciones Hombre Nuevo, 1976. 231p.

A popular history emphasizing United States influence in Panama as well as in other parts of Central America. There is also some treatment of intervention by other powers such as Great Britain and Germany. The book is based on French archival material not always accessible to writers on Latin American affairs.

212 Historic American Buildings Survey. Part II. Canal Zone.
Alexandra, Virginia: Chadwyck-Healey, 1995. 2 microfiches.

First supplement to the 1980 microfiche publication of *The Historic American Buildings Survey*. This supplement includes reduced copies of the drawings of all the buildings recorded by the Historic American Buildings Survey. Photographs and written historical descriptive data were prepared by the Historic American Buildings Survey, Office of Archeology and Historic Preservation, National Park Service, and reproduced from photographs located in the Prints and Photographs Division, Library of Congress.

213 Latin America since 1930. Mexico, Central America, and the Caribbean.
Edited by Leslie Bethell. Cambridge, England; New York: Cambridge University Press, 1990. 775p. maps. bibliog. (The Cambridge History of Latin America, vol. 7).

Michael Conniff contributes the section 'Panama since 1903', and John Major 'The Panama Canal Zone, 1904-79'.

214 **Nuestra ciudad de Panamá en el año 1935.** (Our Panama City in 1935.)
Jorge Conte Porras. *Lotería,* no. 234 (August 1975), p. 81-109.
This illustrated social and economic history of Panama City includes a brief illustrated
essay on the same theme for the years 1898 and 1935.

215 **A people who would not kneel: Panama, the United States, and
the San Blas Kuna.**
James Howe. Washington, DC: Smithsonian Institution Press,
1998. 390p. (Smithsonian Series in Ethnography Inquiry).
A detailed and readable history of the Kuna [Cuna] which includes a good deal of
Panamanian history as well. Topics considered are: earliest times; missionization and
turmoil, 1903-12; Panama enters San Blas, 1913-18; the contest for control, 1918-20; the
conquest of San Blas, 1921-24; the white Indians, 1923-24; the Kuna Rebellion, 1925 and
after. This is an interesting account of how a strong and rich traditional culture encounters
the modern world.

216 **Our country and its resources; what we ought to know about
agriculture – fisheries – forests – Panama Canal – railroads –
manufactures – automobiles – industrial preparedness – the new
navy – the army – our money – aeronautics – motion pictures –
the weather – astronomy – the nation's capital – the President –
Congress – all about the government.**
Albert A. Hopkins. New York: Munn & Co., 1917. 598p. maps.
(Scientific American Series).
A statistician describes, among other parts of the US infrastructure, the Panama Canal as
it was seen in 1917. The pertinent pages are 109-18.

217 **Rails to the diggings: construction railroads of the Panama Canal.**
Charles S. Small. Greenwich, Connecticut: Railroad Monographs,
1981. 223p.
A technological history of the construction and management of the railways that built
modern Panama. The first railway, completed in 1855, provided the land link that was
chiefly used to move from the Gulf of Mexico and Atlantic ports of the United States to
the gold-fields of California. In 1904 a second railway evolved; it was used to move men
and materials to construct the canal. The author describes the latter railway in full detail,
illustrating his text with diagrams and contemporary photographs.

218 **Remaking the world: adventures in engineering.**
Henry Petroski. New York: Alfred A. Knopf, 1997. 239p.
Henry Petroski has written a book describing a variety of engineering marvels. His
description of precisely what it is that makes the Panama Canal the embodiment of
engineering triumph (p. 157-70), namely the carrying of the canal system of transport to
its most technological extreme for its era, is an excellent corrective to the flood of
politically oriented material that forms the general awareness of the canal.

Biography

Collective

219 Diccionario biográfico de Panamá. (Biographical dictionary of Panama.)
Jorge Conte Porras. *Boletín de la Academia Panameña de la Historia Panamá*, vol. 21/22, 3rd series (January/June 1980), p. 169-222.
The first sections (A to C) of a biographical dictionary that will list 2500 Panamanians.

220 Esbozos biográficos. (Biographical sketches.)
Ricardo Joaquín Alfaro. Panama City: Instituto Nacional de Cultura, 1974. 304p.
Medium-length biographies of Panamanians and other persons important to Panama. These sketches by a Panamanian journalist were first published in several periodicals.

221 Galeria de presidentes de Panamá. (A gallery of Panamanian presidents.)
Ernesto J. Castillero Reyes. Panama City: [Tipografía y casa editorial La Moderna], 1936. 95p.
Brief biographical sketches of leaders from the junta of 1903 to the ninth president, 1940. Most entries include portraits and emphasize the political aspects of their subject.

222 **Los héroes olvidados de la panameñidad.** (Forgotten heroes of Panamanianism.)
Jorge Conte Porras. *Lotería,* no. 210 (July 1973), p. 1-16.
A series of biographical notes concerning the major indigenous Panamanian chiefs who fought the Spanish rulers during the colonial period.

223 **Mi Panamá de ayer.** (My Panama of yesteryear.)
Manuel J. Castillo. Panama City: Published by the Author, 1990. 154p.
The author gives his personal recollections of noted Panamanian personalities.

224 **Middle American governors.**
Glen W. Taplin. Metuchen, New Jersey: Scarecrow Press, 1972. 204p.
'This volume [supplies] a concise, factual, objective recital of the leaders and their times and places in the history of the countries of Middle America.' Panama is covered on pages 4-41 by a listing of leaders, of whatever title, together with pertinent dates and major achievements. Time covered begins with Columbus and his son in the early 16th century, through the colonial period to the Departamento de Panamá (Colombia) and the republic up to 1964.

225 **Panameños de la época colonial en el Archivo General de Indias de Sevilla.** (Panamanians of the colonial period in the General Archive of the Indies, Seville.)
Juan Antonio Susto. *Lotería,* no. 205 (January 1973), p. 47-51; no. 206 (February 1973), p. 56-61; no. 208 (April-May 1973), p. 130-36; no. 228 (February 1975), p. 90-101; no. 233 (July 1975), p. 49-66.
A five-part series identifying Panamanians of the colonial period for whom records exist in the archives in Seville. A brief commentary on the person's importance to Panamanian history and some indication of the kind of record extant in the archives follow each name.

Individual

226 **El abate Domingo de Pradt y el Congreso de Panamá.**
(Abbé Dominique de Pradt and the Congress of Panama.)
José Rafael Arboleda. *Boletín de Historia y Antiguedades,* vol. 63 (January-March 1976), p. 3-32.
A vivid description of the life and times of Abbé de Pradt, this article focuses on the abbé's participation in the Congress of Panama, especially his suggestion that the Latin American Catholic Church should seek some degree of independence from Rome.

227 **America's prisoner: the memoirs of Manuel Noriega.**
Manuel Noriega, Peter Eisner.   New York: Random House, 1997.
293p.
General Noriega presents his case to the public, a story of his being unfairly vilified as a miscreant of the order of Saddam Hussein, of being pilloried by the United States government after having been used by it – he identifies specifically William Casey, the head of the CIA and Oliver North. His chapters are encapsulated by an introduction and an afterword by Peter Eisner, an experienced journalist who has extensively covered events in Central America. Noriega's account of the events that led to his trial in Florida add details not elsewhere considered. A collection of materials appended flesh out some parts of his story.

228 **Bolívar.**
Lotería, no. 243-44 (May-June 1976). whole issue.
This double issue of Panama's leading cultural publication celebrated Simón Bolívar, and contains several essays about Panama during the independence period. The text is in Spanish.

229 **Bolívar en Panamá: génesis y realidad del Pacto Americano; las actas extraviadas del Congreso de Bolívar de 1826.** (Bolívar in Panama: genesis and reality of the American Pact; the misleading acts of Bolívar's congress of 1826.)
Ernesto J. Castillero Reyes.   Panama City: Editorial de la Nación, 1976. 187p. bibliog.
In spite of the revisionist tone of the title, Castillero gives an objective collection of extracts from the session minutes, texts of agreements and similar documents knit together with his own comments. Many facsimiles and plates of illustrations are included.

230 **Buccaneer: Admiral Sir Henry Morgan.**
H. R. Allen.   London: Arthur Barker, 1976. 193p. bibliog.
This biography of Morgan is meant as a partial rehabilitation of the privateer, to which end the role of the British government in sponsoring and encouraging the buccaneers is emphasized. The tortuous movement of Morgan's army across the isthmus to Panama City makes exciting reading, as does the destruction and looting of the old capital. Morgan's role in history, however glamorized, remains villainous.

231 **Carlos Antonio Mendoza, father of Panama's Independence Act.**
George W. Westerman.   Panama City: Education Department. 83p.
Mendoza (1856-1916) was a statesman instrumental in the formation of the young republic of Panama. This memoir is one of the few sources of information about him in English.

232 Christopher Columbus.
Ernle Bradford. London: Michael Joseph; New York: Viking, 1973. 288p. bibliog.

An attractive biography of Columbus, profusely and colourfully illustrated. The account of the fourth voyage, which included the isthmus of Panama, is recounted on pages 237-78.

233 Columbus and the conquest of the impossible.
Felipe Fernández-Armesto. London: Weidenfeld & Nicolson, 1974. 224p. bibliog.

Pleasing illustrations, taken mostly from old manuscripts and engravings, make the historical Columbus attractive to readers. Columbus's relations with Panama are discussed on pages 180-91, and excerpts from his diary translated into modern English enhance this section.

234 Columbus: his enterprise.
Hans Konig. New York: Monthly Review Press, 1976. 129p. bibliog.

Konig purposes to remove the false trappings given to Columbus when he is presented as a boy's hero. He shows him rather to be an explorer in an age of exploration, a geographer who put, however unwittingly, the New World on the map. The discovery of the Panamanian isthmus during the fourth voyage, one of the darker episodes of Columbus's life, is dramatically retold in 'The last move' on pages 107-16.

235 Divorcing the dictator: America's bungled affair with Noriega.
Frederick Kempe. New York: Putnam, 1990. 469p.

Frederick Kempe, once diplomatic correspondent for *The Wall Street Journal*, has produced an account of the relationship between Noriega and the United States based primarily on personal accounts cross-checked with other sources. The combination of his journalist's eye and network has provided a rich and exciting account of a world of intrigue and betrayal set in Panama and Washington that seems (but for the documentation supplied in the notes section) to be the stuff of fiction. The author sees the treatment of Noriega as a significant failure of US diplomacy.

236 Eusebio A. Morales.
Lotería, no. 276 (February 1979). whole issue.

Morales (d. 1929) was a founder of the republic and kept a copious record of the stirring days through which he lived. These essays, speeches and letters are impressions filtered through a trained and disciplined mind.

237 From Panama to Verdun.
Philippe Bunau-Varilla. Philadelphia: Dorrance, 1940. 277p.

The memoir of the Frenchman who has been variously described as the hero or villain of the 1903 treaty between Panama – recently become a sovereign state – and the United States for the purpose of building a transoceanic canal. Bunau-Varilla, after the decision of the French to withdraw from the canal project, was determined that the canal would be completed, that the French would be recompensed and their honour salvaged. This book, published just after Bunau-Varilla's death in his eighties, has a somewhat annoying bombastic tone, but it remains, as it were, Bunau-Varilla's final word.

238 **General Benjamin Ruiz el revolucionario.** (General Benjamin Ruiz, the revolutionary.)
Ernesto J. Castillero Reyes. *Lotería,* no. 234 (August 1975), p. 49-53.

A participant in the war of secession is given a modern interpretation.

239 **Getting to know the general: the story of an involvement.**
Graham Greene. London: Bodley Head, 1984. 223p.

General Torrijos was president of Panama from 1968 until his death in an aviation accident in 1981. In his inimitable style, Greene describes in travel book fashion his conversations and recreations with Torrijos and his intimates over a period of some seven years. Greene adds a literary and humanistic aspect to a man known to the world as a strong dictator.

240 **Harry Morgan's way: the biography of Sir Harry Morgan, 1635-1684.**
Dudley Pope. London: Secker & Warburg, 1977. 379p. bibliog.

Treated as a hero in London after the sack of Panama, Morgan was knighted, although more as future lieutenant-governor of Jamaica than for his deeds in Panama. Morgan in Panama is treated in detail on pages 219-52.

241 **Juan Demóstenes Arosemena.**
Jorge Conte Porras. *Lotería,* no. 280 (June 1979), p. 89-104.

An essay on the life of Juan D. Arosemena (1879-1939), member of the Panamanian government from 1903 to 1939. Conte Porras is editor of *Lotería* and an outstanding contemporary Panamanian. Two important writings by Arosemena reprinted here are *Relaciones con los Estados Unidos* (Relations with the United States) and the text of his presidential acceptance speech. There is also a useful chronology of his life.

242 **The keen edge of Ruben Blades; he is a lawyer, essayist and ... oh, yes – a terrific musician.**
Jay Cocks. *Time,* vol. 124 (2 July 1984), p. 82.

A breezy, readable article about the careers and expectations of Ruben Blades.

243 **Life and letters of Vasco Nuñez de Balboa.**
Charles Anderson. New York: Fleming H. Revell, 1941. 368p. map.

Not only a biography of Balboa but also an extensive history of the settlement of Panama, this work is meant by its author to be a 'history of the first years of the introduction of Christian civilization on the continent of America'. Anderson makes much use of his own experience in Panama to interpret this episode in history.

244 The life of Admiral Christopher Columbus by his son Ferdinand.
Ferdinand Columbus.   New Brunswick, New Jersey: Rutgers University Press, 1959. 316p. maps.

Samuel Eliot Morison said of this account that it 'needs no more discounting than does any biography of a distinguished father by a devoted son'. There are explanatory notes in this edition, and Panama, called by its first name, Verabua, is described on pages 241-62. The map gives both modern names of locations and those provided by Columbus.

245 Maya explorer; John Lloyd Stephens and the lost cities of Central America and Yucatán.
Victor M. Van Hagen.   Norman, Oklahoma: University of Oklahoma Press, 1947. 324p. bibliog.

One of the builders of the Panama Railroad, Stephens (1805-52) was also a lawyer, businessman, explorer and travel writer. The author gives a vivid account of Stephens's negotiations with Colombia for the right to build the isthmian railway, the struggles in building the right of way through the jungles and swamps, and the final triumph when the California gold rush made the railroad profitable beyond the investors' wildest dreams. The book is a complete biography, the Panama episode marking the end of Stephens's life.

246 Nuñez de Balboa, el tesoro del Dabaibe. (Nuñez de Balboa, treasure of the Dabaibe.)
Octavio Mendez Pereira.   Madrid: Ediciones Nuestra Raza, 1936. 212p.

Octavio Mendez Pereira (1887-1954), a Panamanian educator, was the first president of the University of Panama published in a variety of genres. This biography of Balboa is considered to be the 'best historical narrative in Panamanian letters'. His educational writings are described in the education section.

247 La vida ejemplar de Justo Arosemena; biografia. (The exemplary life of Justo Arosemena.)
José Dolores Moscote, Enrique J. Arce.   Panama City: Departamento de Bellas Artes y Publicaciones del Ministerio de Educación, 1956. 424p.

A substantial account of Justo Arosemena (1817-96), leader of the intellectuals of his time, who discussed in several works the evolution of the Panamanian consciousness and, as early as 1864, the need for a canal.

248 William Crawford Gorgas, warrior in white.
Edward F. Dolan, Jr., H. T. Silver.   New York: Dodd, Mead, 1968. 269p.

A somewhat fictionalized biography suitable for all ages of Dr William Gorgas, public health official who achieved a level of general health in the early days of the Canal Zone that added considerably to the knowledge of preventive measures leading to good health in the tropics.

Population

249 Demographic diversity and change in the Central American isthmus.
Edited by Anne R. Pebley, Luis Rosero-Bixby.   Santa Monica, California: Rand, 1997. 736p. maps.

These papers were originally presented at the International Conference on the Population of the Central American Isthmus organized by the Central American Population Program at the University of Costa Rica. Topics relating to Panama are regional studies of knowledge of health technologies, family size, and fertility transition. A useful set of estimates of the indigenous population of Central America from the 16th to the 20th century is also included.

250 Los elementos humanos de Panamá y su parte a la panameñedad. (The human elements of Panama and their part in the Panamanian spirit.)
Armando Fortune.   *Lotería,* no. 208 (April-May 1973), p. 26-35.

A discussion of what constitutes the spirit of Panama, emphasizing the role of the black Panamanian.

251 Hombres y ecologia en Panamá. (Man and ecology in Panama.)
Omar Jaén Suárez, preface by Olga F. Linares.   Panama City: Editorial Universitaria: Smithsonian Tropical Research Institute, 1981. 157p. maps.

The distinguished Sorbonne-trained scholar Omar Jaén Suárez presents in this work an overview of man's impact on the physical geography of Panama and that of the environment on the people who live there. Especially useful is a discussion of the impact of the Panama Canal on the environment, followed by some considerations of the difference a sea-level canal would make to the geography.

252 Is population policy necessary? Latin America and the Andean countries.
Carlos Aramburu. *Population and Development Review,* vol. 20, no. 1 (supplement) (March 1994), p. 159-78.
A comparative study of the family planning policies and fertility rates of several countries, including Panama. Panama is one of those countries adopting a national population policy. In comparing these countries with those that have used non-policy means to reduce fertility, the author concludes that policy *per se* is not the deciding factor.

253 Mestizaje en el istmo de Panamá al comienzo del siglo XVII.
(Mestizo in the isthmus of Panama at the beginning of the 17th century.)
Armando Fortune. *Lotería,* no. 253 (March 1977), p. 1-18.
A historical study of people of mixed race by a Panamanian who frequently publishes articles on blacks in Panama.

254 The people of Panama.
John Biesanz, Mavis Biesanz. New York: Columbia University Press, 1955. Reprinted, New York: Greenwood Press, 1977. 418p.
A vivid, cheerful account of the peoples who make up present-day Panama – Panamanians white and black, West Indians, and the American expatriates in the Canal Zone. The authors, both sociologists, discuss such aspects as the economy, agriculture and rural life, the impact of the canal on general Panamanian economic life, social structure, health and nutrition, educational patterns, career preparation and both urban and rural recreational activities. The effect of the rising expectations that have resulted from increased information and contact with Americans from the zone is well described.

255 Through Afro-America; an English reading of the race problem.
William Archer. Westport, Connecticut: Negro Universities Press, 1970. 295p.
An Englishman's study of black–white relations in America. Panama is discussed on pages 276-91 and the emphasis is on the allocation of jobs in the building of the canal. This has been reprinted from the London 1910 edition.

Nationalities

General

256 Una controversia científica: los pigmeos en América. (A scientific controversy: pygmies in America.)
Leopoldo Veloz Duin. *Boletín Histórico, Fundación John Boulton* (Caracas), vol. 37 (January 1957), p. 83-91.

This article explores the current schools of thought concerning the origin of the pygmies of Panama and other Latin American countries. One position is that the New World pygmies were a separate group migrating more or less together to the Latin American continent; the other is of the opinion that the pygmies are a natural evolution of a short-statured people. The author is of the latter opinion.

257 Convenio 169 y los indígenas de Panamá. (Agreement 169 and the Indians of Panama.)
Panama City: Centro de Capacitación Social, 1995. 2nd ed. 71p. bibliog.

This monograph includes the text of the agreement passed in 1989 by the International Labor Organization, concerning the rights of indigenous peoples. It sets forth standards of the rights of national minorities, updating the United Nations declaration of 1957. It provides guidelines for safeguarding land tenure and expands the notion of civil rights to include both preservation of traditions and access to education and means of communication and health and welfare services. The 30-page introduction surveys the position of nearly 200,000 Panamanians who form this group, and touches briefly upon the efforts of the Indians to recover their traditional lands, and the role of international organizations, such as the United Nations and the ILO. The final part of the introduction details the tasks that must be accomplished in order to guarantee these human rights.

258 Frontier adaptations in lower Central America.
Edited by Mary W. Helms, Franklin O. Loveland. Philadelphia:
Institute for the Study of Human Issues, 1976. 178p. maps. bibliog.

This collection of papers was presented at the Southern Anthropological Society's annual meeting in 1974. The sections are: pre-Columbian themes, black population and the Anglo frontiers, and native adaptations to an economic hinterland. The editors place the individual papers in an enlightening ethnological and historical context. The following sections on the Cuna and Guaymí Indians give details of specific papers in this collection (see items 268-69, 286-87).

259 Hail.
J. M. G. Le Clezio. Geneva: Skira, 1971. 170p.

A beautifully illustrated essay on the Indian civilization of Panama which the author, in the style of Rousseau, compares to modern European civilization. Le Clezio visited the Embera Indians of Panama several times in the course of three years. The emphasis is on magic, folklore and art.

260 Handbook of Middle American Indians.
Edited by Robert Wauchope. Austin, Texas: University of Texas
Press, 1964-75. 15 vols. maps. bibliog.

Panama is discussed in volumes 1, 6-9, 15. The first volume deals with the early culture and ecology of Panama and other areas of Middle America, volume 6 with demography, volumes 7 and 8 with various aspects of ethnology, and volume 9 with physical anthropology. The last four volumes are bibliographies, for the most part of unpublished research reports. There is no country index.

261 Las historias aberrantes y los autores panameños. (Deviant
history and Panamanian authors.)
Alberto Smith Fernandez. Lotería, no. 230 (April 1975), p. 40-54.

An attempt at revisionist history dealing with the treatment of Panama's Indians in the colonial period.

262 The Indians of Panama; their history and culture.
Frank Theodore Humphries. Panama City: Panama American
Publishing Co., 1944. 132p.

The author, who lived as an independent medical practitioner among the Guaymí Indians, has written a highly personal account of the Indians of Panama and their similarities to and differences from other primitive societies. His purpose is to extol the value of the Indian contribution to Panamanian culture, and the value of the author's account to present-day readers is his description of a Panama now historical.

263 Requiem pare los indios. (Requiem for the Indians.)
Felicitas Barreto. Rio de Janeiro: Editoria Ground, 1979. 152p.

An indictment of modern social and economic planners for destroying the traditional way of life of the Indians.

Cuna/Kuna

264 Among the San Blas Indians of Panama, giving a description of their manners, customs and beliefs.
Leon Sylvester De Smidt. Troy, New York: Published by the Author, 1948.

The author provides a lively description, with photographs, of the traditional way of life of the Tule Kuna as he observed it in the 1940s. Religious, economic, political and social practices are described. A brief history includes some description of the direct impact the Second World War had on this coastal society.

265 Anna Coope, sky pilot of the San Blas Indians; an autobiography.
Anna Coope. New York: American Tract Society, 1931. 193p. map.

Coope, born in Lancashire, England, in 1864, emigrated to the United States in her late teens. In her early thirties she left her weaving job to proselytize in the West Indies, moving to Panama in 1907 and settling among the San Blas Indians where she lived for twenty years. Her fresh observation of the San Blas Islands and her spiritual odyssey were first written in 1917. Her work among the Indians is responsible in part for the openness of the San Blas towards anthropologists in those early days that made so much research possible; and her teachings were a partial cause of the uprising of 1925 that put the San Blas Cuna into the political mainstream.

266 The art of being Kuna: layers of meaning among the Kuna of Panama.
Edited by Mari Lyn Salvador. Los Angeles, California: UCLA Fowler Museum of Cultural History, 1997. 353p. map.

The editor has brought the leading scholars of Panamanian life and thought together to inform her presentation of the art of the Kuna in this heavily and beautifully illustrated record. The Kuna have a particularly rich culture that has withstood the incursions of the postmodern world. Photographs, many of them full page, vividly chronicle the environment. The exhibited materials, *molas* (appliquéd blouses) and other crafts, show how the Kuna have absorbed what they have found of interest into their art. The art objects are carefully arranged to reveal their important points. The art photographs are of the highest quality. Although most of the book is devoted to *molas*, there are also chapters on Kuna picture-writing, language and literature, music, domestic artefacts, and the Kuna world-view. The publication served as the exhibition catalogue.

267 Coastal adaptations as contact phenomena among the Miskito and Cuna Indians of lower Central America.
Mary W. Helms. In: *Prehistoric coastal adaptations; the economy and ecology of maritime Middle America.* Edited by Barbara L. Stack, Barbara Voorhies. New York: Academic Press, 1978, p. 121-46. maps. bibliog.

A comparison of 'the pre and postcontact [with Europeans] indigenous societies'. Contemporary adaptations are extensively discussed.

268 **Communal land tenure and the origin of descent groups among the San Blas Cuna.**
James Howe. In: *Frontier adaptations in lower Central America.* Edited by Mary W. Helms, Franklin O. Loveland. Philadelphia: Institute for the Study of Human Issues, 1976, p. 151-63. bibliog.
A description of how this Indian tribe has modified its traditional land-holding patterns to meet new economic needs. The increasing population has made land scarce while at the same time the capability of raising a cash crop can raise the standard of living.

269 **Cuna household types and the domestic cycle.**
Regina E. Holloman. In: *Frontier adaptations in lower Central America.* Edited by Mary W. Helms, Franklin O. Loveland. Philadelphia: Institute for the Study of Human Issues, 1976, p. 131-49. bibliog.
A discussion of the factors that contribute to the retention of a traditional household, in which the parents live in a house owned by the mother. With them live their married daughters, sons-in-law and unmarried sons. The men do the work of subsistence farming together and the women share the household work. Because the work is relatively easy, the men have leisure to pursue their own interests and there is no pressure to change to a life-style more compatible with modern economic principles.

270 **Curing among the San Blas Kuna of Panama.**
Norman Macpherson Chapin. PhD thesis, University of Arizona, 1983. 601p. (Available from University Microfilms, Ann Arbor, Michigan, order no. AAT 8319716).
The thesis is summed up in the Abstract as 'An ethnographic account of the belief system surrounding disease and curing among the Kuna Indians of San Blas, Panama'.

271 **Darién: etnoecologia de una region histórica.** (Darien: the ethnoecology of an historic region.)
Reina Torres de Arauz. Panama City: Dirección Nacional del Patrimonio Histórico, Instituto Nacional de Cultura, 1975. 377p. bibliog.
A thorough survey of what is known about the archaeology, ethnohistory and ecology of the area. Peoples discussed include the Cuna, Choco and Negro mestizo as well as more recent immigrants into the area. At the time of writing the author was director of the Instituto Nacional de Cultura.

272 **Etnohistoria cuna.** (Cuna ethnohistory.)
Reina Torres de Arauz. Panama City: Dirección Nacional del Patrimonio Histórico, Instituto Nacional de Cultura, 1974. 51p. bibliog.
Dr Torres, director of the National Institute of Culture, has frequently written about the history and prehistory of Panama, especially Darien province. A more concise version of this report was published in *Lotería*, July 1974 (see below).

273 **Etnohistoria cuna.** (Cuna ethnohistory.)
Reina Torres de Arauz. *Lotería*, no. 221 (July 1974), p. 1-13.
This concise informative survey of the Cuna Indians in Darien has been abbreviated from the official report of the same name.

274 **An historical and ethnological survey of the Cuna Indians.**
Erland Nordenskiold, in collaboration with the Cuna Indian Rubén
Pérez Kantule, edited by S. Henry Wassen. Göteborg, Sweden:
Göteborgs Museum, Etnografiska Andelningen, 1938. Reprinted,
New York: Arno Press, 1979. 686p. (Comparative Ethnological
Studies, vol. 10).
A comprehensive study of Cuna history and culture including political and family organization, religion, customs and traditions, music, and the like. There are various documents translated from Cuna to Spanish. Illustrations include black-and-white photographs of Cuna picture-writing with some explanations. See also Stout's *Ethnolinguistic observations on the San Blas Cuna* and Sherzer's *Namakke, Sunmakke, Kormakke...*, items 240 and 241 in the first edition of *Panama*.

275 **The houses of the Bayano Cuna Indians of Panama.**
Charles F. Bennett. *Antropológica*, vol. 20 (June 1967), p. 37-52.
map. bibliog.
Photographs and diagrams illustrate the design and construction of dwellings of the Bayano Cuna. The author's style is entertaining and appropriate for non-specialist reading, although the primary audience is specialist.

276 **I married a San Blas Indian; the story of Marvel Elya Iglesias.**
Christine Hudgins Morgan. New York: Vantage Press, 1958. 81p.
Marvel Iglesias was the wife of a San Blas Cuna leader, Lonnie Iglesias. Her story is an example of acculturation and tradition in the first half of the 20th century.

277 **Los indios cunas de San Blas; su origen, tradiciones, costumbres,
organización social, cultura y religión.** (San Blas Kunas; their
origin, traditions, customs, social organization, culture and religion.)
Manuel Maria Puig. Panama City: Published by the Author,
[194?]. 229p.
A general work about the Cuna and their environment written by a missionary. One value of the book is its short, annotated bibliography of Cuna writings and language.

278 **The Kuna gathering: contemporary village politics in Panama.**
James Howe. Austin: University of Texas Press, 1986. 326p.
bibliog. (Latin American Monographs, 67).
A detailed study of Kuna society, with a close look at the political systems, specifically the community power structure as manifested in the village gathering, which the author characterizes as 'a remarkable example of democratic self-management'. Topics that include political symbols, influence and alignment, process and outcomes, adjudication

and conflict are covered in separate chapters. An appendix briefly describes some historical examples.

279 Land of the moon-children, the primitive San Blas culture in flux.
Clyde E. Keeler.   Athens, Georgia: University of Georgia Press, 1956. 207p. map.

A popular account by a scientist who went to Panama to study the 'moonchildren' – the fair-haired, white-skinned Indians born from time to time as albinos, but about whom many stories were told to account for their condition. The author concluded from the evidence available to him that the cause of the mysterious children (those who survive childhood often darken as they age) was albinism and perhaps blond genes acquired from some early shipwrecked mariners. The author is a geneticist.

280 La leyenda de los indios blancos del Darién y su influencia en la etnografía y la historia política del istmo. (The legend of the white Indians of Darien and its influence on the ethnography and political history of the isthmus.)
Reina Torres de Arauz.   *Hombre y Cultura* (Panama), vol. 2 (September 1973), p. 5-67.

The curiosity of the world to see the white Indians of Darien had a profound effect on the Cuna, argues the writer. The white-skinned Indians, now generally considered albinos, hastened the acculturation of the Cuna into the mainstream of Panamanian life.

281 El matrimonio entre los indios Cuna. (Matrimony among the Cuna Indians.)
José Manuel Reverte.   Panama City: Published by the Author, 1966. 52p.

This is an illustrated and documented study of the role of the Cuna woman, her preparation for and expected conduct during marriage. Some comparisons are made with other cultures.

282 San Blas; an account of the Cuna Indians of Panama.
Fred McKim, edited by S. Henry Wassen.   In: *Comparative Ethnological Studies,* vol. 15.   Göteborg, Sweden: Etnografiska Museet, 1947, p. 1-113.

A description of the Cuna Indians of the San Blas Islands, based on personal observation. The author describes social, political and economic aspects of their life.

283 White Indians of Darien.
Richard Oglesby Marsh.   New York: Putnam, 1934. 6p. map.

A travel account studded with disaster, treachery and sudden death, whose title does not indicate its contents. The author's purpose in exploring Darien's dense jungles was a study of the terrain for possible development as rubber plantations, undertaken at the behest of Henry Ford and Harvey Firestone. The author emphasizes the savagery of the

Indians, the corruptness of the central government in its handling of local affairs, and the courage of the Cuna Indians. The chapter dealing with white-skinned (albino or partially albino) Indians is neither scientific nor objective. The value of the book lies in the author's assessment of the economic value of Darien and his perceptions of the political tensions and problems of the Cuna during the 1920s that led to the uprising of 1925.

Guaymí

284 The Cerro Colorado Copper Project and the Guaymí Indians of Panama.
Chris N. Gjording. Cambridge, Massachusetts: Cultural Survival, 1981. 50p. bibliog.

The monograph is written from a 'holistic perspective that insists on the need to analyze large-scale development projects' in terms of their impact on various economic sectors. The author is particularly concerned with the Guaymí Indians who live over large but low-grade copper deposits and who represent 3 per cent of the population, the largest indigenous group. Impact studies on the effect of a vast open-pit mine were not carried out by the government agency concerned because they had not budgeted for the very high cost of such a study. Gjording continues to develop his assessment in *Conditions not of their choosing* (item no. 285).

285 Conditions not of their choosing: the Guaymí Indians and mining multinationals in Panama.
Chris N. Gjording. Washington, DC: Smithsonian Institution Press, 1991. 409p. maps.

A developed account and analysis of the impact of an attempt to develop a low-grade copper mining project in an area inhabited by an indigenous Panamanian people. The major players in this scenario include the Panamanian and US governments, especially CODEMIN, the Panamanian government mining corporation, the Intergovernmental Council of Copper-Exporting Countries and the World Bank, which was encouraging mining in less developed countries. The author, a Jesuit anthropologist, argues that in their confrontation with the Guaymí, the government, struggling to raise itself economically, defined the problem incorrectly. The government felt that the economic welfare of the country was paramount, even if the Guaymí had to be sacrificed. Father Gjording argues that what the government failed to see was the damage this project was doing to the ecology, and, indeed, the financial and economic health of the country.

286 The expression of harmony and discord in a Guaymí ritual: the symbolic meaning of some aspects of the Balseria.
Philip D. Young. In: *Frontier adaptations in lower Central America.* Edited by Mary W. Helms, Franklin O. Loveland. Philadelphia: Institute for the Study of Human Issues, 1976, p. 37-53. bibliog.

Young 'argues that the stick game of the Guaymí expresses both harmony and discord'. The game, dating from prehistoric times, uses two teams (each with a leader) which engage in territorial struggle. It seems to have been used by chiefs to impress their neighbouring, competing fellow chiefs. Much information for the report was provided by 20th-century informants in a now egalitarian society.

287 Mesoamerican influences among Talamanca and western Guaymí Indians.
Laura Laurencich Minelli. In: *Frontier adaptations in lower Central America.* Edited by Mary W. Helms, Franklin O. Loveland. Philadelphia: Institute for the Study of Human Issues, 1976, p. 55-65. bibliog.

Provides a description of linguistic, mythological and social factors emanating from Mesoamerica and adopted by the Talamanca and western Guaymí. Myths mentioned include a variant of Kukulcan, the culture hero of Mesoamerica.

288 Ngawbe: tradition and change among the western Guaymí of Panama.
Philip D. Young. Urbana, Illinois; London: University of Illinois Press, 1971. 256p. maps. bibliog. (Illinois Studies in Anthropology, 7).

The Guaymí live in the rugged mountains of Veraguas, Chiriquí and Bocas del Toro in western Panama. This well-written and scholarly book can be appreciated by specialist and non-specialist alike. It describes the social structure, showing the strength of the family, and discusses continuity and change in terms of their effect on family cohesiveness. There is an extended treatment of the impact of the Mama Chi cult as emphasizing tradition over change.

289 Proceso de cambio en la sociedad ngobé (guaymí) de Panama.
(Process of development in the Guaymí society of Panama.)
Francoise Guionneau Sinclair. Panama City: Universidad de Panama, 1988. 155p. maps. bibliog. (Serie Realidad Nacional (Panama City, Panama), 2).

A survey of the life of the Ngobe, essentially an agrarian people, and the modern institutional mechanisms that threaten them, especially agribusiness – above all growing bananas for export. Statistics for the group studied include data on demographics and agricultural production. The maps are especially well designed to show graphically the ethnic group distributions. Conclusions include suggestions for combining traditional and modern social techniques and values to maintain a satisfactory life-style for the Ngobe.

Other

290 A cultural geography of the Embera and Wounan (Chocó) indians of Darien, Panama, with emphasis on recent village formation and economic diversification.
Peter Harry Herlihy. PhD thesis, Louisiana State University and Agricultural and Mechanical College, 1986. 328p. (Available from University Microfilms, Ann Arbor, Michigan, order no. AAT 8710562).

This thesis is a 'a traditional cultural geography [that] documents Chocó life in Panama, with emphasis on the process of recent village formation'.

291 Embera (Chocó) village formation: the politics and magic of everyday life in the Darien forest.
Stephanie Candice Kane. PhD thesis, University of Texas at Austin, 1986. 658p. (Available from University Microfilms, Ann Arbor, Michigan, order no. AAT 8706036).

The author focuses 'on the complex articulation of political economic structures, where differences are ordered by gender and race, and where the contradictory pressures of economy and ecology are mediated by both cosmological schemes and offices of state'.

292 Los indios de Panamá; los indios Tule de San Blas. (The Indians of Panama; the Tule of San Blas.)
Reginald Gordon Harris. Panama City: Imprenta National, 1926. 27p.

Harris was director of the Biology Laboratory, Cold Spring Harbor in the 1920s. This work is an example of the ethnography of the period.

293 Keep out of paradise.
Marjorie Mills Vandervelde. Nashville, Tennessee: Boardman Press, 1966. 127p.

A swiftly moving account of visits to two of Panama's three remaining Indian groups: the Chocó and the Cuna. The emphasis is on women's roles in these societies as studied by two women, the author and her niece. This short work is a pleasant, popular introduction to the subject.

294 Notes on Chocó ecology in Darien province.
Charles F. Bennett. *Antropológica,* vol. 24 (December 1968), p. 26-55. map. bibliog.

'The ecology of culture groups still living in an intimate association with their biophysical environments is of interest for its own sake and for the light that such information can cast upon earlier ecological conditions.' Several Panamanian Indian groups retain much of their original life-style – by choice – and thus provide information on early primitive man's interaction with his environment.

295 The phantom gringo boat: shamanic discourse and development in Panama.
Stephanie C. Kane. Washington, DC: Smithsonian Institution Press, 1994. 241p. map. bibliog. (Smithsonian Series in Ethnographic Inquiry).

In the Darien provinces where most of the Embera peoples live, modern life is deeply imbued with tradition. In this eminently readable book, however scholarly, Kane shows how these traditions, in the forms of myth and magic mesh with the modern world that is intruding upon the old culture. The phantom gringo boat of the title is the Embera metaphor for development. After an introductory chapter, Kane describes the imaginary Indian influenced by the Conquest, colonialism and natural phenomena. Other cultural aspects are realized in events and projects of the Embera people which are described in detail. The particular role of the male is exemplified in a cooperative boat-building venture, while the role of the woman is seen as fundamental both to the traditional culture and the development of the modern. The book ends with an Embera version of the global *realpolitik* in the retelling of the Bush–Noriega confrontation. There is a short glossary of Embera words.

West Indians and others of the Black diaspora

296 The African experience in Spanish America, 1502 to the present day.
Leslie B. Rout. London; New York: Cambridge University Press, 1976. 404p. bibliog. (Cambridge Latin American Studies, 23).

Although Panama is discussed only briefly on pages 273-79, those pages provide a succinct, documented summary of the racial situation in Panama today with some indication of its historical roots. It may be necessary to consult the glossary in the front of the book for definitions of such terms as 'chumbo' and 'zonite'.

297 Between alienation and citizenship: the evolution of Black West Indian society in Panama, 1914-1964.
Trevor Evan O'Reggio. PhD thesis, University of Chicago, 1997. 311p. (Available from University Microfilms, Ann Arbor, Michigan, order no. AAT 9720055).

The Abstract sums up the thesis thus: 'The construction and operation of the Panama Canal by the United States involved three principal groups – Americans, Black West Indians and Panamanians – whose interrelationships and interaction from the completion of the canal in 1914 to 1964 are chronicled here.'

298 Black Latin America.
Latin American Studies.   Los Angeles: California State University, 1977. 73p. bibliog.

An unannotated listing of books and periodical articles about the black experience in Panama as well as other countries in Latin America. Panama is represented by about a dozen publications.

299 Globalization and survival in the Black diaspora: the new urban challenge.
Edited by Charles Green.   Albany, New York: State University of New York Press, 1997. 396p. (SUNY Series in Afro-American Studies).

George Priestly writes on 'Post-invasion Panama: urban crisis and social protests' in this collection discussing the Black diaspora.

300 Historical notes on West Indians on the isthmus of Panama.
George W. Westerman.   *Phylon*, vol. 22 (Winter 1961), p. 340-50.

Westerman covers the whole history of West Indians in Panama, from the 19th century. The author's emphasis is on social justice.

301 Memorias de un criollo bocatoreño = Light in dark places.
Carlos Reid, edited by Stanley Heckadon Moreno.   Panama City: Asociación Panameña de Antropologia, 1980. 199p. maps. (Monografias Antropológicas, no. 1).

Reid is a Creole from Bocas del Toro, whose forebears were West Indians come to work on the canal. In collaboration with the anthropologist Heckadon Moreno, he recounts his memories from 1919 to the mid-1960s, describing his native province in colourful detail. The book is bilingual but Stanley Moreno, who is also editor, says that it was first written in English and then translated. Appendices list male residents of Old Bank, later Bastimentos, women and the governors under whom Reid worked as a minor civil servant.

302 Panama's blacks: a U.S. responsibility.
Steve C. Ropp.   *New Leader*, vol. 60 (7 November 1977), p. 7-8.

The black residents and employees of the Canal Zone are West Indian in origin, English-speaking and Protestant. Although technically Panamanian citizens, they are cultural aliens. The author argues that the US government has a special obligation to safeguard their future.

303 Perspectivos sobre el afro-panameño. (Perspectives on the Afro-Panamanian.)
A. Faulkner Watts.   *Lotería*, no. 234 (August 1975), p. 36-48.

An essay exploring the black experience in Panama at a relatively early point in scholarly interest in the Black Diaspora.

304 The problem of West Indian offspring in Panama; a study of the relationships between ethnic and cultural groups in a cosmopolitan setting.
George W. Westerman.   Panama City: Published by the Author, 1944 309p. bibliog.

The political as well as the socio-economic status of West Indian life-styles are described. Westerman has written frequently on this matter since this work was published, but this title provides insight into his perspective at that time.

305 Race relations in Panama.
Justo Arroyo.   In: *African presence in the Americas*. Edited by Carlos Moore, Tanya R. Saunders, Shawna Moore.   Trenton, New Jersey: Africa World Press, 1995, p. 155-62.

Arroyo briefly discusses the historic and current situation of race relations in Panama.

306 Resisting state violence: radicalism, gender, and race in U.S. culture.
Joy James.   Minneapolis: University of Minnesota Press, 1996. 265p. bibliog.

The author includes his essay 'Hunting prey: the U.S. invasion of Panama', a condemnation of the invasion as an unregulated gendered act.

307 West Indian workers on the Panama Canal: a split labor market interpretation.
Raymond Allan Davis.   PhD thesis, Stanford University, California, 1981. 236p. (Available from University Microfilms, Ann Arbor, Michigan, order no. AAT 8108909).

As declared in the Abstract, 'Bonacich's theory of ethnic antagonism is explicated and applied to the split labour market on the Canal Zone between 1904-1958. Competition between West Indians, Panamanians, and Americans (management and 'workers') is analyzed as a determinant of ethnic relations.'

308 The West Indian in Panama.
Lancelot S. Lewis.   PhD thesis, Tulane University, New Orleans, 1975. 243p. bibliog. (Available from University Microfilms, Ann Arbor, Michigan, order no. DCJ 76-13594).

The West Indians in Panama were one of several black groups imported as labour for constructing the Panama Railroad and the Canal. Lewis's theme in this economic and social study is racism.

Languages

Language and culture

309 Ensayo de semántica general y aplicada al lenguaje panameño.
(An essay on semantics as applied to the Panamanian tongue.)
Octavio Mendez Pereira. Panama City: Published by the Author,
1934. 37p.
An early discussion of Panamanian word usage by Octavio Mendez Pereira (1887-1954),
this study was sponsored by the Academia Panameña de la Lengua.

310 El español de Panamá; estudio fonético y fonológico. (The
Spanish of Panama; phonetics and phonology.)
Elsie Alvarado de Ricord. Panama City: Editorial Universitaria, 1971.
170p. bibliog. (Editorial Universitaria. Sección: Linguistica. Serie).
A description and analysis of the Panamanian dialectical sounds and pronunciations.

311 Estudios de linguística descriptiva; temas panameños. (Studies in
descriptive linguistics; Panamanian themes.)
Pedro I. Cohen. Panama City: Universidad de Panamá, 1971. 67p.
A collection of articles on dialectical language that were first published in *Estudios* from
1961 to 1964.

**312 An exploration of Panamanian Creole English: some syntactic,
lexical and sociolinguistic features.**
Leticia C. Thomas Brereton. PhD thesis, New York University,
1993. 239p. (Available from University Microfilms, Ann Arbor,
Michigan, order no. AAG 9317686).
The recorded speech of eighteen informants was used to describe some features of the
English-based Panamanian Creole. Brereton concludes that the language includes 'many

typical Caribbean English-based Creole features' and 'words which have been borrowed or adapted from Spanish as well as words which appear to be particular to Panamanian Creole alone'.

313 The interplay of social and linguistic factors in Panama.
Henrietta Cecilia Jonas Cedergren. PhD thesis, Cornell University, Ithaca, New York, 1973. 162p. (Available from University Microfilms, Ann Arbor, Michigan).
A sociolinguistic study of provincialisms in Panamanian Spanish is the subject of this thesis.

314 Kuna ways of speaking: an ethnographic perspective.
Joel Sherzer. Austin, Texas: University of Texas Press, 1983. 260p. bibliog. (Texas Linguistics Series).
The San Blas Indians, the Kuna, traditionally rely on speech for daily work, for cultural transmission, for sharing news and for entertainment. In order to transmit all the necessary knowledge and to provide pleasure, all work is done where possible in groups and accompanied by conversation. Although now written in transcription, it was not a language that developed as both an oral and a written one. Sherzer examines the Kuna way of using speech, integrating his findings with other anthropological approaches such as the Kuna use of space, the rites of passage, and healing rites. He ends with a chapter discussing the inroads of modern technology, a key example of which is the tape recorder which mimics the speaking–listening mode of the traditional society, and illustrates the ways the Kuna are adapting to modern life.

315 Lenguaje popular. (Popular speech.)
Angel Revilla. Panama City: USMA, 1982. 40p. (Cuadernos La antigua, 7).
A quick reference tool that defines in Spanish neologisms, anglicisms and indigenous words that have become incorporated into ordinary speech. Revilla has taught in both the United States (at the University of Colorado) and in Panama and has published his linguistic studies in those countries and in Spain. A good resource for West Indian English, such as *madama* (West Indian woman) and *chombo* (West Indian canal labourer).

316 Panamanian English Creole in its sociolinguistic and syntactic contexts.
Antonio Rafael Howell Brathwaite. DA thesis, State University of New York at Stony Brook, 1996. 191p. (Available from University Microfilms, Ann Arbor, Michigan, order no. AAG 9722390).
Argues that Panamanian English Creole, 'rooted in the history of West Indian immigrants, Panamanian blacks, Hispanic Panamanians, and Americans in the Republic of Panama', had a special association that allowed the development of the modern dialect. Brathwaite looks especially at the way pronominal constructions developed and are used today.

317 **Panameñismos.** (Panamianisms.)
Baltasar Isaza Calderón, Ricardo J. Alfaro.   Panama City:
Impresora Panamá, 1968. 2nd ed. 117p.
Sponsored by Academia Panameña de la Lengua, this collection remains useful for the
expressions of the period.

318 **The speech of the *negros congos* of Panama.**
John M. Lipski.   Amsterdam; Philadelphia: J. Benjamins, 1989.
159p. bibliog. (Creole Language Library, 0920-9026, vol. 4).
The *negros congos* of the Caribbean coast which form part of the Carnival celebrations
have a historical element, in which the stories of the black slaves of Panama are told,
while a Hispanic component (the music) and the drumming and dancing (the African
component) contribute much. This monograph examines the question as to where the
speech, precisely identified as *hablar en congo* contains African elements and gives
extensive examples of the speech.

319 **Syntactic innovation in a Caribbean Creole: the Bastimentos
variety of Panamanian Creole English.**
Michael Aceto.   *English World Wide: A Journal of Varieties of
English,* vol. 17, no. 1 (1996), p. 43-61.
Aceto describes the variation that occurs in the past tense in Bastimentos Creole, as one
tense marker is now in the process of being replaced by another. Bastimentos Creole is a
form of Panamanian Creole English.

320 **Take and tell: a practical classification from the San Blas Cuna.**
James Howe, Joel Sherzer.   *American Ethnologist,* vol. 2 (August
1975), p. 435-60.
The San Blas Cuna Indians classify agricultural and forest products according to the way
a person must relate to them. The relationships are governed by rules depending on
whether the products are owned by God or by humans. The authors argue that the words
associated with these concepts influence behaviour.

321 **Tres estudios sobre la cultura nacional.** (Three studies of the
national culture.)
Diogenes Cedeno Cenci.   Panama City: [Universidad de Panamá],
1993. 72p. bibliog.
Three essays dealing with literature, language and politics. Of special note is the essay on
Panamane, an artificial language.

322 **Variation in a variety of Panamanian Creole English.**
Michael Jay Aceto.   PhD thesis, University of Texas at Austin,
1996. 231p. (Available from University Microfilms, Ann Arbor,
Michigan, order no. AAG 9633070).
Panamanian Creole English as spoken on the Caribbean island of Bastimentos is
examined, the researcher concluding that, in general, structural variations in the language

as used today 'existed within the original migrant community in several [forms]' and that these variations are not the result of adopting metropolitan Creole variants.

323 Verbal art in San Blas: Kuna culture through its discourse.
Joel Sherzer. Cambridge, England; New York: Cambridge University Press, 1990. 281p. bibliog. (Cambridge Studies in Oral and Literature Culture, 21).

This book is the outcome of extended residence and study among the Kuna Indians, and offers an array of textual examples of the rich and varied culture of the Kuna. In this treatment the author demonstrates 'the ways in which grammatical, discourse, social, cultural, and personal factors intersect and interact in the creation and structuring of verbal art'. Chapters provide the texts and contexts of a Kuna myth, two stories and discourses of healing (traditional healer) and power (the counselling of a new chief). A guide to the sounds of the language and the phonetic transcription conventions are provided for the specialist.

Dictionaries

324 Diccionario de anglicismos: enumeración, análisis y equivalencias. (Dictionary of anglicisms: enumeration, analysis and equivalents.)
Ricardo J. Alfaro. Panama City: Imprenta Nacional, 1950. 849p.

A collection of English borrowings into Panamanian Spanish, described by the scholar-politician Alfaro who disapproves of these usages as implying a sort of linguistic colonialism. It has also been published in Madrid under the title *Diccionario de anglicanismos*.

325 Diccionario de anglicismos para estudiantes. (Dictionary of anglicisms for students.)
Roberto Jaén y Jaén. Panama City: Published by the Author, 1969. 191p.

This compilation is intended for university and secondary school students.

326 Diccionario de sinónimos hispanoamericanos, con un apéndice sobre algunos vicios de dicción, pleonasmos y americanismos.
(Dictionary of Spanish American synonyms, with an appendix concerning diction, pleonasms and Americanisms.)
Darío Espino Pérez. Caracas, 1969- .

Only Volume 1, 'Terminos de estructura semejante', has appeared. Although no more volumes have as yet been published, this work remains valuable.

327 **Diccionario de terminos panameños.** (Dictionary of Panamanian terms.)
Arnoldo Higuero Morales.   Chicago, Illinois: Allied Enterprises, 1993. 97p.

This is a collection of Spanish words used in Panama that fall into two categories. The first contains Spanish words with specialized Panamanian meaning and words from indigenous and immigrant languages commonly used. The second is a list of words in common use in Panama that are to be found in the standard *Diccionario de la Real Academia* and thus are to be considered standard Spanish.

328 **Dictionary of Panamanian English.**
Leticia C. Thomas Brereton.   Brooklyn, New York: Published by the Author, 1993. 82p.

The listing of Panamanian Creole English, defined in English, includes bibliographical references (p. 7).

Cuna language

329 **Discourse grammar: studies in indigenous languages of Colombia, Panama and Ecuador.**
Robert E. Longacre, Frances Woods.   Dallas, Texas: Summer Institute of Linguistics and University of Texas at Arlington, 1977. 3 vols.

This is a collection of papers dealing with, among other items, various aspects of Cuna and Teribe languages.

330 **Ethno-linguistic Cuna dictionary.**
Nils M. Holmer.   Göteborg, Sweden: Etnografiska Museet, 1952. 193p. (Comparative Ethnological Studies, vol. 19).

A Cuna-to-English dictionary with illustrations. There are important references to other volumes in the series, notably *A critical and comparative grammar...*(Comparative Ethnological Studies, vol. 14) and *Cuna chrestomathy* (Comparative Ethnological Studies, vol. 18).

331 **Outline of Cuna grammar.**
Nils M. Holmer.   *International Journal of American Linguistics*, vol. 12 (October 1946), p. 185-97.

The article covers parts of speech, pronunciation and the like, and serves as a short introduction to the language.

332 **Picture writing and other documents.**
Provided by the Paramount Chief of the Cuna Indians Nele, the
Cuna Indian Rubén Pérez Kantule, edited by Erland Nordenskiold.
Stockholm: Ethnological Museum, 1928, 1930. 2 vols. Reprinted
New York: AMS Press, 1979. 2 vols in 1. (Comparative
Ethnological Studies, vol. 7, parts 1 and 2).

Part 1 is a long essay on the production of the documents of the Cuna here collected. The
picture-writing is first transcribed into spoken Cuna and then into Spanish. Part 2 brings
together original documents, relating to Cuna mythology as transcribed into English and
Cuna by English-speaking Cuna Indians, Charlie Nelson and Charles Slater. Pictures were
also drawn as part of the explanation given by the two Cuna, and these are reprinted here.

333 **Tummat ikar par soik malat kus malatti.** (Bible. New Testament.
Acts of the Apostles. Cuna [San Blas].)
P. Miller (et al.).   New York: Sociedad Bíblica Americana, 1956. 148p.

This is a translation of the Acts of the Apostles into Kuna. It has been included in this
bibliography as an example of the Kuna language. There is a Spanish-language version
supplied with each verse. The Kuna version is by P. Miller *et al.* and the Spanish is the
Reina-Valera Revised version.

Other languages

334 **Chocó I: introduction and bibliography.**
Jacob A. Loewen.   *International Journal of American Linguistics,*
vol. 29 (July 1963), p. 239-63. map. bibliog.

This overview of the Chocó language which is spoken by some 25,000 Indians discusses
geographical distribution of variants and dialects, and surveys scholarship. See also the
following entry.

335 **Chocó II: phonological problems.**
Jacob A. Loewen.   *International Journal of American Linguistics,*
vol. 29 (October 1963), p. 357-71.

This is the continuation of the above overview of Chocó grammar.

336 **Cursillo de asimilación – Teribe.** (A short assimilation course in
Teribe.)
Carol Heinze.   Panama City: Instituto Lingüístico de Verano, 1979.
48p. bibliog. (Lenguas de Panamá, 6).

This short grammar of Teribe is divided into six lessons, with emphasis on idiomatic
speaking. There is a preface by the chief of the Teribe, Simeón Santana.

337 **Una gramática pedagógica del Waunana: primer parte.**
(A teaching grammar of Waunana: part 1.)
Reinaldo Binder.   Panama City: Instituto Lingüístico de Verano,
1975. 175p. (Lenguas de Panamá, 3).
This is a basic introduction to Waunana.

338 **Guaymí grammar and dictionary with some ethnological notes.**
Ephraim S. Alphonse.   Washington, DC: Smithsonian Institution,
1956. 128p. (Bureau of American Ethnology, Bulletin 162).
The Guaymí greeting is 'How did you dream?' to which the polite response is 'I didn't
have any dreams'. This detailed grammar explains the Guaymí language in English and
Spanish and much vocabulary is given. Some short essays on customs of the Guaymí are
included. The compiler lived among this Indian tribe for twenty years, and uses a
traditional method of language analysis.

339 **Languages of Chiriquí and Darién: various authors collected
in MS.**
Edited by Karl Herman Berendt.   Los Angeles: Scholarly Data,
1975. 260p.
Berendt has put together a collection of studies on Waunana and other indigenous
languages of Panama.

Religion

Policy and overviews

340 Archbishop Marcos Gregorio McGrath: the renewal of the Panamanian church.
Notre Dame, Indiana: Ave Maria Press, 1995. 39p.

A short biographical essay is included in this collection of translations of and excerpts from the writings and sermons of Archbishop McGrath of Panama City. The Archbishop was a strong and appreciated leader in the changes in the Catholic Church encouraged by the Second Vatican Council.

341 Congrès de Panamá. (Congress of Panama.)
Dominique Georges Frédéric de Riom de Prolhiac de Fout de Pradt.
Caracas: Edición Homenaje del Congreso de Venezuela, 1976.

With a preliminary note in Spanish by Gonzalo Barrios to give its setting, this work is a reprint of the 1825 Paris edition of the French text of the Abbé de Pradt's ideas regarding the nature of the Latin American ecclesiastical establishment within the context of an independent Latin America. His work discusses the agenda for the Congress of Panama, and this reprint commemorates its 150th anniversary.

342 Conquista, evangelización y resistencia: triunfo o fracaso de la política indigenista? (Conquest, evangelization and resistance: triumph or disaster of the pro-Indian policy?)
Alfredo Castillero Calvo. Panama City: Editorial Mariano Arosemena: Instituto Nacional de Cultura, 1995. 494p. maps. bibliog. (Colección Ricardo Miró. Premio ensayo, 1994).

A detailed study of the indigenous populations of Panama druing the colonial period. The author, who has taught at universities in Panama, the United States and Costa Rica, has made extensive use of the materials from the Archivo General de Indias (Seville). He explains the resistance of the indigenous population to Christianity as a refusal to make basic changes in their culture. In making this point, Castillero provides a detailed history of the organization of the colonial church and rural aspects of colonial rule. There are many useful statistics bolstering his arguments.

343 **Hacia una economía más humana y fraterna: la economía nacional, el desarrollo humano y la doctrina social de la Iglesia Panamá.** (Having a more human and fraternal economy: the national economy, development and the social doctrine of the Panamanian Church.)
José Guillermo Ros-Zanet.   Panama City: Editorial Portobelo, 1971. 47p.

A sociological discussion of a Christian economic policy for Panama is the subject of this short work.

344 **Panamá: la iglesia y la lucha de los pobres.** (Panama: the Church and the struggle of the poor.)
Andres Opazo Bernales.   San José: Editorial DEI, 1988. 213p. bibliog. (Colección Sociologia de la Religión. Iglesia y Pueblo).

This sociological examination of the role of the Catholic Church in Panama from 1968 to 1983, gives some examples of urban pastoral activities and takes a brief look at the current state of popular religion. The social focus is on poverty and the role of the Church in ameliorating the condition of the poor.

345 **Le Protestantisme en Amérique latine: une approche socio-historique.** (Protestantism in Latin America: a socio-historical approach.)
Jean-Pierre Bastian.   Geneva: Labor et fides, 1994. 324p. bibliog. (Histoire et société, 27).

Bastian contextualizes Protestantism in Panama.

346 **We make the road by walking: Central America, Mexico and the Caribbean in the new millennium.**
Washington, DC: Ecumenical Program on Central America and the Caribbean (EPICA), 1998. 236p.

Within the context of contribution from the churches in Central America, Panama is represented by an essay by Conrado Sanjur, 'Defending the poor in Panama: aftermath of the US invasion'. The book in general discusses most issues immediately relevant to Panama.

Special topics, local churches

347 5757.
Stanley Fidanque B. Panama: Published by the Author, 1997. 76p.
This is a genealogical history of the Fidanques, a prominent Jewish family in Panama.

348 A church in search of itself: a counter-hegemonic experiment.
Gail D. Keeney-Mulligan. DMin thesis, New York Theological
Seminary, 1995. 204p. bibliog. (Microform available from New York
Theological Seminary).
The author reports the results of a demonstration project at the English-speaking
Episcopal Church in Colón.

349 Colón y Kunayala: desafío para la Iglesia y el gobierno. (Colón
and Kuna Yala: challenge for church and government.)
Agustín Jaén Arosemena. Panama City: Diócesis Misionera de
Colón, 1992. 318p. map. bibliog.
A report prepared at the Institute for National Studies, University of Panama at the request
of the Missionary Diocese of Colón.

**350 Identity and millenarian discourse: Kuna Indian villagers in an
ethnic borderland.**
Eric J. Moeller. PhD thesis, University of Chicago, 1997. 251p.
bibliog.
The author argues that millenarian discourse among the Kuna is used not to effect social
change but to maintain established boundaries and to legitimate the Kuna way of life as
distinct from Panamanian Latino society.

**351 Movimiento profético e innovación política entre los ngobe
(guaymí) de Panama, 1962-1984.** (Prophetic movement and
political innovation among the Ngobe [Guaymí] of Panama,
1962-84.)
Françoise Guionneau Sinclair. Panama City: Universidad de
Panama, 1987. 222p. bibliog. (Serie Realidad Nacional, 1).
A sociological study of the millenarian sect of Mama Chi to be found in the Ngobe sector
of the Guaymí people, of whom nearly 25 per cent are practitioners, according to a 1978
census. The impact of the sect was to develop political action to assure more land for the
expanding population in face of the demand for land from agribusiness interests. The
author has also written *Proceso de cambio en la sociedad ngobe* (Developmental process
in Ngobe society).

352 Notas histórico-religiosas sobre el Darién Sur. (Historical and religious note about southern Darien.)
Mauro Ocharan. Colón, Panama: Diócesis de Colón-Kuna Yala, 1998. 129p. bibliog.

These brief notes, as the title suggests, provide information about the missionary presence in Darien from earliest times. While some of the notes repeat generally known information, many references are to persons, some indigenous to the area, who engaged in church work, but who have been lost in the standard retelling of the region's history.

353 Pab Igala: historias de la tradición Kuna. (Pab Igala, stories from the Cuna tradition.)
Edited by Mac Chapin. Quito, Ecuador: Ediciones Abya-Yala; Rome: MLAL, 1989. 183p. (Colección 500 años, 5).

In this collection of Creation stories and other legends of Kuna heroes up to the Age of Discovery, the tales are retold by Kuna informants Nele Kantule, W. Archibol, William Smith, H. Méndez, L. Stócal, L. Valdez, Olomaniiligiña. This edition includes an informative introduction, a glossary of Kuna terms and a brief schema of the Kuna Creation myth.

Social Organization and Groupings

General

354 Clase y nación: problemática latinoamericana.
Ricaurte Soler.   Barcelona, Spain: Fontamara, 1981. 145p.
This study of social classes in Latin America is by Panama's noted Marxist philosopher
(b. 1923).

355 Cities of hope: people, protests, and progress in urbanizing Latin America, 1870-1930.
Edited by Ronn F. Pineo, James A. Baer.   Boulder, Colorado:
Westview Press, 1998. 285p. map. bibliog.
Sharon Phillipps Collazos's 'The cities of Panama, sixty years of development' is
included in this collection about Latin American urbanization. The focus is on the
working classes in urban settings.

356 Household composition in Latin America.
Susan M. De Vos.   New York: Plenum, 1995. 251p.
Using data from the mid-1970s De Vos examines family and non-family living
arrangements of all age groups in several Central and South American countries.

Women

357 El acceso de la mujer a la tierra en Panamá. (Women's access to land in Panama.)
Edited by Vielka Bolanos. San José, Costa Rica: Fundación Arias para la Paz y el Progreso Humano; Panama City: Centro de Estudios Acción Social Panameño, 1995. 196p. bibliog.

A sociological study of under what conditions rural Panamanian women hold rights to land ownership. It is far-reaching and looks at the educational characteristics, the political activism and the profitability of engaging in agricultural business activities. The survey ends with some recommendations.

358 Compañeras: voices from the Latin American women's movement.
Edited by Gaby (Gabriele) Kuppers. London: Latin American Bureau, 1994. 188p.

In this collection of interviews and articles of Latin American women talking about their political activism, Panama is represented by Margarita Muñoz of the Coordinadora Nacional de la Mujer (CNM), an organizational outgrowth of the trade union movement. She discusses the impact of the US invasion of Panama and Panamanian men's attitudes towards women workers on current social and economic problems and describes the role of CNM in ameliorating them. It is a translation of: *Feministamente: Frauenbewegung in Lateinamerika*.

359 Diseño y ejecución del Plan Nacional Mujer y Desarrollo: un caso de incidencia: Panamá. (Design and execution of the national plan for promoting the role of Panamanian women in development.)
Edited by Tania Palencia. San José, Costa Rica: Fundación Arias para la Paz y el Progreso Humano, 1997. 1 vol.

A description of the Panamanian national-level plan suggesting areas and modes in which the state and women will be mutually benefited by development.

360 Entre silencios y voces: género e historia en América Central, 1750-1990. (Between silence and shouts: class and history in Central America, 1750-1990.)
Edited by Eugenia Rodriguez Saenz. San José, Costa Rica: Centro Nacional para el Desarrollo de la Mujer y la Familia, 1997. 254p.

In this collection of papers from the Third Central American Congress of History, Professor Yolanda Marco Serra contributes 'Feminism at 20 years and the redefinition of feminism in Panama', pages 183-96. She describes the contributions of Angélica Chávez (education and family life) and Clara González in politics and the ideas of self-realization and professionalization of the Panamanian woman.

361 **Gendered jobs, gendered earnings in the Panamanian labor force.**
Amelia Márquez de Pérez. PhD thesis, Brandeis University, Massachusetts, 1996. 171p. (Available from University Microfilms, Ann Arbor, Michigan, order no. 9629777).
Gender discrimination is measured in earnings, together with other variables. This quantitative study looks at nearly 15,000 questionnaires.

362 **Ho for California!: Women's overland diaries from the Huntington Library.**
Edited and annotated by Sandra L. Myres. San Marino, California: Huntington Library, 1980. 314 p. bibliog.
The isthmus of Panama section (p. 1-33), consists of excerpts of a diary kept by a passenger from California to the East Coast, Mrs Jane Mcdougal, via the isthmus. Her gritty account of her travels from the Pacific side of the country, to Chagres, the Atlantic port, make interesting reading in the literature of women adventurers. The women rode astride over the bad roads, beginning and ending their journey in the dark, and for the most part contended not only with the unusual language and culture, but also a demanding climate and terrain.

363 **Homenaje póstumo a valores femeninos panameños.** (Homage to noteworthy Panamanian women.)
F. Zentner, Jr. Panama City: Published by the Author, 1975. 31p.
These are the biographies of twenty-one important Panamanian women, of the late 19th and 20th centuries.

364 **Mujeres de maiz: programa de análisis de la política del sector agropecuario frente a la mujer productora de alimentos en Centroamérica y Panamá.** (Women of Corn: program of political analysis of the commercial agriculture sector: women as food producers in Central America and Panama.)
Manuel Chiriboga, Rebeca Grynspan, Laura Pérez E. San José, Costa Rica: Banco Interamericano de Desarrollo (BID): Instituto Interamericano de Cooperación para la Agricultura (IICA), 1995. 384p. bibliog. (Serie Publicaciones Miscelaneas, 0534-5391, no. A1/SC-95-10. Miscellaneous Publications Series, no. A1/SC-95-10).
A series of studies of the condition of women in agriculture for several Central American countries. Panama is discussed on pages 249-84. Each country is described in terms of its growing of basic foodstuffs, the participation of women in agricultural production, food production and technology transfer, and marketing.

365 **Panama: children and women at the crossroads of year 2000.**
Panama City: Ministry of Planning and Economic Policy; United
Nations Children's Fund, 1996. 87p. bibliog.

Also published in Spanish as *Panamá: la niñez y la mujer en la encrucijada del año
2,000*, this report details nutritional needs, health care, education and family planning
goals and statistical projections.

366 **Perceptions of couple decision making in Panama.**
Sharon M. Danes, Ramona F. Oswald, Sylvia Arce de Esnaola.
Journal of Comparative Family Studies, vol. 29, no. 3 (Autumn
1998), p. 569-70.

In this study of Panamanian families, women who had more education had more influence
in major family decisions. Generally, sex determined the level of decisions.

367 **The role of Panamanian grandmothers in family systems that
include grandchildren with disabilities.**
Avraham Scherman, Maria S. Efthimiadis, J. Emmett Gardner.
Educational Gerontology, vol. 24, no. 3 (April/May 1998),
p. 233-46.

The study reported in this article investigated the role of Panamanian grandmothers who
cared for disabled children. Their styles of child care were compared to those of US
grandmothers. The authors make some recommendations for training these caregivers.

368 **Situación de la mujer en Panamá.** (The situation of women in
Panama.)
Elsie Alejandra Madrid.   Panama City: Departamento de
Sociologia, Universidad de Panama, 1989. 137p. bibliog. (Serie
Realidad Nacional [Panama City, Panama], 3).

The work comprises six research studies and accompanying documents and research
notes. The studies include 'La mujer negra en nuestra historia' (The black woman in our
history) by Agatha Williams; 'Las organizaciones de mujeres: La alternativa feminista'
(The women's organizations: the feminist alternative) by Urania Ungo; 'Situación de la
mujer panameña en la coyuntera actual' (Situation of Panamanian women at this current
juncture) by Elsie Madrid and Urania Ungo; 'Algunas reflexiones sobre la alienación de
las mujeres' (Some reflections on the alienation of women) by Yolanda Marco Serra;
'Mujer joven e estructura del empleo en Panamá' (Young women and the employment
structure in Panama) by Briseida Allard; and 'Mujer e ideologia: ¿Reproducción o cambio
social?' (Women and ideology: Reproduction or social development?) by Vicky Balaños.

Poverty

369 Panama's poor: victims, agents, and history makers.
Gloria Rudolf.   Gainesville, Florida: University Press of Florida, 1999. 224p.

The author, who spent some twenty years in the Coclé village of Loma Bonita, provides a sociologist's view of how the rural poor of this community live.

370 Poverty theory and policy: a study of Panama.
Gian Singh Sahota.   Baltimore, Maryland: Johns Hopkins University Press, 1990. 393p. bibliog. (The Johns Hopkins Studies in Development).

A full national study of poverty in a developing country. Poverty in urban, Indian and rural areas is described. Data from the 1983 National Socioeconomic Survey is included. The author concludes from the data that relief of poverty, however limited, is generally consistent across the country in terms of access to schooling and medical care, and that the government policy is consistently applied.

371 Staff appraisal report: Panama: rural poverty and natural resources project.
Central America Department. Latin America and the Caribbean Regional Office.   Washington, DC: World Bank, 1997. 1 vol. bibliog.

The World Bank study looks at sustainable development in its relation to the rural poor. A certain priority is given to the integration of the needs of this segment of the population into national-level planning.

372 You can do something! Forming policy from applied projects, then and now.
Robert A. Hackenberg, Beverly H. Hackenberg.   *Human Organization,* vol. 58, no. 1 (Spring 1999), p. 1-2.

The Malinowski Award Lecture for 1999 used, among other instances, the case of squatter communities in Panama City to reinforce the concept of the efficacy of applied anthropology.

Health

373 Dengue type 3 infection – Nicaragua and Panama, October-November 1994.
JAMA, The Journal of the American Medical Association, vol. 273, no. 11 (15 March 1995), p. 840-42.

Dengue fever is transmitted by mosquitoes and the disease seems to be on the increase. This article from the Centers for Disease Control and Prevention describes the epidemiology of this disease in Nicaragua and Panama. The population most at risk consists of children under the age of sixteen.

374 The ecology of malnutrition in Mexico and Central America: Mexico, Guatemala, British Honduras, Honduras, El Salvador, Nicaragua, Costa Rica and Panama.
Jacques M. May, Donna L. McLellan. New York: Hafner, 1972. 395p. (His: Studies in Medical Geography, vol. 11).

Panama shares with the other countries of the region the same problems of malnutrition, usually a function of poverty. More urban than its neighbours, the diet of the poor whether in the cities or the countryside is typically protein, mineral and vitamin deficient, especially for children. The authors, however, are optimistic that Panama has both the resources and the national will to overcome problems of malnutrition. Panama is discussed on pages 333-82.

375 Human T-lymphotropic virus type II among Guaymí Indians – Panama.
Morbidity and Mortality Weekly Report, vol. 41, no. 12 (27 March 1992), p. 209-12.

HTLV-II is one of a group of immunodeficiency virus infections. In 1989-90 Guaymí Indian households were studied for this infection which is common in the Caribbean basin. Social information was gathered to profile infected persons.

376 The profession of medicine and health policies in the Republic of Panama.
Otto Soren Wald Bocharel. PhD thesis, University of Texas at Austin, 1985. 219p. (Available from University Microfilms, Ann Arbor, Michigan, order no. AAT 8527665).

Bocharel explores the question of whether the training of physicians in the School of Medicine of the University of Panama is in accordance with the country's health care needs.

377 The Republic of Panama: Rural Health Project.
Washington, DC: World Bank, 1994. 146p.

The authors provide an overview of health policies that work towards the goals of economic development.

378 **The triumph of American medicine in the construction of the Panama Canal.**
J. Ewing Mears. Philadelphia: W. J. Dornan, 1913. 3rd ed. 46p.

The author, who from personal experience is able to compare health maintenance during the building of the Panama Canal to the health care of the troops in the Spanish-American War, published three editions of this essay, microfilmed for preservation by the National Library of Medicine.

Drug traffic

379 **Drug prevalence in Latin America and Caribbean countries: a cross-national analysis.**
Joel M. Jutkowitz, Hongsook Eu. *Drugs: Education, Prevention and Policy*, vol. 1, no. 3 (1994), p. 199-252. bibliog.

The authors compare patterns of drug use in ten representative countries including Panama. Substances analysed include tobacco, alcohol, marijuana, cocaine, and their derivatives.

380 **International handbook on drug control.**
Edited by Scott B. MacDonald, Bruce Zagaris. Westport, Connecticut: Greenwood Press, 1992. 454p. bibliog.

With numerous contributors, this handbook surveys the problems of international drug control, provides a country-by-country account of drug activities, and looks at the international organizations and drug control policy. For each area it looks at the structure of the drug trade, the government's response, societal reaction, and international linkages for control. The Panama section by Laura Vasquez and Barbara Jahansoozi (p. 193-206) highlights Panamanian society's anti-drug stand, blaming the United States and Europe for creating the market. There is a bibliography of sources, mostly from journalistic publications.

381 **Mountain high, white avalanche: cocaine and power in the Andean states and Panama.**
Scott B. MacDonald. New York: Praeger, 1989. 153p. bibliog. (The Washington Papers, 137).

A description of the cocaine industry in the Andean states and Panama with emphasis on the relation between cocaine and power, that is, 'the linkages that exist between political and economic power of those in the cocaine trade...and the governments in the region'. The final section of the book suggests options for creating an effective US and international policy to cope with the problem. Dr Macdonald is a senior international economist and has travelled extensively in Latin America. His discussion of the economics of drug production and the need for effective policy is highly suggestive.

382 Panama, 16 years of struggle against drug traffic.
Panama City, 1986. 306p.

This collection of documents describes the actions Panama has taken to control drug trafficking.

Political Organization, Law and Politics

Regional

383 América Latina, para entenderte mejor. (Latin America, to understand you better.)
Eduardo Galeano, Agustín Cueva.   Panama City: Universidad de Panama, 1990. 64p. (Serie Realidad Nacional [Panama City, Panama], 4).

Two essays comprise this work: 'La crisis en América Latina (Crisis in Latin America)' by Agustín Cueva; and 'América Latina, comunicación y cultura (Latin America, communication and culture)' by Eduardo Galeano. The first paper was presented at a conference held at the university of Panama in 1989 with the theme 'Crisis actual de América Latina' (Present crisis in Latin America) and that of Galeano includes his responses to a question-and-answer period. Galeano is a Uruguayan writer and journalist who has extensively published on Latin American politics. Cueva has lived in several Latin American countries and now teaches political science at the University of Mexico.

384 The Central America fact book.
Tom Barry, Deb Preusch.   New York: Grove Press, 1986. 357p.

The politics, foreign relations, and government of Panama are treated in this work. It also deals with the other countries of Central America.

385 Democratic transitions in Central America.
Edited by Jorge I. Dominguez, Marc Lindenberg.   Gainesville, Florida: University Press of Florida, 1997. 210p. bibliog.

In this collection of essays on various Central American countries, two essays discuss Panama. They conclude with a note of cautious optimism that new coalitions are being formed that promise democratic movement. José I. Dominguez is the Frank G. Thomson professor of government at Harvard University. In 'Democratic transition in Central America and Panama' (p. 1-31), he points to the fact that in four Central American

89

countries, former leaders of the opposition are now leading the country, a fact that he sees as a strong indicator of strengthening democratic institutions. Nicolas Ardito-Barletta in 'The political and economic transition of Panama, 1978-1991' (p. 32-66) surveys Panama's transitions during the 1980s and looks to a future which, if sound strategic economic planning is maintained and political processes develop, should be for the benefit of Panama.

386 Elections and democracy in Central America, revisited.
Mitchell A. Seligson, John A. Booth. Chapel Hill: University of North Carolina Press, 1995. New & enlarged ed. 299p.

There are references to Panama throughout these essays, but two deserve special note. First, 'Elections under crisis: background to Panama in the 1980s' by Orlando J. Pérez (p. 123-47). Panama, Pérez writes, has struggled throughout this century for a stable government. It was not until the post-US invasion election of 1994 that a truly free election was held. Up to that time, the commercial élite and US government interests unduly affected political outcomes. The article surveys the political climate in the 1980s. The other is 'The impact of election observers in Central America' by Margaret E. Scranton (p. 183-201), which has brief discussions of the events of the Panamanian elections of 1984, 1989 and 1994, and of the role of external observers in assuring honest ballots, open discussion of the process, and the corollary of lessened violence, possibly due to the presence of international observers. The author concludes that the authority of the external observers had a very strong weight in these elections.

387 Political parties and democracy in Central America.
Edited by Louis Wolf Goodman, Leo Grande, William M. Forman, Johanna Mendelson. Boulder, Colorado: Westview Press, 1992. 407p. bibliog.

A collection of essays to which David A. Smith contributed 'Panama: political parties, social crisis, and democracy in the 1980s'.

Panama

388 Elites, power, and ideology: the struggle for democracy in Panama.
Orlando J. Pérez. PhD thesis, University of Pittsburgh, Pennsylvania, 1996. 404p. (Available from University Microfilms, Ann Arbor, Michigan, order no. AAT 9728689).

As explained in the Abstract, 'The dissertation focuses on the struggle to build democratic governance in Panama and is the first attempt to use both qualitative and quantitative methods to analyze the political culture of Panama's political elites'.

389 Fundación de la nacionalidad panamena. (Foundation of Panamanian nationality.)
Justo Arosemena. Caracas, Venezuela: Biblioteca Ayacucho, 1982. 514p.

A modern selection of the writings of Justo Arosemena (1817-96), and other early Panamanian republicans, chosen, extracted and introduced by Ricaurte Soler. A chronology and extensive bibliography is included. Reproduction of the title pages of these early writings enhance the text.

390 In the time of the tyrants: Panama, 1968-1990.
R. M. Koster, Guillermo Sanchez. New York: W. W. Norton, 1990. 430p. map.

Guillermo Sanchez, the co-author, cooperated on this book while in exile in Florida. He has since resumed his journalistic career in Panama. Essentially a tale of corruption in high places, events are narrated with dramatic force fuelled in part by the treatment of Sanchez by the Noriega government, and bolstered with data from the Centro de Investigaciones de Derechos Humanos y Socorro Jurídico. A readable book not intended for a scholarly audience but for readers who wish to get a sense of these climactic events. It includes bibliographical references and index.

391 Military government and popular participation in Panama: the Torrijos regime, 1968-75.
George Priestley. Boulder, Colorado: Westview Press, 1986. 166p. bibliog. (Westview Special Studies on Latin America and the Caribbean).

Priestley gives a detailed description and analysis of General Omar Torrijos Herrera and his government.

392 Our man in Panama: how General Noriega used the United States – and made millions in drugs and arms.
John Dinges. New York: Random House, 1990. 402p.

A frequently cited reconstruction of General Noriega's involvement with drug trafficking and with several US government agencies whose sources include interviews, the Kerry hearing transcripts, documents released under the Freedom of Information Act, and other substantial secondary accounts of the events described. The author concludes that the whole Noriega case was the result of US government policy based on the more extreme and less documentable facts presented. That the US overall Central American policy dictated the actions taken in Panama, ultimately rejecting, indicting and convicting 'Our man in Panama'.

393 **Panama, 15 meses de lucha por la democratización y los derechos humanos, junio '87-agosto '88.** (Panama, 15 months of struggle for democratization and for human rights, June '87-August '88.)
Guatemala City: Instituto Centroamericano de Estudios Políticos, 1988. 200p. (Cuadernos de Derechos Humanos, no. 3).

This is a gathering of primary materials in the form of manifestos, press releases and other communications relating to the Cruzada Civilista Nacional. A detailed chronology of events leading to the electoral reform, a summary of the report of Americas Watch and the declaration of the Organization of American States about human rights in Panama add value to this collection.

394 **Panamá, nación y oligarquía, 1925-1975.** (Panama: nation and oligarchy, 1925-75.)
Ricaurte Soler. Panama: Ediciones de la Revista Tareas, 1982. 3rd ed. 62p.

A pamphlet in the Marxist tradition, whose author places the blame for Panama's failure to progress economically on the middle-class attitudes of *laissez-faire* and reluctance to give the proletariat a real voice in the government.

395 **Panama: the whole story.**
Kevin Buckley. New York: Simon & Schuster, 1991. 304p.

A journalist who is deeply immersed in the political life of Panama, directly and through a network of friends, gives an account of the events leading up to the US invasion in the style of an adventure novel. The author's sources are personal observation and reporting by many journalists known to him. He provides a good range of estimates as to damage and casualties and exposes the US indifference to redressing the civilian damage wrought by the invasion and the general lack of interest shown by Washington. A chronology and a list of sources for each chapter, many of which are direct interviews or newspaper accounts, are provided.

396 **Panamanian politics: from guarded nation to national guard.**
Steve C. Ropp. New York: Praeger; Stanford, California: Hoover Institution Press, 1982. 151p. bibliog.

Ropp's overview of politics in Latin America includes some discussion of the Panama Canal Treaties of 1977.

397 **Realidad o artificialidad histórica de la nación panameña.** (Historical reality or artificiality of the Panamanian nation.)
Ricaurte Soler. *Lotería*, no. 181 (1970), p. 38-50.

Soler argues that Panama evolved as a result of nationalism rather than as a convenience of the United States in its search for a neutral site to build an interoceanic canal.

398 Things fall apart: Panama after Noriega.
Steve C. Ropp. *Current History*, vol. 92, no. 572 (March 1993),
p. 102-05.
Ropp here compares the pre-1994 election political climate with the period preceding the
Torrijos coup of 1968.

Law

**399 The case against the general: Manuel Noriega and the politics of
American justice.**
Steve Albert. New York: Charles Scribner's Sons; Maxwell
Macmillan International, 1993. 456p.
Albert uses the materials of the trial, the transcripts, court pleadings, Congressional
transcripts and news coverage to provide a detailed account of the trial and conviction in
a US federal court of General Manuel Noriega for drug trafficking and money laundering.
In the aftermath of the US invasion of Panama for the purpose of capturing General
Noriega, an extraordinary act of one sovereign nation inside another, the involvement of
the Central Intelligence Agency, and the convoluted political machinations are all detailed
in this competent work of journalism.

400 Código penal (1982). (Penal Code, 1982.)
Edited by Carlos E. Muñoz Pope. Panama City: Impretex, 1986.
119p.
The editor of this text, Professor of Law at the University of Panama, served on the
Comisión Revísora del Código Penal that produced this updating of the Panamanian penal
code.

**401 Compilación de leyes y decretos sobre la circunscripción de San
Blas.** (Compilation of laws and decrees concerning the district of
San Blas.)
Panama Republic. Statutes. Panama City: Imprenta Nacional,
1915. 33p.
This is a collection of decrees emanating from the National Assembly of the Republic of
Panama under President Belisario Porras with a view to implementing the modernization
of the government and bringing all indigenous people into the modern world. It is of
historical interest.

402 The corporation under Panamanian law: advantages, incorporation, legislation.
Panama City: Morgan & Morgan, 1989. 56p.

In the 1980s climate of encouraging external capitalization of business activities, Morgan and Morgan issued an English-language guide to the legal climate of Panama.

403 Derechos humanos: aspectos procesales y jurisprudenciales.
(Human rights: aspects of trial procedures and jurisprudence.)
Ricaurte Soler Mendizabal. Panama City: Editorial Portobelo, 1997. (Colección Pequeño Formato. Derecho, 32).

A basic overview of the legal framework that protects human rights in Panama, placed within the context of the Comisión Interamericana de Derechos Humanos (Inter-American Commission for Human Rights). The author is professor of law and an editor of the intellectual-oriented magazine *Tareas*. He has written frequently on constitutional reform.

404 Estado constitucional y mechanismos de defensa constitucional.
(The constitutional state and constitutional defence mechanisms.)
Rigoberto Gonzalez Montenegro. Panama City: Instituto de Estudios Políticos e Internacionales, 1997. 126p. bibliog.

A professor of constitutional law at the University of Panama looks at what recourse defendants have in assuring judicial review of their cases. After a survey of what is generally available in constitutional governments, the author discusses in some depth what the Panamanian law provides.

405 Human rights in Panama.
New York: Americas Watch, 1988. 71p. bibliog. (An Americas Watch Report).

An overview of human rights and violations in Panama towards the end of the Noriega regime. The country is a signatory to many of the international laws regarding human rights. Its own laws provide for many rights. The findings of this report are that the laws are not applied, the judicial system is so under-funded and under-equipped that it cannot carry out its mandate, and the prisons fall far below the standard set by the United Nations.

406 The invasion of Panama and international law.
John Quigley. Vienna: International Progress Organization, 1990. 28p. (Studies in International Relations, Vienna, Austria, 16).

This short work discusses the legal aspects of the US intervention in Panama and concludes that the United States was in violation of international law and its own treaties in taking this action. It also suggests that the mechanisms of international law need to be strengthened so that it can be upheld in this case.

407 Is Panama still an iron-clad secrecy jurisdiction?
Enrique M. Illueca. Panama City: Bufete Illueca, 1989. 1 vol.
Laws controlling and defining secrecy in Panama have not been codified but affect every sector where the law must be considered. The author, himself a lawyer, covers secrecy as it relates to commercial law, banking, labour, corporation law, and civil and criminal law. Various international agreements in force are also discussed. Particularly valuable in its discussion of the difference between US and Panamanian disclosure, the work is in both English and Spanish.

408 Militarismo y administración de justicia. (Militarism and the administration of justice.)
Miguel Antonio Bernal. Panama City: Ediciones Nari, 1986. 111p. bibliog.
Bernal discusses justice as it was applied in Panama, with special reference to the effect of the military government of General Torrijos.

409 Report on the situation of human rights in Panama.
Washington, DC: General Secretariat, Organization of American States, 1979. 122p.
Part of a series of reports in a standardized format that sets forth the laws of the country regarding human rights, such as due process and fair trial, the right to freedom of expression and dissemination and the right to vote. For each section there is a brief reference to each case that has been alleged to be in violation of the law. Before publication, the report is given to the government in question, in this case Panama, and the response of the government is included as a separate section of the report.

410 Trusts: legislation in force in the Republic of Panama.
Panama City: Arosemena, Noriega & Castro, 1989. 64p.
This explains the law on trusts and trustees in Panama as of 1984. The text of Ley no. 1 (1984) is provided in English and Spanish. These revisions of the law are part of the modernization of the legal and fiscal systems of Panama.

411 We answer only to God: politics and the military in Panama, 1903-1947.
Thomas L. Pearcy. Albuquerque, New Mexico: University of New Mexico Press, 1998. 232p.
Argues that neither Torrijos not Noriega made the police Panama's dominant force, but rather made use of it to further their political ends, and in so doing were merely doing what had been done for decades. Pearcy digs into the past to describe the impact of the building of the canal upon Panama, the government of the 1930s, and then the 1940s with emphasis on how the police were used to maintain power and further political aims. The work is enriched by numerous tables of data, such as number of arrests by causes, and defence sites acquired by the Defense Treaty of 1942.

Administration

412 Cultural expression and grassroots development: cases from Latin America and the Caribbean.
Edited by Charles David Kleymeyer.   Boulder, Colorado:
L. Rienner Publishers, 1994. 293p.

Marc Chapin, director of the Central American Program for Cultural Survival, wrote the paper 'Recapturing the Old Ways: Traditional knowledge and Western science among the Kuna Indians of Panama' (p. 83-102). Here he relates the establishment of the first indigenous conservation project in the Americas, that of the Kuna, which seemed to have been based on concepts shared by Western science and Kuna tradition. Since the young people of the Kuna are being educated along Western lines, and the parents are not passing on the traditional beliefs, no true fusion of beliefs can occur. Chapin leaves the reader with the question as to whether, in becoming acculturated, the Kuna will continue to treat the earth with the respect that is part of their tradition.

413 El hispanoamericanismo en la independencia panameña de 1821.
(Hispano-Americanism in the Panamanian independence of 1821.)
Ricaurte Soler.   *Lotería,* no. 190 (December 1971), p. 1-13.

Soler, a neo-Marxist writer, examines early regionalism and its impact on the political climate of Panama in 1821.

414 Mensaje dirigido por el presidente de la Republica de Panamá a la Asemblea Nacional al inaugurar sus sesiones ordinarias.
(Messages sent by the president of the Republic of Panama to the
National Assembly to inaugurate ordinary sessions.)
Panama City: Office of the President, 1906- . biennial.

The work comprises presidential policy messages regarding budget and political matters. It is primary material for scholars tracing governmental policy.

415 Panama's Canal: what happens when the United States gives a small country what it wants.
Mark Falcoff.   Washington, DC: AEI Press, 1998. 168p.

Falcoff looks at the treaties of 1977 twenty years later. He notes that ridding Panama of the US military presence, so attractive in 1977, now seems to be something that Panamanians would like to reconsider, a change that would require a new treaty. He describes the groups in the United States, such as the prestigious Atlantic Council, who also would like to revise these provisions. With the reversion of the former Zone properties to the government has come a tendency to consider selling the properties to outside investors, mostly from outside the Western hemisphere, giving rise to security concerns. Falcoff concludes that the intent of the Torrijos–Carter treaties was to leave Panama free to make such choices as it deems best, and that the United States should adhere strictly to this agreement.

416 Teoría de la nacionalidad por Justo Arosemena y Gil Colunje.
(Theory of nationality as held by Justo Arosemena and Gil Colunje.)
Compiled by Ricaurte Soler. Panama City: Ediciones de la Revista
'Tareas', 1968. 304p.

Rogelio Miró wrote the preface to this volume, which brings together writing by Justo
Arosemena (1817-96) and Gil Colunje (1831-99) concerning early federal planning and
treaties. Both writers were known for their far-seeing ideas for Panama and Latin
America.

**417 The transformation of a frontier: state and regional relationships
in Panama, 1972-1990.**
Alaka Wali. *Human Organization*, vol. 52, no. 2 (Summer 1993),
p. 115-27.

Modernization processes, Wali argues, affect the citizens of the Third World in significant
ways. 'The problems involve changing patterns of organization, political economy
configurations, and cultural adaptation to new ecological systems.' The Bayano
Hydroelectric Project is studied for its impact on residents of the area.

Foreign Relations

General

418 Beneath the United States: a history of U.S. policy toward Latin America.
Lars Schoultz.   Cambridge, Massachusetts: Harvard University Press, 1998. 476p. bibliog.

A hegemonic model is used to analyse US policy in those of its aspects that are infused by elements of racism and nationalism.

419 Canalgate: a Panama Canal brief for the American people.
Samuel J. Stoll.   Livingston, New Jersey: Policy Press, 1989. 589p.

Stoll confronts the administration policies that led to the treaties of 1903 and 1977 with documents, many of which appear in full text versions, which suggests that a more widespead and careful study of material such as these would have led to changes in the treaties now in force.

420 Communism in Central America and the Caribbean.
Edited by Robert Wesson.   Stanford, California: Hoover Institution Press, 1982. 177p. bibliog. (Hoover International Studies).

'Costa Rica, Honduras, and Panama' was contributed by Neale J. Pearson, a scholar who has specialized in political movements, especially those of the Left.

421 The good neighbors: America, Panama, and the 1977 Canal treaties.
Edited by G. Harvey Summ, Tom Kelly. Athens, Ohio: Ohio University Center for International Studies, Latin American Studies Program, 1988. 160p. bibliog. (Monographs in International Studies. Latin American Series, no. 14).

A series of papers, written before the US invasion of Panama by persons affiliated with the prestigious graduate School of Foreign Service at Georgetown University, Washington, DC. The papers are arranged chronologically but move all preceding events and political documents towards the treaties of 1977.

422 Latin America: its problems and its promise.
Edited by Jan Knippers Black. Boulder, Colorado: Westview Press, 1998. 658p. bibliog.

Using multi-disciplinary approaches, the essays explore various topics, among them US–Panamanian relations.

423 Panama and the United States: divided by the Canal.
Edmund Lindop. New York: Twenty-First Century Books, 1997. 127p. maps. bibliog.

Lindop discusses foreign policy issues between the United States and Panama, specifically regarding the Canal and the Canal Zone. The intended audience is older children and young adults.

424 The Panama Canal.
Barbara Gaines Winkelman. New York: Children's Press, 1999. 32p. (Cornerstones of Freedom).

Writing for children aged 9-12, Winkelman tells the story of the Panama Canal incorporating all the current political thinking about the venture. The book is illustrated with historical photographs and furnished with a timeline.

425 Panama, the Canal, and the United States: a guide to issues and references.
Thomas M. Leonard. Claremont, California: Regina Books, 1993. 132p. maps. bibliog. (Guides to Contemporary Issues, 9).

A useful book for generalists studying current Panamanian history, with summaries of the key topics of Panama's political history, the United States and Panama in their changing relationships over the years, and the causes and effects of the 1989 invasion. The aim of the book is to provide a context for the bibliographical essay that ends it. Highly selective in its material, the point of view is always to present the transactions within a relationship, first of an enabling and then a stifling major power in its dealings with a client state.

426 Panama Canal Commission. Annual Report.
Washington, DC: Panama Canal Commission: for sale by the
Superintendent of Documents, US Government Printing Office,
1982- . annual.

Operating data with full details as to cargoes and ports of origin and destinations are given
in these reports mandated by the US executive branch during the time it was responsible
for the operation of the Panama Canal. The canal is fully under the control of Panama as
from the end of 1999.

427 Tres ensayos sobre la cuestión canalera. (Three essays about the
Canal question.)
Diogenes A. Arosemena G. Panama City: Instituto de Estudios
Políticos e Internacionales, Editorial Portobelo, c. 1996. 1 vol.

A pamphlet that makes available the thinking of a leading Panamanian intellectual about
matters relating to the Panama Canal.

Before the Canal Treaties of 1977

**428 The banana wars: a history of United States military
intervention in Latin America from the Spanish-American War
to the invasion of Panama.**
Ivan Musicant. New York: Macmillan, 1990. 470p.

This is a readable retelling of the history of US involvement in Latin America from 1898
to the Panama Invasion, which forms the afterword on pages 390-417. The original tale
of President Teddy Roosevelt's 'taking' of the Canal Zone is recounted. Other countries
discussed include Cuba, Haiti, the Dominican Republic and Nicaragua. The theme
throughout is how the United States tried on the mantle of empire, emulating its European
cousins. Panama is covered on pages 79-136, 390-417.

429 Central America.
Mario Rodriguez. Englewood Cliffs, New Jersey: Prentice-Hall,
1965. 178p. bibliog. (Modern Nations in Historical Perspective).

Panama is historically oriented towards South America rather than Central America, says
the author, but through its very location cannot help but have some influence in the rest
of Central America. Panama's role is discussed in several chapters.

430 Commentary on Pan American problems.
Ricardo J. Alfaro. Cambridge, Massachusetts: Harvard University
Press, 1938. 98p.
The work comprises 'Three Oscar S. Straus memorial association lectures delivered at
Harvard University on February 28, March 2, and March 4, 1938'. The Spanish title is
Panorama internaciónal de América.

**431 Conflict resolution and democratization in Panama: implications
for U.S. policy.**
Edited by Eva Loser. Washington, DC: Center for Strategic and
International Studies, 1992. 95p. (Significant Issues Series, vol. 14,
no. 2).
In this series of papers the topics discussed include: 'The Panama debacle' by Frederick
Kempe; 'The failure of Panama's internal opposition, 1987-1989' by Richard L. Millett;
'Panama's troubled resuscitation as a nation-state' by Andres Oppenheimer; 'Foreign
assistance and reconstruction efforts' by Eusebio Mujal-León and Christopher Bruneau;
'Panama: national shadow without political substance' by Irving Louis Horowitz ; and
'Comparative perspectives on promoting democracy in Panama' by Thomas Carothers.
The issues relate to the efforts of the opposition to oust the Noriega government, the
failure of which led to the US invasion of Panama, the reasons that can be adduced and
the results of the installation of the opposition as the new government by the more
powerful partner.

**432 Cultural imperialism and the development of the Panama Canal
Zone, 1912-1960.**
Stephen Wolff Frenkel. PhD thesis, Syracuse University, New
York, 1992. 350p. (Available from University Microfilms, Ann
Arbor, Michigan, order no. AAT 9312610).
The Abstract explains that 'The dissertation examines and interprets the development of
the Panama Canal Zone, an American administrative and suburban enclave built
alongside the Panama Canal'.

**433 The dynamics of foreign policymaking: the President, the
Congress, and the Panama Canal treaties.**
William L. Furlong, Margaret E. Scranton. Boulder, Colorado:
Westview Press, 1984. 263p. bibliog.
The signing of the 1977 Panama Canal Treaties was the crown of the Carter presidency.
The authors explain what went into the making of these treaties, focusing on the
interaction of the President and Congress, the implications for domestic politics and the
handling of big power small power negotiations at the end of the twentieth century. A
keynote of this last was the way in which the Senate proceeded to ratify these documents,
and the impact of the House of Representatives. An appendix contains the text of the
treaties.

434 The era of U.S. Army installations in Panama.
Dolores De Mena. Fort Clayton, Panama: Headquarters US Army
South History Office, 1996. 216p. maps.

A history of the army bases in Panama that have been such bones of contention, and
which have become such valuable developmental areas in the post-Zonal period.

435 France and Panama: the unknown years, 1894-1908.
James M. Skinner. New York: P. Lang, 1989. 310p. (American
University Studies. Series IX, History, vol. 50).

The expectations of instant wealth held by the investors in the building of the Panama
Canal were dashed at the demise of the first company, headed by Charles and Ferdinand
de Lesseps and Gustav Eiffel. But hopes were raised again when the second, the
Compagnie Nouvelle du Canal de Panama took over in 1894. This company would
continue the building of the canal started by de Lesseps and finally, in 1904, hand it over
to the United States, Panama having successfully seceded from Colombia. This readable
account focuses on the history of the company that was at the centre of the developments
that led to a modern Panama.

436 Panama and the United States: the forced alliance.
Michael L. Conniff. Athens, Georgia: University of Georgia Press,
1992. 201p.

A survey for the general reader of US–Panama relations for the past 170 years with
interpretations for key events. The 'forced alliance' of the title refers to the aspirations of
Panama from earliest times to be a commercial crossroads and the need of the United
States to link its Atlantic and Pacific coasts, a joint alliance forced by circumstances. In
another sense it is also the force suggested by an alliance between strong and weak
partners. For the United States it was a matter of the very entangling alliance foreign
policy traditionally avoided. For Panama it was a matter of being Americanized to the
detriment of the Hispanic traditions. Conniff suggests that the final decision is in the
hands of the people, not the diplomats.

437 The Panama Canal: the crisis in historical perspective.
Walter LaFeber. New York: Oxford University Press, 1989. 270p.

The author states in his preface that his aim is to present the history of US and
Panamanian relations so that readers will be better equipped to understand the current
situation. The original edition has been updated in this present publication to include
events up to the tenure of President Reagan. The chapters centre on the presidential
administrations of William Howard Taft, Woodrow Wilson, Franklin Roosevelt, Dwight
D. Eisenhower, Lyndon B. Johnson, Jimmy Carter and Ronald Reagan which are seen to
have significant dealings with Panama. The exposition is even-handed in its presentation
with the conflicting needs and aspirations of the two countries and the resolution of the
problems.

438 The Panama Canal in American national consciousness, 1870-1990.
Alfred Charles Richard, Jr.   New York: Garland, 1990. 378p.
(Foreign Economic Policy of the United States).

The bulk of this monograph covers the early decades of US involvement in Panama. A brief new introduction brings it up to 1990. The work is invaluable for its collection of political cartoons from influential newspapers in the early part of the 20th century, such as the *New York World* and the *Oregonian*, and accompanying commentary. It examines US public opinion as reflected in widely read publications such as *The North American Review*, the *Nation* and the *Literary Digest*. This is a revision of the author's PhD thesis, Boston University, 1969.

439 The Panama Canal in American politics: domestic advocacy and the evolution of policy.
J. Michael Hogan.   Carbondale, Illinois: Southern Illinois University Press, 1986. 291p.

Only the Treaty of Versailles had a more prolonged debate in the US Senate than the Panama Treaties. The author looks at the impact of language in the shaping of public opinion during the period of drafting and approving the treaties with Panama. Always considering language, the author devotes the first third of the book to the early history, dwelling on Theodore Roosevelt's infamous boast of 1911, 'I took the Canal' (p. 61). The rest of the book looks at the debate that occupied the public and the politicians, detailing the methods used by the State Department to 'educate the American people' who by and large wanted to retain the status quo on the isthmus. Techniques used to lobby Congress are extensively discussed. Hogan concludes that the ambiguities in the treaty about defence may be the source of new difficulties in the early decades of the 21st century.

440 Panamá: historia de una crisis. (Panama: the history of a crisis.)
Ricaurte Soler.   Mexico City: Siglo Veintiuno Editores, 1989. 119p.

Soler, who has long written about Panamanian nationhood, looks again at United States and Panamanian relations.

441 Panama odyssey.
William J. Jorden.   Austin, Texas: University of Texas Press, 1984. 746p.

A detailed account of the Panama Canal Treaties of 1977 by an author who is a former senior staff member, Latin American Affairs, of the National Security Council and US ambassador to Panama during four key years. The basic documents of this history have been augmented by interviews and conversations with the major players in the treaty negotiations, a list of whose names is given in the sources. The book contains photographs and two useful maps, one of which graphically shows the changes in governance of the Canal Zone.

442 Portrait of the Panama Canal.
William Friar. Portland, Oregon: Graphic Arts Center, 1996. 1 vol.

Friar's lively presentation of the building and operation of the Panama Canal is lavishly illustrated by both historical and current photographs. This title provides a good contrast to readers who are examining older photographs of the area.

443 Prize possession: the United States and the Panama Canal, 1903-1979.
John Major. Cambridge, England; New York: Cambridge University Press, 1993. 432p.

A comprehensive history of US Panama Canal policy from 1903 to 1979 based on primary sources from archives that include the State Department, the Department of Defense, and the Panama Canal Commission. Major draws strong parallels between the US Canal and the British-controlled Suez Canal activity of the 1950s.

444 Red, white, and blue paradise: the American Canal Zone in Panama.
Herbert Knapp, Mary Knapp. San Diego, California: Harcourt Brace Jovanovich, 1985. 306p.

A first-hand account of an extended residence in the Panama Canal Zone by two high-school teachers. The Zone had been designed in the early part of the century to be a workers' utopia, but instead, is seen by the authors as a 'peaceful, rational, coherent, non democratic system', 'the unintended consequences of which were limited access to predestined forms of success, a diminished value placed on the individual, and a static quality that could not adapt to change.' This book, although based on personal experience is better than a diary as a primary resource because it can also draw on other resources, such as student work. One chapter refutes assertions of international authors about the Zone, among them Paul Theroux, who felt qualified to explain the Zonians to themselves. These New Yorkers were disconcerted to learn from him that they were from the Deep South, and thus racists. A work that will be of value to historians for some time to come.

445 Searching for Panama: the U.S.-Panama relationship and democratization.
Mark Falcoff, Richard L. Millett, foreword by Georges A. Fauriol. Washington, DC: Center for Strategic and Internatioal Studies, 1993. 42p. (Significant Issues Series, vol. 15, no. 6).

These two essays consider Panama's future. Dr Falcoff discusses the impact of independence for the close control exercises by the United States in the past, the development of a fuller democracy and the modernization of the economy, especially the Canal, in light of the loss of the US government subsidies. Dr Millett looks at the shaky political structure and the economic and security needs of the country. A useful short summary of policy issues just prior to the 1994 elections is included.

446 Simulating sovereignty: intervention, the state, and symbolic exchange.
Cynthia Weber. Cambridge, England; New York: Cambridge University Press, 1995. 147p.
Weber applies the deconstruction methods of Michel Foucault and Jean Baudrillard to an analysis of several episodes of intervention as practised by such groups as the Concert of Europe, NATO and the administrations of Presidents Reagan and Bush.

447 Theodore Roosevelt's Caribbean: the Panama Canal, the Monroe Doctrine, and the Latin American context.
Richard H. Collin. Baton Rouge, Louisiana: Louisiana State University Press, 1990. 598p.
The foreign policy of Roosevelt referenced Europe almost exclusively, so that the US action in Central America was essential to deny European control over an isthmian canal. This detailed work, mainly based on primary documents, argues that in the context of isolationist, racist politicians in the United States, expansionist colonizers in Europe must also consider the Latin American aspirations of José Martí, Simón Bolívar and other South American nationalists. These elements combined to form the movement that resulted in the formation of an independent Panamanian state. Insularity, racism and the low esteem in which the United States was held by the European powers contributed to this policy and its reception.

448 Understanding the Central American crisis: sources of conflict, U.S. policy, and options for peace.
Edited by Kenneth M. Coleman, George C. Herring. Wilmington, Delaware: SR Books, 1991. 240p. (Latin American Silhouettes).
In this collection of essays various aspects and themes that are key to Central American politics are discussed. Richard L. Millett contributes an early essay on post-invasion conditions, 'The aftermath of intervention: Panama, 1990'. This material is designed to be accessible to students.

449 U.S.-Panama relations, 1903-1978: a study in linkage politics.
David N. Farnsworth, James W. McKenney. Boulder, Colorado: Westview Press, 1983. 313p. bibliog.
Linkage politics is defined by the author (p. 3), citing James N. Rosenau, as 'any "recurrent sequence of behavior that originates in one system and is reacted to in another"'. The foreign policy links between the United States and Panama are examined from the inception of the canal-building project under US auspices, with emphasis on defining problems and their attempted solutions, and always looking forward to the 1977 treaty. This work is especially valuable for the links identified and described that existed between 'the Two Panamas' and a discussion of the politics of the Zone, from the beginning to the eve of the treaty. Although much has been written about the administration of the Canal, it is generally seen as a free-standing entity. Here the interrelationships between the republic and the Zone are discussed, described and evaluated.

The 1980s

General

450   Civil military operations in the New World.
John T. Fishel.   Westport, Connecticut: Praeger, 1997. 269p.
The author believes that civil military operations (CMOs) are the most essential aspect of successful termination of conflict in the post-Cold War world. Civil military operations are those activities enjoined by international law on an occupying, liberating force in the aftermath of actual war. These operations include the maintenance of law and order, providing food and health care, care of displaced civilians and the re-establishment of public education. One of the major lessons of the 1989 invasion of Panama by the United States is that the US military was not properly trained to carry out these requirements. The author calls for better cross-training of all government agencies likely to be working in CMOs.

451   Comando Sur, poder hostil. (Southern Command, hostile power.)
Raul Leis.   Panama City: Centro de Estudios y Acción Social Panameño, 1985. 124p.
Raul Alberto Leis Romero (b.1947), who writes as Raul Leis, has written prize-winning plays, including *El nido del Macuá* (1982) (The Macuá nest), and *Mundunción* (1988), as well as other works listed here.

452   In the aftermath of war: US support for reconstruction and nation-building in Panama following Just Cause.
Richard H. Shultz.   Maxwell Air Force Base, Alabama: Air University Press, 1993. 73p.
A description and evaluation of the United States government's role in reconstructing Panama after the US invasion in 1989. Another version of this report with the same name was issued during the same year by the Office of the Assistant Secretary of Defense for Special Operations and Low Intensity Conflict.

453   Letter from Panama.
Alma Guillermorprieto.   *The New Yorker*, vol. 68, no. 26 (17 August 1992), p. 60-72.
President Bush visited Panama in June 1992, an event which focuses this extended essay on the impact of the US involvement with Manuel Noriega in Panama and subsequent events.

454 **The limits of victory: the ratification of the Panama Canal treaties.**
George D. Moffett, III. Ithaca, New York: Cornell University Press, 1985. 263p.

Written under the auspices of the Center for International Affairs, Harvard University, this detailed study of the process that led up to the ratification of the Panama Canal treaties, looks at the reasons behind the high political cost to the Carter administration of achieving senate ratification and how, in a climate of anti-ratification, the administration finally succeeded in achieving the necessary two-thirds majority, possibly at the cost of the re-election of the president. The American public in general looked at the negotiations as a failure of resolve on the part of the government to retain what was, by right of development, American. The author has made extensive use of primary sources, including taped interviews with the major negotiators, public opinion polls, and presidential papers.

455 **The Noriega mess: the drugs, the Canal, and why America invaded.**
Luis E. Murillo. Berkeley, California: Video-Books, 1995. 1096p. maps.

Murillo writes for a general audience a readable and vivid account of the Noriega government in Panama. He is able to supply details, some running contrary in part to those reported in government reports, because he is personally related to members of that government and has access to sources not available to outsiders. Most of his sources are either personal or journalistic, but his appendices include much basic data, such as economic tables, and the Noriega indictment. He supports the invasion of Panama and gives his reasons, essentially because it was desired by the Panamanian people and was necessary to give a chance at economic growth within a democratic framework.

456 **The Noriega years: U.S. Panamanian relations, 1981-1990.**
Margaret E. Scranton. Boulder, Colorado: Lynne Rienner Publishers, 1991. 245p.

Since the author states that this book, an explanation of US policy during the 1980s, cannot be understood without the Panamanian context, she has drawn in the view from the Panamanian side and supplied salient formative details. Her analysis occurs at three levels: international systems, the nation-state, and the decision-making process. Her conclusions are based on what she sees as a lack of interest in the well-being of Panama as a state during the 1970s and 1980s that contrasted sharply with the developmental interest of the preceding 20 years. The final chapter lists the crucial issues facing the country, among them the need for institutional reforms and creating consensus by constitutional means, and seriously addressing the race and class divisions that mark its society.

457 **An old canal's new life.**
The Economist (US), vol. 351 (12 June 1999), p. 29.

The Panamanian Canal Authority's structure and powers are described in this brief article. Additional information is given about how the Authority is quarantined from political interference.

458 Panamanian militarism: a historical interpretation.

Carlos Guevara Mann. Athens, Ohio: Ohio University Center for International Studies, 1996. 221p. (Monographs in International Studies. Latin American Series, no. 25).

The author distinguishes two types of militarism, predatory and institutionalized, and describes both, finally concluding that militarism and corruption infuse the Panamanian sub-culture. He considers the militarism that existed in Panama's early history to be predatory, while that of the twentieth century has become institutionalized. Both types are discussed at length in this scholarly exposition. Guevara argues that Panamanian militarism is deeply rooted in the political system, and that the abolition of the Defense Forces in 1989 did not eradicate it. He predicts that it will return as a dominant force.

459 The Panamanian problem: how the Reagan and Bush administrations dealt with the Noriega regime.

Godfrey Harris, Guillermo de St. Malo Arias. Los Angeles, California: Americas Group, 1993. 352p. bibliog.

The authors founded the Associación Panameña de Relaciones Internacionales (Foreign Policy Association of Panama) in the 1980s, believing that the United States and Panama enjoyed a special relationship, but that the American public needed more information about Panama. In this book are narrated the events that led to the US invasion and its aftermath. It is especially strong in its identification of the many players who wielded power on both sides, and supplies or emphasizes some factors that are omitted or played down in other accounts.

460 United States policy in Latin America: a decade of crisis and challenge.

Edited by John D. Martz. Lincoln, Nebraska: University of Nebraska Press, 1995. 407p.

This collection is useful for its survey and analysis of key political developments in Latin America during the 1980s and 1990s. Steve C. Ropp contributes an essay 'The Bush Administration and the invasion of Panama: explaining the choice and timing of the military option'.

461 U.S. influence in Latin America in the 1980s.

Edited by Robert Wesson. New York: Praeger, 1982. 242p. (Politics in Latin America).

Steven Ropp's essay on Panama, subtitled 'Restive client', partakes of the theme of the whole work, which is an 'assessment of levels of influence', of 'means and magnitude of U.S. influence in Latin America'. He finds in his essay (p. 120-40) that the epithet 'neo-colonial' no longer suffices and explores new dimensions, especially generational changes and psychological distancing. The collection is based on papers from a conference held at the Hoover Institution, Stanford University.

462 The U.S. military bases: will they stay or go?
John Lindsay-Poland. *NACLA Report on the Americas*, vol. 29, no. 5 (March-April 1996), p. 6-10.

This detailed and thoughtful article by John Lindsay-Poland, the Coordinator of the Fellowship of Reconciliation Task Force on Latin America and the Caribbean, and editor of the quarterly *Panama Update*, takes up each of several possibilities as to the nature of the US military presence in Panama, examining the benefits and dangers of each of the options. As originally constituted, bases accounted for thousands of jobs and represented 4.5 per cent of the Gross Domestic Product. Alternatives are discussed.

463 World wonder risks.
José Luis Salinas, Stavros Costarangos. *Risk Management*, vol. 45 (December 1998), p. 44-45.

The authors, Dr José Luis Salinas – risk manager for the Panama Canal Commission – and Stavros Costarangos, president of Istion Managers Panama, Inc., describe the area of risk to the Panama Canal and suggest means to contain insurance costs by prevention and training. The risks discussed are to assets, liabilities, and loss of revenue.

Treated in fiction

464 Panama, a historical novel.
William Young Boyd, II.   Herndon, Virginia: Capital Books, 1999. 196p.

In a panoramic historical novel which covers the time from the building of the Canal to the present, the necessarily multiple protagonists, the male line of a well-connected family, witness and participate in the stirring events. There is general reviewer agreement that the novel does not work well, but the history is readable, with details acquired from Boyd's early life in Panama.

465 The tailor of Panama.
John Le Carré.   New York: Knopf, 1996. 331p.

A fast-paced and superbly written satire about a plot to void the 1977 Panama Canal Treaty in which a British citizen now resident in Panama is blackmailed into working for British intelligence.

466 Target: Panama.
Mack Tanner.   New York: Kensington Publishing, 1993. 318p.

A novel of suspense using Panama as the focal point for an act of political revenge.

The US military intervention, 1989

Personal accounts and reportage

467 Assembly demands immediate halt of United States intervention in Panama; similar text vetoed in Security Council.
UN Chronicle, vol. 27 (March 1990), p. 67.
The article reports and summarizes the action of the United Nations Security Council and General Assembly in reacting to the US invasion of Panama.

468 Battle for Panama: inside Operation Just Cause.
Edward M. Flanagan, Jr. Washington, DC: Brassey's, 1993. 251p.
(AUSA Institute of Land Warfare Book).
A retired general of the US Army who has written several works of military history, builds the background of the US invasion of Panama in 1989, then describes in detail each of the separate operations. His sources include a large number of primary items: interviews, private papers, letters and personal communications, all of which are identified in the Sources (p. 241-44). His evaluative sections are thoughtful and do not conflate military and political aspects of history.

469 The enemy within: casting out Panama's demon: illustrated with 320 photos.
Kenneth J. Jones. El Dorado, Panama: Focus, 1990. 132p.
Jones's heavily illustrated book gives detailed information about Operation Just Cause.

470 Esta es la Causa Justa: testimonios de un pueblo ante una tragedia vigente: la invasión de Estados Unidos a Panamá. This is the Just Cause; breaking the silence: testimony of the Panamanian people, resulting from the U.S.A. invasion.
Comissión para la Defensa de los Derechos Humanos en Centroamérica. San José, Costa Rica: CODEHUCA, 1990. 118p. bibliog.
With materials in both English and Spanish, a collection of eyewitness accounts of the violence attending the US invasion of Panama, 1989.

471 Invasion: the American destruction of the Noriega regime in Panama.
Photographs by David S. Behar, narrated by Godfrey Harris, prologue and epilogue by Ross W. Simpson. Los Angeles, California: Americas Group, 1990. 144p.
A heavily illustrated book that looks at the invasion of Panama from three perspectives: the photographs depict the historical event, the narrative describes US–Panama relations, and the prologue and the epilogue discusses the US. military experience. This book is an

early look at the events described by two experienced men; Behar is a Panamanian businessman and author of several other titles about Panama; Simpson is a veteran radio news correspondent. The authors argue that as a show of force and as a military operation it was successful in upholding the provisions of the 1977 treaty.

472 Just Cause: Marine operations in Panama, 1988-1990.
Nicholas E. Reynolds. Washington, DC: History and Museums Division, Headquarters, US Marine Corps; for sale by the US Government Printing Office, 1996. 50p. maps.

Reynolds is a military historian. This is his account of Marine Corps policies and actions in Panama for the period covering Operation Just Cause.

473 Just Cause: the real story of America's high-tech invasion of Panama.
Malcolm McConnell. New York: St. Martin's Press, 1991. 307p.

This is a tightly written and dramatic account of the US invasion of Panama. The author makes the point in this collection of episodes, by means of which he builds his case, that much of the use of military technology tested in Panama was later used against Iraq, and by implication, that that was why is was first used against militarily unsophisticated Panama.

474 El libro de la invasión. (The book of the invasion.)
Pedro Rivera, Fernando Martinez. Mexico City: Fondo de Cultura Económica, 1998. 356p.

An oral history, in part, the work recounts some experiences of the American invasion of 1989.

475 May the world know it = Que el mundo lo sepa.
Luis Humberto Gonzalez. Havana: Editorial José Martí, 1990. 31p. 40p. of plates.

Although published in Cuba, this work is by a Mexican photographer whose work has been published widely. He describes his experiences in covering the US invasion of Panama in 1989 in this bi-lingual edition and includes a selection of photographs of the war. The work is in English and Spanish.

476 Operation Just Cause: Panama, December 1989, soldier's eyewitness account.
Clarence E. Briggs, III. Harrisburg, Pennsylvania: Stackpole Books, 1990. 155p.

A detailed account of one man's experience, this book might well belong with most other personal accounts except for Briggs's recommendations at the end of his adventure. Briggs suggests that, in limited warfare where the fighting is not separated from civilians, soldiers be better trained to cope with civilian needs in a war zone, such as traffic control, civil order and civil emergencies. The current separate specialists, possibly based on the Second World War model are too few and not available where and when needed.

477 Operation Just Cause: the storming of Panama.
Thomas Donnelly, Margaret Roth, Caleb Baker. New York: Lexington Books; Toronto: Maxwell Macmillan Canada; New York: Maxwell Macmillan International, 1991. 453p.

In terms of a military operation alone, Operation Just Cause has generally been considered a success in supporting the US foreign policy of the time. This account relies on military journalism sources, and many parts of the book are undocumented, but the author's writing seems steeped in military science. Tactical maps assist in understanding the battle orders.

478 Panama invaded: imperial occupation vs struggle for sovereignty.
Compiled and edited by Philip E. Wheaton. Trenton, New Jersey: Red Sea Press, 1992. 188p. bibliog.

A compilation, by an Episcopal priest with 35 years' experience in Central American and Caribbean affairs, of eyewitness accounts of Panamanians' experiences during the 1989 invasion by the United States and some comments and discussion by important but non-establishment leaders. Although Wheaton's thesis that Panama was a testing-ground for advanced weapons can probably be refuted on the grounds that Panama was too small for such a use, his concern for the welfare of people who have no voice is well expressed here.

479 Panama: made in the USA.
John Weeks, Phil Gunson. London: Latin American Bureau, 1991. 131p.

A short, concise history of the US invasion of Panama in 1989. The authors develop the case against the United States government and show little interest in the country as such. Material is selected to support the authors' contention that the United States abused its power in its actions in Panama; the factual material, however, is useful and well presented.

480 Support from Panama for U.S. invasion.
Society, vol. 27, no. 3 (March-April 1990), p. 2-4.

The article consists of an early look at Panamanian popular support for the 1989 invasion.

Analytical

481 Beyond the storm: a Gulf crisis reader.
Edited by Phyllis Bennis, Michel Moushabeck, foreword by Edward Said, introduction by Eqbal Ahmad. Brooklyn, New York: Olive Branch Press, 1991. 412p.

A short esssay 'The Panama paradigm' by a noted journalist Barbara Ehrenreich – who is also the author of the well-received *Blood rites: origins and history of the passions of war* – describes the US invasion of Panama in the light of the Gulf War on pages 88-91.

She argues that the Panama action may well prove to have been just as poor a decision as the prolongation of the Vietnam War.

482 A country in fragments.
Bessy Reyna. *The Women's Review of Books*, vol. 9, nos. 10-11 (July 1992), p. 14.
The author of this essay examines the paradox of neo-colonialism at work in Just Cause where the invaders see themselves as rescuers, and the rescued, the citizens of Panama, come to see themselves as being unexpectedly worse off than under the oppressive Noriega regime.

483 The laws of war and the conduct of the Panama invasion.
New York: Human Rights Watch, 1990. 53p. (An Americas Watch Report).
The Human Rights Watch presents arguments against the US invasion of Panama in 1989.

484 The "man question" in international relations.
Edited by Marysia Zalewski, Jane Parpart. Boulder, Colorado: Westview Press, 1998. 219p.
In her essay 'Something's missing: male hysteria and the U.S invasion of Panama' (p. 150-68), Cynthia Weber, a political scientist at Purdue University (USA), argues that Noriega and Bush exhibited hysteria (a feminine attribute) because both, in different ways, lacked the Panama Canal. Because of this shared phenomenon, both used excessively masculine imagery in their invasion discourse. If one accepts her equation, 'domestic = feminine, international = masculine' and her assertion that Operation Just Cause was justified on domestic grounds alone – that is, to the American people and without reference to international organizations such as the Organization of American States – the value of such criticism of the discourse is useful primarily to linguistic scholars and political scientists. The book as a whole is a collection of essays applying feminist criticism to international affairs. Weber's essay was also published in *Sexual artifice: persons, images, politics*, edited by Ann Kibey (New York: New York University Press, 1994).

485 Operation Just Cause: lessons for operations other than war.
Jennifer Morrison Taw. Santa Monica, California: Rand, 1996. 40p.
Taw's detailed study of the military aspects of the US invasion of Panama identifies the implications for similar future operations. These operations, known as Military Operations Other Than War, are characterized by the use of high technology, mixed small units, restrictive rules of engagement, and preservation of infrastructure and public utilities. From this analysis, which the author prepared for the United States Army, there develops a series of recommendations including the need for better intelligence and more effective and less destructive operations in urban areas.

486 Operation Just Cause: the U.S. intervention in Panama.
Edited by Bruce W. Watson, Peter G. Tsouras. Boulder, Colorado: Westview Press, 1991. 245p.
This collection of essays written by intelligence experts and academics examines several aspects of the US intervention in Panama. It is an early and successful attempt to go

beyond the reportorial and evaluate the operation. One essay discusses how the Panamanians came to believe themselves not only owners but also builders of the Canal. Another discusses the government's role in narcotics and money-laundering. One section deals with the operation as a military phenomenon, and includes many comparisons with recent US military operations.

487 Panama: casualties of the US invasion.
Peter Kandela. *The Lancet*, vol. 335, no. 8696 (28 April 1990), p. 1025.
The death count in the US invasion of Panama in 1989, and its aftermath, has been a matter of bitter controversy. This editorial discusses the work of the Physicians for Human Rights which investigated the matter.

488 Panama: made in the U.S.A.
Bernard A. Weisberger. *American Heritage*, vol. 40, no. 7 (November 1989), p. 24-25.
This condemnation of the US invasion of Panama was written as it was occurring. It was bolstered by a rather cursory overview of US–Panama history, but the article is useful as representative of media dissent.

489 State crime, the media, and the invasion of Panama.
Christina Jacqueline Johns, P. Ward Johnson. Westport, Connecticut: Praeger, 1994. 157p. (Praeger Series in Criminology and Crime Control Policy).
The presence of this title in the Praeger series in criminology and crime control policy suggests that the emphasis is on what constitutes a state crime and how it should be handled. The authors have limited themselves to pinpointing the areas of conflict, such as the use of military power, a diplomatic arm, in the drug enforcement area which is a criminal law violation. They also discuss those underlying assumptions that would help in understanding the relationship between criminal law and international law. It provides a good introduction to the conflict between the two legal approaches for a reader who is not a legal specialist.

490 This is the Just Cause: breaking the silence: testimony of the Panamanian people, resulting from the U.S.A. invasion.
New York: Apex Press, 1991. 2nd ed. 79p.
The material was gathered by the Comisión para la Defensa de los Derechos Humanos en Centroamérica. This second edition is in English only.

491 The U.S. invasion of Panama: the truth behind Operation 'Just Cause'.
Independent Commission of Inquiry on the U.S. Invasion of Panama. Boston, Massachusetts: South End Press, 1991. 133p.
This collection of documents from various groups dissenting from the official assessment of the US invasion of Panama represents opinion from within Panama and in the United States. Any student of this event will find this a useful book for the points of view expressed and also as an indicator of sources of further information.

Economy

General

492 Analysis of WFS data in Colombia, Panama, Paraguay, and Peru: highlights from the CELADE Research and Training Seminar.
Arthur M. Conning, Albert M. Marckwardt.   Voorburg,
Netherlands: International Statistical Institute; London: World
Fertility Survey, 1982. 34p. (Occasional Papers [World Fertility
Survey], no. 25).

The material in this item represents in-depth analysis of data gathered in the 1980s for the World Economic Survey for purposes of economic planning. Findings suggest that for most Panamanian women economic needs rather than fertility are the key factors in joining the workforce after marriage. A second study of infant mortality showed a strong decline in overall infant mortality ascribed to better neonatal care and the control of parasitic diseases.

493 Background notes: Panama.
US Department of State.   Washington, DC: US Government
Printing Office, 1980- . bibliog.

Updated frequently, this publication supplies basic information about Panama and a selective reading list of readily available materials. Essential reading for any traveller, but slanted towards the business community.

494 Censos nacionales de 1990. IV censos económicos, abril-junio 1993. (National censuses of 1990. Fourth economic censuses, April-June 1993.)
Panama City: República de Panama, Contraloría General de la República, Dirección de Estadística y Censo, 1999. Vol. 1- .
This series is in process of production. Volume 1, 'Estructura productiva y financiera de las industrias manufactureras y la construcción' (Production and financial structures of the manufacturing and construction industries), is the first to appear.

495 Country Profile. Panama.
EIU, the Economist Intelligence Unit. London: EIU, annual.
An annual country profile that provides political and economic background about Panama. It is updated quarterly. Topics covered include political background, resources, the economy and economic infrastructure, production, and the external sector. It is the companion publication to *Country Report. Panama*.

496 Foreign Economic Trends and their Implications for the United States. Panama.
US Department of Commerce. Washington, DC: US Government Printing Office, 1968- . semi-annual.
In this overview of general economic activity, current outlook and new and future developments, the emphasis is on the early stages of new or expanded economic activity.

497 Panama at the crossroads: economic development and political change in the twentieth century.
Andrew Zimbalist, John Weeks. Berkeley, California: University of California Press, 1991. 219p.
Each of the topics covered in this book is carried from early beginnings to the present. The first chapter looks at political power as it affects economic development. Later chapters survey institutions in the service economy, such as the Free Zone, banking and the ship registry. In their conclusion the authors call for debt restructuring and a broader-based economy as the way forward for Panamanian economic development.

498 Panamá en América: ensayo de economía poética. (Panama in America: essay of poetic economics.)
Pedro Rivera. Panama City: Ediciones Formato Dieciseis, 1997. 48p.
As Panama entered the decade of its assumption of full control of its destiny, Rivera, a writer and cinematographer, offered some thoughts about Panama's economic future. His humanistic approach to development is evident throughout. 'Panama holds the key to its own destiny', he writes, but 'Latin America and the world, in its turn, must understand that Panama constitutes its own great national resource'.

499   Panama: structural change and growth prospects.
Latin America and the Caribbean Regional Office.   Washington,
DC: World Bank, 1985. 307p. (A World Bank Country Study).

Designed to assist in the major economic policy development at national and international levels, this report covers all aspects of the economy – employment, agriculture, industry and trade, and the role of the government – public employment, national indebtedness, and social security. It is also basic to the planning of anyone doing business in Panama. The statistics conveniently quantify the points covered in the text. A summary of major conclusions precedes the supporting content. The accompanying map displays key items in the infrastructure: roads and type of surface, pipelines, railroads, airports, and seaports.

500   Socioeconomic conditions in Panama.
Princeton, New Jersey: Princeton University Library; Wilmington,
Delaware: Scholarly Resources, 1989. 1 reel. (Princeton University
Latin American Pamphlet Collection).

Pamphlets in English, French and Spanish housed in the Princeton University Libraries have been published in microform, thus making this invaluable and rare collection of source materials on the Panama Canal more widely available.

**501   The soft war: the uses and abuses of U.S. economic aid in
Central America.**
Tom Barry, Deb Preusch.   New York: Grove Press, 1988. 304p.
bibliog.

US economic aid to Panama is discussed in the context of regional policy.

Regional and local

**502   The Cerro Colorado Copper Project: Panama, multinational
corporations and the Guaymí Indians.**
Chris N. Gjording.   PhD thesis, New School for Social Research,
New York, 1985. 408p. (Available from University Microfilms,
Ann Arbor, Michigan, order no. AAT 8607154).

According to the Abstract, the thesis comprises a 'description and analysis of social, economic, political and cultural dimensions of the Cerro Colorado copper mining project in Panama'.

503 **Cooperativismo de Panamá en cifras.** (Statistics of Panamanian cooperatives.)
Silma Pinilla, Wim Dierckxsens. San José, Costa Rica: Confederación de Cooperativas del Caribe y Centro America (CCC-CA), 1993. 106p.

A survey history of the cooperative movement in Panama examines its administrative structures, evaluates its effectiveness, and makes recommendations. Most of the data are provided in map or tabular form as well as being discussed in the text.

504 **Kuna crafts, gender, and the global economy.**
Karin E. Tice. Austin, Texas: University of Texas Press, 1995. 232p.

The author's concern in this work is the effect of craftswomen's access to economic resources. Kuna women are famous for their appliquéd blouse, the *mola*. 'The first six chapters situate San Blas and *mola* commercialization historically within the global political economy.' They treat of such topics as gender and class and ethnicity. The final chapters of the book describe the regional *mola* cooperative, families active in it and its impact on their lives. This scholarly work is eminently useful to a wide range of readers, from feminists to economists.

505 **One is none and two is one: development from above and below in North-central Panama.**
Luz Graciela Joly. PhD thesis, University of Florida, 1981. 336p. (Available from University Microfilms, Ann Arbor, Michigan, order no. AAT 8127435).

As explained in the Abstract, 'This dissertation evaluates the development process in its two major dimensions; namely, planning and programming for "development from above" by bureaucratic systems and the "development from below" of indigenous socio-cultural systems in their process of community development.'

506 **Panama City cost of living survey.**
Stanford, Connecticut: Rector Press, July 1995. 60p.

The publisher specializes in this kind of information used to set salary scales and the like. The publication is frequently updated.

507 **Panama in transition: local reactions to development policies.**
Edited by John R. Bort, Mary W. Helms. Columbia, Missouri: Museum of Anthropology, University of Missouri–Columbia, 1983. 198p. (Monographs in Anthropology, 6).

The 1950s and 1960s, the period covered by these papers, were decades of development in Panama. This collection of papers on human demographic and capitalistic expansion explores the wide range of reactions from the Naturales of the Caribbean who wish to assimilate, to the extreme separatism of the Guaymí. Techniques employed by each group include migration and reorganization for survival. Other topics include the impact of mining operations on the ecology, and modern versus traditional modes of politics.

Finance and Banking

508 The economic impact of offshore banking centers on the host countries: with special reference to the feasibility of establishing an offshore banking center in Korea.
Soon Young Chang. DBA thesis, George Washington University, Washington, DC, 1986. 268p. (Available from University Microfilms, Ann Arbor, Michigan, order no. AAT 8613063).

The purpose of this study was to evaluate the economic impact of an offshore banking centre (OBC) on its host country. One of the countries subject to examination for this study was Panama.

509 Emerging financial centers: legal and institutional framework: Bahamas, Hong Kong, Ivory Coast, Kenya, Kuwait, Panama, Singapore.
Robert C. Effros. Washington, DC: International Monetary Fund, 1982. 1150p.

Published by the International Monetary Fund, this compilation of relevant legislation for several financial centres is preceded, for each, by an overview of the financial system of the country. Panama's financial system is discussed and evaluated on pages 799-815. Following the essays are the texts of some dozen laws and decrees.

510 Historia completa y documentada de la moneda panameña.
(Complete and documented history of Panamanian money.)
Guillermo E. Diez Morales. Panama City: Diez Morales, 1974. 386p.

In this documentary history of Panamanian money and its regulation up to the year of publication, see especially 'Leyes y decretos' (Laws and decrees) on pages [107]-256.

511   La moneda panamena. (Panamanian money.)
José Daniel Crespo.   Panama City: Imprenta Nacional, 1953. 56p.

This discussion of appropriate monetary policy for Panama is now of historical interest only.

512   Panama: Latin America's best-kept secret.
William Chislett.   London: Euromoney Publications PLC, in association with Private Asset Management Group, 1995. 164p.

Chislett's overview of Panama stresses the promise it holds for investors and developers. General information on the infrastructure, the economy, several chapters devoted to banking, tourism, the free trade zone and privatization add detail. Ernst and Young, the accounting multinational, provided the chapter on the fiscal environment and the Private Asset Management Group provided a survey of the governmental structure.

513   Panama offers investment opportunities as Canal treaties take effect.
Latin Trade, vol. 7, no. 7 (July 1999), p. 74.

Under the terms of the 1976-77 Panama Canal Treaties, 7,000 former US military buildings and more than 300,000 acres of prime real estate are being transferred to the Panamanian government which has decided to privatize much of it. The article summarizes what has been done to date with this land.

Trade

Guides and directories

514 Cracking Latin America: a country-by-country guide to doing business in the world's newest emerging markets.
Allyn Enderlyn, Oliver C. Dziggel. Chicago: Probus, 1994. 403p.
The material for this concise compendium of information about trading in Panama and other countries is taken from official government sources, mostly the US government, but also from the host government and central bank. For each country there are brief historical and geographical contexts; socio-economic and market demographics, statistics and contracts of interest to business. Two useful features are an introduction that covers regional themes such as the North American Free Trade Agreement and the commercial implications of narcotics trafficking.

515 Decrees regulating the representation, agency, and/or distribution of products or services of local and foreign manufacturers in the Republic of Panama.
Panama City: Morgan & Morgan, Attorneys at Law, 1987. 2nd ed. 24p.
These are the texts of the administrative laws regulating agencies and distributors.

516 Directorio de Investigadores Activos Especializados en Banano.
(Directory of Banana Industry Researchers.)
Panama City: Union of Banana-Exporting Countries. annual. 300p.
A worldwide directory of approximately 400 individuals conducting research in banana agriculture. Entries include: Researcher name and title, education, name and address of sponsoring institution, general and technical experience, field of interest, published works. Arrangement is alphabetical, and the text appears in both Spanish and English.

517 Doing business in Latin America.
Dover, New Hampshire: Kogan Page, 1998. 2nd ed. 352p.

This country-by-country survey has some general information chapters that discuss business climate, government incentives and restrictions, and the commercial scene.

518 Doing business in Latin America and the Caribbean, 1993.
Lawrence W. Tuller. New York: AMACOM, 1993. 385p.

Hemispheric free trade agreements offer a variety of business opportunities, including those providing environmental clean-up and protection. Tuller marshalls data for the countries of Latin America with the intention of fostering mutually profitable business activities. Panama is treated specifically on pages 176-85, and other sections describe regional organizations, such as CACM, the Central American Common Market.

519 International directory of importers south/central America.
Poulsbo, Washington: Interdata, 1999.

Panama is treated on pages 239-41. This very succinct statement of required information includes a directory of companies on pages 242-47. The work is useful for identifying companies who import particular products, general importers, for verifying company data, and for strategic and general business planning.

520 Market survey in Mexico and Panama: selected engineering & chemical products.
New Delhi: Latin American Cell, Indian Institute of Foreign Trade, 1980. 137p.

This market survey looks at the strategic importance of the Colón Free Zone in the profitable distribution of goods throughout the region. Specifically, the study is about Indian exports to Mexico, a major trading partner, using the Free Zone.

521 Panama Annual Directory.
Washington, DC: US Chamber of Commerce, International Division Publications. annual.

The directory gives details of some 300 companies in Panama engaged in international trade. As with several other annual publications, it is not clear when publication began.

522 Que Pasa Panamá!
Brooklyn, New York: Viaful Dynamics, 1992- . bi-monthly.

A newsletter for overseas Panamanians and others that provides news on Panama and the Panamanian communities in the United States and abroad. It provides community and cultural information, and business and networking opportunities offered to Panamanians, with emphasis on business opportunities. It is published in English and Spanish.

Exports and imports

523 ANS oil trade sends ripples to Panama, Virgin Islands plant.
Alan Kovski.   *The Oil Daily*, vol. 45, no. 116 (19 June 1996),
p. 1-2.

An article about Panama's role in moving crude oil from Alaska to markets sheds light on the problems that must be faced in a changing market.

524 Bridging the Pacific; Panama and China.
The Economist, vol. 319, no. 7711 (15 June 1991), p. 44.

Panama as a well-positioned export-processing locale has become attractive to Chinese investors. The article surveys the legal and tax benefits and some of the industries that have been established.

525 Dollars & dictators: a guide to Central America.
Tom Barry, Beth Wood, Deb Preusch.   New York: Grove Press,
1983. 2nd ed. 282p. bibliog.

This is an overview of business operations within the context of the political and economic climate of Central America.

526 Ice cream, in Central America?
Charles R. Bertsch.   *AgExporter*, vol. 10, no. 6 (June 1998),
p. 12-14.

The article describes the new and growing market for American ice cream products in Panama, coming in after European companies developed an interest. It is written for US businesses interested in the Panamanian consumer market.

Industry

527 IV Censos Económicos Nacionales: directorio de establecimientos de actividades económicas, año 1990. (National economics statistics: directory of economic establishments for the year 1990.)
Panama City: La Dirección de Estadística y Censo, 1992.
Vols. 1, 3, 4.

These industrial statistics are published in three volumes: Vol. 1 Características económicas, cifras definitivas (Economics characteristics; final figures); Vol. 3 Directorio de establecimientos, provincia de Panamá (Directory of establishments, province of Panama); Vol. 4 Directorio de establecimientos, resto de la República (Directory of establishments, the rest of the Republic).

528 Directorio Commercial e Industrial de Panamá. (Commercial and Industrial Directory of Panama.)
Panama City: Camara de Comercio, Industrias y Agricultura de Panama, 1954- . annual. 400p.

Formerly *Directorio Comercial e Industrial de la Ciudad de Panamá*, this directory provides company name, address, phone and line of business for 1,250 firms in Panama and the Colón Free Zone. The arrangement is alphabetical by company name. Indexes give access by product and service.

529 Latin American and Caribbean International Moving – Membership.
Panama City: Latin American and Caribbean International Moving. annual.

A bi-lingual Latin American and Caribbean moving, packing, and storage company directory that lists firms that are not subsidiaries of foreign firms.

124

530 North Americans buy Panama power stakes.
Petroleum Times Energy Report, vol. 18, no. 23 (4 December 1998), p. 6.

Four leading North American energy groups – Enron, AES Corporation, Hydro-Quebec and Coastal Power – have bought into Panama's four power-generating companies. This is part of the Panamanian government's plan to privatize some of its industry.

531 Panama.
A. Notholt. *Mining Magazine*, 1991, p. 65.

In 1990 the Panamanian government rescinded restrictions in the national mining reserve areas. Mineral mining has been mostly centred on limestone, clay and salt. The interest of international companies has recently been aroused by gold and copper deposits thus made available.

532 Panama pursues slot as offshore equipment manufacturer.
Sam Fletcher. *The Oil Daily*, vol. 46, no. 119 (24 June 1996), p. 2.

The fact that Panama's top priorities for development are its maritime industry and its tax-free trade zones is the key point made in this report of an interview with Nicolas Ardito-Barletta, now head of the Interoceanic Regional Authority, which takes over the land and infrastructure reverting from US control under the 1977 Panama Canal treaties. One activity planned is offshore equipment manufacturing.

533 Privatization of Panama's electricity generation.
Petroleum Times Energy Report, vol. 18, no. 6 (27 March 1998), p. 6.

The article reports on the government's restructuring of the Panamanian electric power industry, including privatizing half of it.

Agriculture

534 Censos nacionales de 1990: IV censo agropecuario, 21 a 28 abril de 1991: cifras preliminares. (National census, 1990. Commercial agriculture census, 21-28 April, 1991: preliminary data.)
Dirección de Estadística y Censo.   Panama City: La Dirección, 1991. 16p.

These commercial agricultural statistics are of value in governmental and business sectors. Quantities and value of various foodstuffs, exports and the like are provided. This is a good example of the rationalization of quantitative data required to develop effectively a modern economy and social fabric.

535 The conversion of rain forests to pastures in Panama.
Luz Graciela Joly.   In: *The human ecology of tropical land settlement in Latin America.*   Boulder, Colorado: Westview Press, 1989, p. 86-130. maps. bibliog. (Westview Special Studies on Latin America and the Caribbean).

Joly examines the impact that domesticated animals have on the rain forest.

536 The demise of a rural economy: from subsistence to capitalism in a Latin American village.
Stephen Gudeman.   London; Boston, Massachusetts: Routledge & Kegan Paul, 1978. 176p. Reprinted, 1998. (International Library of Anthropology).

A narrative account of how the *campesinos* (country people) of Los Boquerones, Panama, made the transition from subsistence rice and maize farming to sugar cane, a cash crop. The detailing of this event is preceded by a description of Panama's general economic situation at the time of writing. The development of changes such as the substitution of competition for cooperation, and the growing awareness of political empowerment make this scholarly work nearly as exciting reading as *Akenfield* or *Village in the Vaucluse*, although in the present work there is no personalization.

537 **Feeding the crisis: U.S. food aid and farm policy in Central America.**
Rachel Garst, Tom Barry. Lincoln, Nebraska: University of Nebraska Press, 1990. 275p.
US economic assistance in the form of food and development is described and assessed in the context of Central America.

538 **Income effects of donated commodities in rural Panama.**
David L. Franklin, Marielouise W. Harrell, Jerry B. Leonard.
American Journal of Agricultural Economics, vol. 69 (February 1987), p. 115-34.
An economist models different modes of delivering food to the poor of rural Panama and finds that food supplements most nearly resembling traditional foods were better received in households. Data used in the study were developed as part of the Panamanian Nutrition Evaluation Project.

539 **Incomes on some agrarian reform *asentamientos* in Panama.**
William C. Thiesenhusen. *Economic Development & Cultural Change*, vol. 35, no. 4 (July 1987), p. 809-31.
The author examines the primary economic data from forty-three agrarian reform settlements (*asentamientos*) to determine the level and sources of income. These projects were fraught with problems, usually families living on credit intended for agricultural development. A description of the National Agrarian Reform Program is given. The author closes with a set of questions he suggests be considered in further projects and research.

540 **Small-scale fishery development: sociocultural perspectives.**
Kingston, Rhode Island: International Center for Marine Resource Development, 1991. 158p.
This collection of papers was published by the International Center for Marine Resource Development (ICMRD) at the University of Rhode Island with support funds from the US Agency for International Development (USAID). It includes contextualizing information and a paper by J. J. Poggie and R. B. Polinac on the conflict of interests between the traditional and commercial fishers.

541 **Sunny sales prospects ahead in Costa Rica and Panama.**
David Young. *AgExporter*, vol. 6, no. 9 (September 1994), p. 20-22.
David Young describes the growth of agricultural exports to Panama from the United States and compares the market with that of Costa Rica. Government regulation, labelling and consumer preferences are discussed.

Transport

542 The canoe: a history of the craft from Panama to the Arctic.
Kenneth G. Roberts, Philip Shackleton.   Toronto: Macmillan of
Canada, 1983. 279p. bibliog.

In this extensive, beautifully illustrated treatment of simple means of water transportation,
Panama's contributions are discussed in various sections. Rafts and dugouts such are the
piragua, are included in this study. Routes along the western and eastern parts of what is
now modern Panama are discussed briefly. The bibliography occupies pages 265-74.

**543 The Panama Canal: a vision for the future: Universal Congress
of the Panama Canal, 7-10 September, 1997.**
Organizing Commission of the Universal Congress of the Panama
Canal, 1997.   Panama City: Published by the Author, 1997. 59p.

This commemorative collection of pictorial materials and text addresses the past, present
and future of the canal.

**544 Panama, a paradise for world wide investors engaged in the
shipping business: maritime laws and administrative
dispositions.**
Panama City: Morgan & Morgan, 1985. 163p.

Necessary information about the registration and transfer of registration of ships is the
subject of this work, along with an overview of Panamanian maritime law.

545 Ships of the Panama Canal.
James L. Shaw, photographs by Ernest Hallen.   Annapolis,
Maryland: Naval Institute Press, 1985. 269p. maps. bibliog.

This work consists of a collection of photographs taken by Ernest Hallen of ships making
the transit of the Canal between 1907 and 1939. US warships are represented as well as
the behemoths of the trading nations. Curiosities include the *City of New York,* used in the

exploration of Antarctica, and the *Tusitalia*, the last commercial sailing vessel to pass through the locks. The appendix includes lists of 'firsts', such as the first ship of a given nationality to use the canal.

546 Sovereignty for sale: the origins and evolution of the Panamanian and Liberian flags of convenience.
Rodney Carlisle. Annapolis, Maryland: Naval Institute Press, 1981. 278p. bibliog.

Carlisle's detailed history of ship transfers to foreign registry compares Panama and Liberia.

Human Resources

General

547 Black labor on a white canal: Panama, 1904-1981.
Michael L. Conniff. Pittsburgh, Pennsylvania: University of
Pittsburgh Press, 1985. 221p.

In his introduction, Conniff tells us that he 'traces the history of the West Indian
predicament on the isthmus under both American and Panamanian masters'. Some
100,000 West Indians came to work and live in Panama before the Second World War,
and, as the West Indies were still under British rule, that government was also concerned
with the treatment of these workers, in the discrimination the West Indians had suffered
from their arrival on the isthmus, including the loss of citizenship and forced repatriation
for some groups just before the Second World War. Panamanians resenting the
employability of the English-speaking West Indians in the Zone, hindered either their
acceptance or assimilation, while American Canal Zone managers exploited them in their
'gold' (white) and 'silver' (black) stratification of workers. With the implementation of
the 1977 treaty came vast improvements, leaving the future post-colonial outlook bright.

**548 El esclavo negro en el desenvolvimiento económico del istmo de
Panamá durante el descubrimiento y la conquista (1501-1532).**
(The black slave in the economic development of the isthmus of
Panama during the discovery and conquest 1501-32.)
Armando Fortune. *Lotería,* no. 228 (February 1975), p. 1-16.
bibliog.

This is the address given by Professor Fortune on his reception into the Panamanian
Academy of History.

549   Ethnicity at work: divided labor on a Central American banana plantation.
Philippe I. Bourgois.   Baltimore, Maryland: Johns Hopkins
University Press, 1989. 311p. (Johns Hopkins Studies in Atlantic
History and Culture).

The author is a cultural anthropologist whose extensive fieldwork resulted in this book describing the life of workers in the banana plantations of Costa Rica and Panama. Bourgois was especially interested in the relationship of ethnicity to the work experience. He looks at three groups: West Indian blacks; Kuna, Bribri and Guaymí Amerindians; and white North Americans and Hispanics, all of which saw the other groups in terms of cultural stereotypes. Work performed conformed to ethnic groupings, with the Indians doing the lowest skilled, most physically demanding work. Each group is studied separately as to its work and life on the plantation. Sources include archival materials of the United Fruit Company describing historical managerial practices, and interviews and other oral communications of the workers, lower and middle management and top management that substantiate the author's correlation of ethnicity to workforce participation. The bibliography occupies pages 279-302.

550   El fenómeno de la esclavitud en la civilización panameña.
(The phenomenon of slavery in Panamanian civilization.)
Roberto de la Guardia.   *Hombre y Cultura* (Panama), vol. 2
(December 1972), p. 27-73.

The author has excerpted documents illustrating various economic and legal activities of slaves in colonial Panama, such as purchasing their freedom or that of members of their families, the sale and exchange of slaves, and the use of slaves as collateral for loans.

551   Foreign Labor Trends. Panama.
US Department of State.   Washington, DC: US Government
Printing Office, 1997- . annual.

Based on reports from the embassy, this series of country studies includes Panama. The data itself comes mostly from host government sources and includes key labour indicators, a summary of the laws covering labour, social security provisions, recent developments and a directory of labour organizations.

552   Indian slavery and the Cerrato reforms.
William L. Sherman.   *Hispanic American Historical Review*,
vol. 51 (February 1971), p. 25-50.

Slaves were imported into Panama from the earliest years of colonization. This thoroughly documented essay discusses the short-lived reforms of Alonso López de Cerrato, president of the Audiencia 1554-55.

553 An investigation of the labor market earnings of Panamanian males.
James J. Heckman, V. Joseph Hotz. *Journal of Human Resources*, vol. 21, no. 4 (Fall 1986), p. 507-42.

Using recent statistical data, Heckman and Hotz develop an argument that family background is a determinant of relatively high earnings and access to higher education. The data for Panama are compared with countries at several stages of economic development. The data are limited to male workers.

554 Jamaican labor migration: white capital and Black labor, 1850-1930.
Elizabeth McLean Petras. Boulder, Colorado: Westview Press, 1989. 297p. bibliog. (Westview Special Studies on Latin America and the Caribbean).

West Indian labour has long played an important role in the development of Panama. This study moves from the end of the colonial era to pre-Second World War times.

555 Negro slavery in New Granada.
James F. King. In: *Essays in honor of H. E. Bolton.* Berkeley, California: University of California Press, 1945, p. 295-318.

A study of colonial Hispanic slavery, with emphasis on the miners and their social and economic conditions.

556 Panama money in Barbados, 1900-1920.
Bonham C. Richardson. Knoxville, Tennessee: University of Tennessee Press, 1985. 283p.

The building of the Panama Canal had a strong economic, demographic and social impact on the whole Caribbean. In the first two decades of the twentieth century, tens of thousands of Barbadian workers emigrated to Panama to work on the canal, the railroad and the infrastructure of the Canal Zone. As they sent money back to Barbados, those remaining at home had capital they would never otherwise have acquired and used it to buy land. This purchasing power created an inflationary surge. In this eminently readable work by an African-American geographer, the story of what he thinks is the most extreme impact is laid out in the context of local events. Sources include governmental and newspaper archives and photographs from Barbados and the official Panama Canal Commission photographer's record of Barbadians at work. The bibliography is found on pages 269-78.

Labour movement

557 Ethnic diversity on a corporate plantation: Guaymí labor on a United Brands subsidiary in Bocas del Toro, Panama and Talamanca, Costa Rica.
Phillippe Bourgois. Cambridge, Massachusetts: Cultural Survival, 1985. 52p. (Occasional Paper, 19).

This paper forms part of the literature of labour relations in Panama, and its thesis is that the Guyamís' ability to organize effectively can be explained in part by the fact that while this large group forms 70 per cent of the unskilled labour force on the banana plantations, it is also the group that suffers most from ethnic discrimination on the part of other workers. Management sees them as the cheapest possible unskilled labourers and they see themselves as men who will work for only a few years before returning to their homes. A description of the 1960 strike against the United Fruit Company includes much direct anecdotal material from the participants.

558 Labor and politics in Panama: the Torrijos years.
Sharon Phillips Collazos. Boulder, Colorado: Westview Press, 1991. 196p. (Westview Special Studies on Latin America and the Caribbean).

Collazos examines the condition of labour and the labour movement in the 1970s with particular reference to the Labor Act of 1972. Topics covered include the context of the political climate of the decade with special reference to the élites, the influence of Torrijos and his government. A particularly valuable chapter discusses the specific costs and benefits of the act. This labour reform was bitterly fought by business interests and considerably weakened, but nonetheless changed society by extending access to economic benefits to a broad sector of the population.

559 Voces de lucha: testimonios del quehacer sindical: en la viva voz de dirigentes obreros panameños. (Voices of the struggle; union workers: living words of leading Panamanian workers.)
Raul Leis. San José, Costa Rica: CEDAL, Centro de Estudios Democráticos de América Latina; Panama City: IPEL, Instituto Panameño de Estudios Laborales, 1984. 201p.

Leis's description and oral history of Panama's labour unions includes testimonies of labour union activists in Panama.

Statistics

560 **Censos nacionales de 1990: IX de población y V de vivienda, 13 de mayo de 1990. Resultados finales ampliados.** (National census of 1990: 9th of population and 5th of housing, 13 May 1990. Final complete results.)
Dirección de Estadística y Censo.   Panama City: República de Panamá, Contralória General de la República, Dirección de Estadística y Censo, 1991-92. 5 vols. map.

Volume 1 includes data regarding the inhabited areas of Panama; the second volume has general characteristics of population; the third details housing and households. Volume 4 provides data on economic activities and the fifth covers migration and fertility.

561 Demographic Yearbook.
United Nations, Statistical Office.   New York: UN, 1948- . annual.

Statistics on population, births, deaths, marriages and divorces are arranged by subject area. As in other international statistics, the broad arrangement is regional, thus allowing meaningful comparisons.

562 FAO Production Yearbook.
Food and Agriculture Organization.   Rome: FAO, 1946- . annual.

Statistics cover land use, population, crops, livestock, food supply and means of production. More detailed information about forestry and forest products can be found in the *FAO Yearbook of Forest Products*. Country summaries are included.

563 FAO Trade Yearbook.
Food and Agriculture Organization.   Rome: FAO, 1964- . annual.

Statistics cover agricultural products as they are imported or exported, their quantities and value. Tables are arranged regionally which makes it easy to compare Panama's figures with those of its neighbours. Data may cover up to twelve years.

564 Statistical Yearbook.
United Nations, Statistical Office.   New York: UN, 1948- . annual.
The yearbook contains general statistical coverage on population, production of raw materials and manufactured goods, construction, trade, transportation, communications, flow of money, health, education, science and technology, and cultural affairs. A country name index refers the user to Panama and to the applicable regional summaries.

565 World Health Statistics Annual.
World Health Organization.   Geneva: WHO, 1962- . annual. 3 vols.
All aspects of health and disease are covered in this series. Volume 1 includes vital statistics and causes of death, volume 2 deals with infectious diseases, and volume 3 with health personnel and health establishments. Regions are larger than in other series and there is usually a delay of several years in publishing the data.

566 Yearbook of National Account Statistics.
United Nations.   New York: UN, 1957- . annual. 2 vols.
Detailed national accounts estimates are contained in volume 1. Volume 2, 'International tables', gives data on gross national product, national income and national disposable income.

Environment

567 Does mammal community composition control recruitment in neotropical forests? Evidence from Panama.
Nigel M. Asquith, S. Joseph Wright, Maria J. Clauss. *Ecology*, vol. 78, no. 3 (April 1997), p. 941-46.

Do mammals distribute seeds in an area and destroy the seedlings, and thus affect germination patterns? This study was carried out in forests bordering Gatún Lake. The authors conclude that protected seedlings are more likely to come to maturity than unprotected seedlings.

568 An ecological survey of the proposed Volcan Baru National Park, Republic of Panama.
Gland, Switzerland: International Union for Conservation of Nature and Natural Resources, 1973. Distributed in USA by Unipub, New York.

This is a rather old report, but it is both thorough in treatment, and also illustrative of environmental thinking of the 1970s.

569 Ecological survey of the U.S. Department of Defense lands in Panama.
Panama City: The Nature Conservancy, Legacy Resource Management Program, ANCON, 1995. 2 vols. maps. bibliog.

A compilation of environmental planning materials for Albrook Air Force Station, Corozal, Fort Clayton, Fort Amador, Quarry Heights, Semaphore Hill, Summit Radio Station, Fort Davis and Fort Gulick.

570 Las estrategias de recursos naturales del Japon y su efecto en la situación ambiental en América Latina. (Natural resources strategies of Japan and their effect on the environmental situation in Latin America.)
Charlotte Elton. Heredia, Costa Rica: Universidad Nacional, 1992. 73p. (Cuadernos de Política Económica, no. 9).
The author is director of CEASPA, Center for Research and Social Action, Panama. This paper presents data about the trading patterns between Japan and Latin America, with special reference to Panama. US data is included for comparison purposes. Elton concludes that benefits of this trade are unequal, benefiting the industrialized nations over the smaller ones, who for the most part contribute mineral resources to the trade.

571 Forest management practices in the Bayano Region of Panama: cultural variations.
Cynthia S. Simmons. *World Development*, vol. 25, no. 6 (June 1997), p. 989-1000.
A survey was conducted in three indigenous and three settler communities in the Bayano region to measure the degree of environmental degradation and deforestation to evaluate their management. The focus was on the differences between the economics of the regions; use of the forest by both groups was similar.

572 Frank goes to Panama.
The Economist (US), vol. 350, no. 8102 (6 January 1999), p. 75.
Frank Gehry, designer of the Guggenheim Museum in Bilbao, Spain, and whose wife is Panamanian, has taken on the task of developing a master plan for the Panama Canal Zone and former US military bases. Included in the plan will be a bridge over the Canal, housing, and historic preservation that emphasizes eco-tourism.

573 Juan Carlos Navarro, 37: A "revolutionary" who has truly put preservation on the map.
Time International, vol. 153, no. 20 (24 May 1999), p. 90.
In the context of young leaders, Panamanian Juan Carlos Navarro is seen as instrumental in the development of that country's national parks and protected areas. This article details what Navarro has done in this area.

574 Kilowatts and crisis: hydroelectric power and social dislocation in eastern Panama.
Alaka Wali. Boulder, Colorado: Westview Press, 1989. 205p. maps. (Development, Conflict and Social Change Series).
The building of the Bayano hydroelectric complex in what had previously been lands inhabited by groups living a traditional life, offers an example of the conflict between the old and the new. For the Kuna Indians who by it lost 80 per cent of their reserved lands, it was a massive disruption of their lives. For the Panamanians in general, it promised needed electrical energy. One outcome of this project was to rewrite regulations so that international funds for development would assure the survival of fragile ecosystems.

575 Latin American urbanization: historical profiles of major cities.
Edited by Gerald Michael Greenfield. Westport, Connecticut:
Greenwood Press, 1994. 536p. maps.

The two major cities of Panama are included in this handbook which provides succinct,
non-interpretive data, enriched by maps, demographic tables and the like. Each country
in Latin America is the subject of a chapter, and for each chapter an overview of urban
development for the nation as a whole. The profiles that follow have an historical
orientation. Because of the wide variance in demographic data collection in Latin
America, the authors and editors have adapted the material enough to allow for
comparisons. A very selective bibliography ends each section. Panama, Panama City and
Colón are profiled on pages 416-26.

**576 The law of the mother: protecting indigenous peoples in
protected areas.**
Edited by Elizabeth Kemf. San Francisco: Sierra Club Books,
1993. 296p.

The law of the mother watches over the land, its preservation as well as its use. Guillermo
Archibold and Sheila Davey contribute 'Kuna Yala: protecting the San Blas of Panama'.

577 'Living coastline' suffers most from oil spills.
Stephanie Pain. *New Scientist*, vol. 141, no. 1907 (8 January 1994),
p. 4-6.

With the increasing development of industry in Panama, oil spills are an increasing threat
to the environment. This study reports on the results of a 5-year study, and documents the
destruction of the ecosystem.

**578 Long-term changes in the avifauna of Barro Colorado Island,
Panama, a tropical forest isolate.**
W. Douglas Robinson. *Conservation Biology*, vol. 13, no. 1
(February 1999), p. 85-97.

Some bird species on Barro Colorado, in Lake Gatún, have become extinct over the last
20 years. This article describes the changes and discusses probable causes.

579 The Panama Canal; will the watershed hold?
Tensie Whelan. *Environment*, vol. 30, no. 3 (April 1988), p. 12-15.

The deforestation of the canal watershed is a danger to the Panama Canal. A new sea-
level canal brings its own problems. Whelan, a writer on environment affairs in Central
America, sees some increasing awareness of this complexity in policy and planning.

580 Parks, politics, and Panama's future.
Juan Carlos Navarro. *Environment*, vol. 30, no. 3 (April 1988),
p. 38.

As an addition to Whelan's article on the canal watershed (see item above) comes this
plea by Navarro, the Executive Director of ANCON, for Panama to safeguard its ecology.

581 Plants and animals in the life of the Kuna.
Jorge Ventocilla. Austin, Texas: University of Texas Press, 1995.
150p.
This translation of *Plantas y animales en la vida del pueblo Kuna* focuses on the interaction of the Kuna people with their environment, including discussions of both fauna and hunting. In the discussions about flora the author examines the use of medicinal plants, and ecological damage to plants on the seabed. The urgency of ecological preservation is discussed by Ventocilla, who also serves as the editor of this collection.

582 Protecting Panama; the land made famous by Noriega needs to protect its rainforests.
Will Nixon. *E*, vol. 5, no. 4 (August 1994), p. 20-22.
The slash-and-burn agriculture still in use in Panama is threatening the 900 bird species and 1200 tree species that flourish there. The Association for the Conservation of Nature is one of the organizations that are looking for alternatives.

583 Settlement vs. environmental dynamics in a pelagic-spawning reef fish at Caribbean Panama.
D. Ross Robertson, Stephen E. Swearer, Karl Kaufmann, Edward B. Brothers. *Ecological Monographs*, vol. 69, no. 2 (May 1999), p. 195-96.
This is a basic biological study of reef fish and how and where they spawn. It is a good example of the kind of research that must precede eco-tourism as well as other incursions into nature.

584 The Smithsonian's tropical niche.
Alun Anderson. *Nature*, vol. 349, no. 6311 (21 February 1991), p. 647-48.
Because of its many significant accomplishments, the Smithsonian Tropical Research Institute in Panama has managed to survive many political upheavals to attain its present status. The author gives a brief history.

585 Successional patterns of mortality and growth of large trees in a Panamanian lowland forest.
Katharine Milton, Emilio A. Laca, Montague W. Demment.
The Journal of Ecology, vol. 82, no. 1 (March 1994), p. 79-87.
The growth of large trees was studied over a 15-year period, concluding that data from young trees cannot be applied to mature trees.

586 Traditional peoples and biodiversity conservation in large tropical landscapes.
Edited by Kent Hubbard Redford, Jane A. Mansour. Arlington, Virginia: Nature Conservancy, 1996. 267p. (America Verde).
Two essays in this collection deal directly with the conservation challenge facing Panama. They are 'The Kuna Indians and conservation' by Jorge Ventocilla, Valerio Núñez,

Heraclio Herrera, Francisco Herrera and Marc Chapin, and 'On common ground: the Nature Conservancy and traditional peoples: The Rio Chagres, Panama Workshop' by Allyn Maclean Stearman. Other essays discuss the impact of social change on biodiversity conservation.

587 Tropical forest gardening: an alternative to destruction.
The Futurist, vol. 23 no. 3 (May-June 1989), p. 53-54.

One of the scientists engaged in developing counter-measures to the destruction of tropical forests is Gilberto Ocana, a biologist at the Smithsonian Tropical Research Institute headquartered in Panama. This article describes the Forest Garden Project that counters the slash-and-burn techniques used in traditional agriculture.

588 United Nations list of national parks and equivalent reserves.
International Commission on National Parks. Brussels: Hayes, 1971. 2nd ed. 601p.

For Panama this directory lists seven proposed national park areas with descriptions: Baru (or Chiriquí) volcano, an extension to the Chepigara Forest Reserve, Tacaruma, the mountain massif of Azuero, Canito, Bayano river basin and Altos de Campaña. This last is now being developed.

589 Urban and regional analysis for development planning.
Richard Rhoda. Boulder, Colorado: Westview Press, 1982. 204p. maps.

The purpose of this introduction to urban and regional planning is limited to practical applications of relevant theories for a readership of persons now at work in the field, such as planners and others in Third World development. Topics covered include microanalysis of beneficiary groups, spatial distribution of development and poverty, urban land use and transport, and urban and regional functions and interactions. The book ends with two case-studies, one of Panama and one of Costa Rica, followed by a comparison of the two studies. The Panama study looks at models of decentralization in western Panama, focusing on urban–rural linkages at market towns, and including not only distribution but also information and training elements.

Education

590 Administración de empresas para la liberación nacional.
(Education in business administration for national liberation.)
Guillermo J. Padilla M., B. Rosas, Roberto A. Lamphrey. Panama
City: Published by the Author, 1989. 162p.

The authors discuss university-level business education in Panama from the standpoint of
national needs and priorities.

591 Las ciencias sociales en Panamá: en vísperas del tercer milenio.
(The social sciences in Panama: on the eve of the third millennium.)
Alfredo Figueroa Navarro. Panama City: Editorial Portobelo, 1998.
119p.

The work comprises updated versions of two texts, *Derrotero de las ciencias sociales en
Panamá a fines del milenio,* originally published as part of the work *Panamá: 90 años de
república,* and an update of the introductory study published in the author's *El desarrollo
de las ciencias sociales en Panamá.*

**592 Implementation of an educational reform plan: an ethnographic
approach to the case in Panama.**
Maritza Yvonne Tason. PhD thesis, Pennsylvania State University,
1985. 204p. (Available from University Microfilms, Ann Arbor,
Michigan, order no. AAT 8526081).

The author states that 'The purpose of this study is to analyze the implementation of the
Panamanian Reform Plan of 1971 utilizing an ethnographic approach' with a view to
providing reasons why the plan was ultimately rescinded.

593 **Inspiraciones de una educadora penonomeña.** (Inspirations of a
woman educator of Penonome.)
Magdalena Herrera de Pezet.   Panama City: Published by the
Author, 1991. 322p.

This collection of articles by the author was first published in the regional periodical
Tierra y dos mares.

594 **Itinerario, selección de discursos, ensayos y conferencias; indice
de las preocupaciones intelectuales del autor.** (Itinerary, selection
of discourses, essays and conferences; an index of the intellectual
preoccupations of the author.)
José Dolores Moscote.   Panama City: Ferguson & Ferguson, 1942.
254p.

Moscote (1879-1956), a professor and educator who founded and edited a variety of
education journals, brings together here a collection of his writings.

595 **Latin America and the Caribbean: A Survey of Distance Education
1991. New Papers on Higher Education: Studies and Research 5.**
Joan Carty.   Milton Keynes, England: International Centre for
Distance Learning of the United Nations University, 1991. 156p.

The country profiles compiled through a survey of distance education in Latin America
and the Caribbean provide basic educational data for Panama and look at the place of
distance learning. For each institution the report also provides: contacts, aims and
objectives, staff size, annual budget, course details, research, and special features. It is
also published by ERIC as ED343015.

596 **Nación y universidad.** (Nation and university.)
Louis Gonzalez Olaciregui.   Panama City: Universidad de Panamá,
Ediciones Formato Dieciseis, Ediciones Campus, 1988. 109p.

The articles were previously published between 1983 and 1987 in the periodical *Campus.*

597 **El nivel inicial y la democratización de la educación.** (Beginning
level and democratization of education.)
Antonella Ponce.   Panama City: Editorial Cronos, 1991. 18p.

In this conference paper on early childhood education the underlying assumption is that
children entering Panamanian schools at this time will need to be prepared for more years
of education to remain viable in the workforce.

598 **Panama Canal College seeks role for era after the U.S.
withdraws.**
Colin Woodard.   *The Chronicle of Higher Education*, vol. 43
(16 May 1997), p. A38.

The *Chronicle* has been carefully tracking higher education in Panama in recent years.
This article discusses the possible fate of Panama Canal College, the only higher

education institution in Panama with US accreditation. One possibility is to become part of the 'City of Knowledge' project, which will be a major research and education centre.

599 Panama hopes to create a 'City of Knowledge' where U.S. forces once ran the Canal Zone.
Colin Woodard. *The Chronicle of Higher Education*, vol. 43 (16 May 1997), p. A37-A38.
One of the vacated military bases, Fort Clayton, is planned for use as a magnet institution for students, researchers and corporations. The institution is to be a 'City of Knowledge', an international university.

600 Panama: issues in basic education.
Washington, DC: World Bank, 1995. 49p. map. (Document of the World Bank).
This document contextualizes the need for education in response to the world economy and makes recommendations.

601 Pensamientos del doctor José Dolores Moscote, seleccionados por Ricardo Jaén, jr. (Reflections of Dr José Dolores Moscote selected by Ricardo Jaén, Jr.)
José Dolores Moscote.   Panama, City: Colegio José D. Moscote, 1961. 23p.
This posthumous homage to the noted educator was sponsored by the institution named in his honour.

602 The politics of language and the survival of indigenous culture: from suppression to reintroduction in the formal classroom.
Monique Fordham. *Equity & Excellence in Education*, vol. 31, no. 1 (April 1998) p. 40-47.
The experiences of the Kuna nation of Panama in reintroducing their native language are described as an example of applying the concept of indigenous rights to language preservation.

603 Privatización de la educación panameña: el plan de las IFIS, CONEP y el gobierno del PRD. (The privatization of Panamanian education: the plan of IFIS, CONEP and the government of the Republic of Panama.)
Virgilio Araúz.   Panama City: Published by the Author, 1997. 96p. bibliog.
This is an analysis of the 10-year plan, 'Strategic plan for the modernization of Panamanian education, 1997-2006', a good deal of which was suggested by a report of the World Bank. The author strongly urges more local and regional input, and much less direction from the United States. The underlying thesis is that education must be designed in such a way that it guarantees jobs for all university graduates and appropriate and continuing technical training for workers.

604   Racionalización y planificación educativa nacional y temas complementarios de educación superior. (Rationalization of and planning for national education and complementary themes of higher education.)
Alberto de Saint Malo Orillac.   Panama City: Editora Sibauste, 1990. 135p. bibliog.

The author discusses national education plans and goals at all levels of education.

605   Regional education profile: Central America.
Institute of International Education.   New York: Published by the Author, 1986. 172p.

A point-in-time profile of Panama is included in this comparative study whose introductory essay by Rene Greenwald, 'Higher Education in Central America: Trends and Developments: 1985-86', develops the points of comparison and discusses common trends. The trends that Greenwald identifies are the increase of in-country graduate education, especially for programmes responding to national priorities, and an overall increase in the level of education for the whole population. For Panama, an overview of the elementary, secondary and higher educational systems is provided. There is a certain emphasis on US-based overseas education utilized by Central American students. It is also available as ERIC document ED276374.

606   Staff appraisal report: the Republic of Panama: basic education project.
Latin American and the Caribbean Regional Office.
Washington, DC: World Bank, 1996. 114p. bibliog.

This World Bank study examines the requirements for an education policy responsive to the needs of an increasingly technology-driven Panama.

607   La universidad autonóma y la universidad cultural: discursos académicos. (The autonomous university and the cultural university: academic discussions.)
Octavio Mendez Pereira.   Panama City: Editorial Universitaria, 1973. 236p.

These essays about the idea of the Panamanian university are by the first president of the University of Panama.

Literature

History and criticism

608 Análisis de la obra literaria de Tristán Solarte. (Analysis of the literary work of Tristán Solarte.)
Víctor Fernández Cañizález.   Panama City: Ediciones Librería Cultural Panameña, 1986. 383p.

A fully developed and scholarly examination of the work of the poet and novelist Tristán Solarte, with an introduction by the poet Elsie Alvarado de Ricord. Much space is given to *Tres imágenes de la muerte en tres edades*, *El Guitarrista*, *El ahogado*, and *Confesiones de un magistrado*.

609 Los aspectos socio-políticos en la trilogia canalera de Joaquín Beleño. (The socio-political aspects in the Canal trilogy of Joaquín Beleño.)
Patricia Watkins.   PhD thesis, Florida State University, 1996. (Available from University Microfilms, Ann Arbor, Michigan, order no. AAG 9719281).

The author's Abstract states that 'The Panamanian novel of the 20th century, particularly the "novela canalera" of Joaquin Beleno, [is] the focus for this study. The Panamanian novel has obtained its best achievements in the socio-political sphere. One of the best known writers of this sub-genre is Joaquin Beleno. His social protest novels represent a landmark in the history of Panamanian "criollismo" because of the examination of two of Panama's most pressing social and political issues: the race question, and the United States presence. The purpose of this investigation is to make an analysis of the "novela canalera" of Joaquin Beleno and its presentation of the racial, economic and social problems that originated with the construction of the Panama Canal.'

610 Blades, la calle del autor. (Blades, the author's street.)
Roberto Cedeno. Panama City: Editorial Panama, 1992. 207p.

Ruben Blades, a popular singer who has shown some interest in poetry and politics, is the subject of this biography.

611 Central American writers of West Indian origin: a new Hispanic literature.
Ian Smart. Washington, DC: Three Continents, 1984. 149p. bibliog.

Smart includes Beleño and Cubeno in his study, although the former is not West Indian. Smart feels he was so influenced by the West Indian presence that it is essential to include him. Cubeno is the paradigm of a black writer who incorporates his African heritage into his world-view and his writing.

612 The Colón people: reading Caribbeanness through the Panama Canal.
Rhonda Denise Frederick. PhD thesis, University of Pennsylvania, 1998. 282p. (Available from University Microfilms, Ann Arbor, Michigan, order no. AAG 9814845).

Using the writings of George Lamming of Barbados, Claude McKay and Michael Thelwell of Jamaica, and Eric Walrond and Maryse Conde of Guadeloupe, Frederick argues that the image of the Colón Man, depicted in Canal histories as the type of the exploited West Indian labourer, is seen in Caribbean literature as a man participating in a project beneficial to the region, a man of stature worthy of emulation. Frederick argues further that what created the Colón Man as a social hero was his depiction in vernacular histories, memories and songs. Colón man as trope was one of complexity, a truer response to post-colonial oppression than mere exploited victim.

613 Encyclopedia of Latin American literature.
Edited by Verity Smith. London; Chicago: Fitzroy Dearborn, 1997. 926p.

Not only Spanish and the other languages of conquest are considered for inclusion but also Mayan and other indigenous literatures. General articles on each genre, such as travel literature, journals, colonial literature, the essay, theatre, nationalism, transculturalization and women's writing are useful to supplement Carmen S. Alverio's general article on Panama (p. 615-19), which covers literature from the beginnings to the present and also suggests the rate of publication of imaginative literature from Panama (25 novels represent the total output for the 1960s). Alverio teaches at Regis University, Denver, Colorado and is currently at work on a lengthy study of Panamanian literature.

614 Handbook of Latin American literature.
Edited by David William Foster. New York: Garland, 1992. 2nd ed. 799p. (Garland Reference Library of the Humanities, 1459).

For an introduction to the literature of Panama, it would be difficult to find a better place to start than with this handbook which covers all the countries of Latin America. María A. Salgado of the University of North Carolina at Chapel Hill wrote the dense survey from earliest times to writers publishing today. She focuses on themes such as the Panama Canal, the transition from the early literature of ideas to the imaginative literature of today.

615 History of the Panamanian novel (modernism, criollism).
Donald Clark Lindenau. PhD thesis, University of California, Berkeley, 1989. 312p. (Available from University Microfilms, Ann Arbor, Michigan, order no. AAT 9028929).

From the Abstract we learn that 'Panama's authors continue to be relegated to marginal status. The reasons for this have less to do with the question of intrinsic worth than with other factors, such as limited access to mass audiences and the absence of a viable publishing industry. This dissertation presents a comprehensive historical survey of the Panamanian novel, and demonstrates that isthmian writers merit more consideration than they have heretofore received.'

616 Lecturas para lectores. (Readings for readers.)
César Young Núñez. Panama City: Ediciones Formato Dieciseis, 1987. 100p.

This collection of studies of Panamanian literature is by a poet described as irreverent in some circles, but as in the literary stream as an antipoet by other critics. Born in 1934, he has also written poems collected in *Poemas de rutina* (Routine poems, 1967) and others.

617 Letra viva. (Living letters.)
Dimas Lidio Pitty. Panama City: Ediciones Formato Dieciseis; Extensión Universitaria, Universidad de Panamá, 1986. 267p. bibliog. (Colección Labrapalabra, 1).

A dozen or so Panamanian writers in all genres, many of whom are represented in this bibliography, were interviewed using a set of questions about the state of Panamanian letters, the answers to which they could prepare in advance. They were asked to comment on strengths and weaknesses in the current crop of writers, their generational differences in style and sense of aesthetics.

618 Mar de fondo: 10 breves estudios en torno a la obra literaria de Enrique Jaramillo Levi. (Groundswell: 10 short studies on the literary works of Enrique Jaramillo Levi.)
Alfredo Figueroa Navarro (et al.). Panama City: Instituto Nacional de Cultura, Dirección Nacional de Extensión Cultural, Departamento de Letras, 1992. 89p.

This *Festschrift* of critical essays on the literary work of Enrique Jaramillo Levi (1944-) includes bibliographical references.

619   La novela del imperialismo en Centroamérica. (The novel of imperialism in Central America.)
Esther Maria Osses.   Maracaibo, Venezuela: Universidad del Zulia, 1986. 174p.

Although this is a literary study, Esther Maria Osses (b. 1914) is more known as a vanguardist poet who wrote *La niña y el mar: poemas* (1956) (The little girl and the sea; poems) and *Crece y camina; poesía* (1971) (Grow and walk; poetry) among others.

620   Octavio Mendez Pereira; una figura cumbre en la litteratura panameña. (Octavio Mendez Pereira, a towering figure in Panamanian literature.)
Matilde de Réal Gonzalez.   Panama City: Ediciones del Ministerio de Educación, Departamento de Bellas Artes y Publicaciones, 1960. 310p.

This is both an appreciation and a study of Octavio Mendez Pereira (1887-1954). The Panamanian educator was the first president of the University of Panama and also published in a variety of genres.

621   Tomás Martín Feuillet; prototip romántico. (Tomás Martín Feuillet, romantic prototype.)
Rodrigo Miró.   Panama City: Published by the Author, 1962. 94p. bibliog.

Tomás Martín Feuillet (1832-62) is important in the history of Panamanian literature for his romantic style, but with frequent excursions into humour. This collection with an introductory essay includes a generous selection of Feuillet's poetry (p. 39-94).

Anthologies

622   Antología esencial.
Demetrio Herrera Sevillano.   Panama City: Ediciones Formato Dieciseis, 1983. 117p.

Demetrio Herrera Sevillano (1902-50) was a self-taught urban poet whose poetry was published between 1924 and 1950. Starting as a Modernist, he experimented with Ultraism, Futurism, and other trends. This edition was selected and introduced by Rafael Ruiloba with a portrait and sketches by Manuel Chong Neto.

623   Cuentos panameños: stories of struggle and hope in rural Panama.
Richard Allen Bower, illustrated by Stephanie Bower.   New York: Friendship Press, 1993. 144p.

This collection of short vignettes and tales that illustrate the modern-day life of the *campesinos* was written by an Episcopalian priest, based on his three years in rural

Panama. Themes such as developing new community modes to cooperate in building a water supply, dependence on the cities as sources of health care, education and work are developed.

624 Dos poetas panameños. (Two Panamanian poets.)
Mercedes G. Dolaños Guevara. Panama City: Ediciones del Ministerio de Educación, Dirrección Nacional de Cultura, 1970. 269p.
This critical edition of two poets, Ricardo Miró (1883-1940) and Gaspar Octavio Hernandez, is primarily intended for students, but is also a good general reader edition.

625 Fireflight: three Latin American poets.
Elsie Alvarado de Ricord, Lucha Corpi, Concha Michel, translated into English by Catherine Rodriguez-Nieto. Berkeley, California: Oyez, 1976. 109p.
Both English and Spanish versions are given in this collection of work by Elsie Alvarado de Ricord, a Panamanian (b. 1928), Lucha Corpi, a Californian (b. 1945), and Concha Michel, the Mexican writer whose first publications appeared in the 1930s.

626 When new flowers bloomed: short stories by women writers from Costa Rica and Panama.
Edited by Enrique Jaramillo Levi. Pittsburgh, Pennsylvania: Latin American Literary Review Press, 1991. 208p. (Discoveries).
Writers in the Third World are seldom read by a larger, even international audience. Indeed, as the editor points out, Panama has no private publishing houses that might be expected to serve as channels for the dissemination of creative writing. Enrique Jaramillo Levi has selected and edited a collection of representative short stories by women writers. The Panamanian authors represented include Lilia Algondona, Giovanna Benedetti, Rosa Maria Britton, Griselda López, Moravia Ochoa López, Bertalicia Peralta, Bessy Reyna, Graciela Rojas Sucre, and Isis Tejeira.

Individual authors

627 A la sombra del Arco (crónicas de Paris). (Under the shadow of the bow.)
Guillermo Andreve. Paris: Editorial Excelsior, 1925. 285p.
Guillermo Andreve (1879-1940), editor of cultural magazines of the *fin de siècle* and first decade of the 20th century encouraged all genres of creative writing and published some of his own. This work is a collection of essays and tales. A novel, *Una punta del velo* (1929) (A corner of the veil), and *Cuatro cuentos* (1933) (Four tales) also are representative of his work.

628 Panamá y nuestra América. (Panama and our America.)
Justo Arosemena. Mexico City: Universidad Nacional Autónoma
de México, Coordinación de Humanidades, 1981. 394p.

Ricaurte Soler introduced and annotated this selection of the writing of Justo Arosemena
(1817-96) for university students. Included are the texts 'Estado Federal de Panamá'
(Federal state of Panama), 'Nuestra América' (Our America) and 'La reacción en
Colombia' (Reaction in Colombia).

629 Capricornio en gris: cuentos. (Capricorn in grey; stories.)
Justo Arroyo. Panama: INCUDE, 1973. 117p.

Short stories include 'El jazzista y su mujer' (The jazz-player and his woman), 'Lo
impossible' (The impossible), 'Geminis' (Twins), 'Capricornio en gris' (Capricorn in
grey), 'Decir manaña' (To say tomorrow), 'Revelación' (Revelation), 'En 33 1/3' (In 33
1/3). Arroyo is associated with the University of Panama and is considered to be a
cosmopolitan writer.

**630 Corazón de aguila: biografía novelada de Marcos Antonio
Gelabert: un heroe panameño.** (Eagle-heart: a fictionalized
biography about Marcos Antonio Gelabert, a Panamanian hero.)
Justo Arroyo. Panama City: Editorial la Boina Roja, 1996. 303p.

This is a novelized biography of the patriot Marcos Antonio Gelabert, born in 1907 or
1908 and living till 1952.

631 Dedos. (Fingers.)
Justo Arroyo. Mexico City: Organización Editorial Novaro, 1971.
165p. (Grandes Escritores Latinoamericanos, 30).

The author's lyrical style is manifested in this evocative novel of the lives and loves of
two young men. The narrative is told though the eyes of one of the pair, a frustrated
novelist. A variety of formal techniques such as multiple viewpoints, changing narrative
styles and not adhering to the traditional chronological order of a novel were all attempted
in this one work.

632 Geografía de mujer. (Geography of woman.)
Justo Arroyo. Panama City: GEE, Grupo Editorial Encuentro,
1982. 161p.

This novel is representative of Justo Arroyo's transition from the fiercely experimental
work he produced in the 1970s to a more controlled style. He has been one of the most
prolific writers in Panama, beginning in the 1970s, peaking in 1995 when a novel –
Semana sin viernes (A week with no Friday) (Panama City: Editorial Mariano
Arosemena, Instituto Nacional de Cultura, Dirección Nacional de Extensión Cultural,
Departamento de Letras, 1995. 194p. [Colección Ricardo Miró. Premio novela, 1995]) –
and a collection of short stories – *Para terminar diciembre* (To end December) (Panama
City: Editorial Mariano Arosemena, Instituto Nacional de Cultura, Dirección Nacional de
Extensión Cultural, Departamento de Letras, 1995. 194p. [Colección Ricardo Miró.
Premio cuento, 1995]) – won the Miró prize in their respective categories.

633 Las aves (The birds.)
Jarl Babot. Panama City: Ediciones Instituto Nacional de Cultura, 1980. 40p.

The play is by Jarl Ricardo Babot (b. 1945) who is a professor of drama as well as a playwright. *Las aves* won the Miró prize in 1979. He has also produced *Poemas de la calle Gorki* (Poems from Gorky Street) (1990) and a collection of writings, *La pequeña orquesta* (The little orchestra) (q.v.).

634 La pequeña orquesta: primera antología personal, 1966-1991.
(The little orchestra: first personal anthology, 1966-91.)
Jarl Ricardo Babot. Panama City: Editorial Mariano Arosemena del Instituto Nacional de Cultura, 1993. 233p.

Babot (b. 1945) is a prolific author as well as professor of dramatic arts.

635 Flor de banana. (Banana flower.)
Joaquín Beleño C. Panama City: Dirección de Cultura del Ministerio de Educación, 1970. 248p.

Joaquín Beleño (b. 1922) has written several novels, among them *Curundú* (1963), *Gamboa road gang* (1959) and *Luna verde* (1951) (Green moon). *Flor de banana* is a novel of social protest attacking the practices of the fruit companies. The first three are a trilogy on the Canal theme. The main character of *Gamboa road gang*, Atá, has been seen as 'one of the most important fictional characters in Panamanian literature'.

636 Delia's way.
Olga Berrocal Essex. Houston, Texas: Arte Publico Press, 1998. 186p.

At Carnival, two teenage sisters confront their life-long competitiveness and jealousy in a novel set in modern-day Panama.

637 El perseguido. (The pursuer.)
César A. Candanedo. Panama City: Instituto Nacional de Cultura, Dirección Nacional de Extensión Cultural, 1991. 170p.

César A. Candanedo (b. 1906), a writer of social protest novels, is also known for *Los clandestinos* (The clandestine ones), Miró Prize 1949, published 1972 – the reason for such a long-delayed publication is unclear, but it seems there may be a connection with the author's political leanings – and *La otra frontera* (The other frontier) of 1967.

638 Marisol and Magdalena: the sound of our sisterhood.
Veronica Chambers. New York: Jump at the Sun, 1998. 141p.

Thirteen-year-old Marisol spends a year with her grandmother in Panama where she secretly searches for her real father and yearns to be with her best friend in Brooklyn. This is a novel of bi-cultural identity.

639 Black Cubena's thoughts.

Cubena, edited and translated by Elba D. Birmingham-Pokorny.
Miami, Florida: Ediciones Universal, 1991. 55p. (Colección Ebano y
Canela).

Based on interviews with Carlos Guillermo Wilson, the writer about the Black Diaspora
who was born in in 1941 and who uses a single *nom de plume* Cubena for his creative
writing – his scholarly work is published under his birth name of Wilson. The translator
of this selection of his terse prose poems with political themes is also the founder and
organizer of a conference on the Black Image in Latin American Literature and co-editor
of the *Journal of Afro-Latin American Studies*.

640 Chombo (novela).

Cubena.   Miami, Florida: Ediciones Universal, 1981. 104p.
(Colección Caniquil).

A novel about West Indian Panamanians in the Canal Zone by the Black Diasporist writer
Carlos Guillermo Wilson who writes as Cubena. 'Chombo' is the non-standard word for
a West Indian labourer on the Panama Canal. The protagonist of *Chombo* is intended to
represent the whole group of West Indians working in Panama. The title also indicates a
category, and it is this category of black labouring man that Cubena represents in his
protagonist.

641 Cuentos del negro Cubena: pensamiento afro-panameño. (Stories of black Cubena: Afro-Panamanian thought.)

Cubena.   Guatemala City: Landivar, 1977. 94p.

In these short stories by the Panamanian writer Carlos Guillermo Wilson, especially to be
noted are the African influences in 'La abuelita africana' (The African grandmother), a
tale with Twi elements; 'La depravada' (The depraved one), a study of interracial and
aberrant relationships; and 'La familia' (The family), again a story in which African
heritage plays a significant part.

642 Los nietos de Felicidad Dolores. (Felicidad Dolores's grandchildren.)

Cubena.   Miami, Florida: Ediciones Universal, 1991. 233p.
(Colección Ebano y Canela).

The novel is by Carlos Guillermo Wilson, the Black Diasporist writer who uses the name
Cubena.

643 Pensamientos del negro Cubena: pensamiento afro-panameño. (Reflections of black Cubena: Afro-Panamanian thought.)

Cubena.   Los Angeles: Published by the Author, 1977. 48p.

The poems by Carlos Guillermo Wilson who writes as Cubena, are, according to Ian
Smart, romantic in feel, in contrast to Cubena's prose.

644 Short stories.
Cubena, translated, annotated and introduced by Ian Isidore Smart.
Washington, DC: Afro-Hispanic Institute, 1987. 103p.
This is a selection of Cubena's short stories for English readers. Carlos Guillermo Wilson writes under the name of Cubena. Smart, who has written extensively about African influences in world literature, and especially about West Indian literatures finds Cubena and his Panamanian writing important in African Diaspora culture. His prose 'expresses bitter recrimination and outrage although the clean, terse prose seems to state facts only'.

645 Obra selecta. (Selected works.)
Armando Fortune, edited and introduced by Gerardo Maloney.
Panama City: Instituto Nacional de Cultura, Dirección Nacional de Publicaciones y Comunicación, 1994. 370p. bibliog. (Colección Dabaibe).
This selection of essays from the pen of Armando Fortune (1921-79) has been selected by Gerardo Maloney. He emphasizes those works that illustrate the impact of the Panama Canal on Panamanian blacks, and on the larger society. Fortune's academic training was in economics and he edited the economy page for the periodical *La Nación*. He also had an international voice in developing awareness about black culture. Much of the material reprinted here first appeared in *Lotería*.

646 Hojas secas. (Dry leaves.)
Amelia Denis de Icaza. León, Nicaragua: Talleres gráficos Robelo, 1926. 186p.
A Romantic poet and one of the early women poets of Panama, Amelia Denis de Icaza (1836-1911) was published in book form only posthumously. Currently receiving notice is her 1906 poem, 'Al cerro Ancón' (To Ancon Hill) in which she laments the loss to a foreign power of territory to build an interoceanic canal. This poem can be seen as the first work of the 'canalera' literary works.

647 El grillo que canto sobre el Canal. (The cricket that sang over the Canal.)
Demetrio Korsi. Panama City: Published by the Author, 1937. 86p.
Demetrio Korsi (1899-1957) found an international audience with his Modernist poems, *El viento en la montaña* (1926) (Wind of the fountain), whose prologue was contributed by Manuel Ugarte. He later wrote *poesía negra*, black poetry, such as the title above and *Cumbia* (1936) (Cumbia, the national dance) and *Los gringos llegan y la cumbia se va* (1953) (The Gringos come and the Cumbia goes).

648 Panamá: luces y sombras hacia el siglo XXI. (Panama: light and shade towards the 21st century.)
Raul Leis. Panama City: Editorial Mariano Arosemena, 1997. 156p.
The collection includes essays in many forms, the themes of which are the social concern of a writer (b. 1947) who feels very much a part of his times.

649 Raices primordiales. (Primordial roots.)
Moravia Ochoa López. Panama City: Departamento de Bellas
Artes y Publicaciones del Ministerio de Educación, 1960. 109p.

With illustrations by Bolivar Rivera, this collection was first published in 1958 when the
poet was seventeen. Other publications include *Circulos y planetas* (Circles and planets)
(1977) and *Cantos para decir la noche* (Songs to convey the night) (1977).

650 Apparently incongruous parts: the worlds of Malcolm Lowry.
Malcolm Lowry with the assistance of Gordon Bowker. Metuchen,
New Jersey: Scarecrow Press, 1990. 230p.

This is not significantly about Panama, but Lowry's name has been associated with the
country.

651 The little painter of Sabana Grande.
Patricia M. Markun, illustrated by Robert Casilla. New York:
Simon & Schuster Children's, 1993. 32p.

This beautifully illustrated story of a little boy who makes a mural in his Panamanian
village describes the whole story, from the gathering of flowers and plants from the forest
to make the colours, to the completion of the work.

652 Aproximación crítica cordial a Ricardo Miró y su obra. (A warm
critical approach to Ricardo Miró and his writings.)
Compiled by Rodrigo Miró Grimaldo, Joaquina Pereira de Padilla,
Ricardo Segura J. Panama City: Editorial Universitaria, 1996.
251p. bibliog.

This book is a project of the Circullo Lingüística Ricardo J. Alfaro (the Ricardo J. Alfaro
Linguistic Circle). It is a gathering of short critical pieces about the writing of Ricardo
Miró (1883-1940) by some twenty authors – university professors, journalists and
creative writers – that was begun in celebration of the centenary of Miró's birth. Events
precluded publication at that time, but this *Festschrift* could be said to have mellowed and
improved with time.

653 Obra literaria de Ricardo Miró: poesia. (Literary works of
Ricardo Miró: poetry.)
Ricardo Miró. Panama City: Editorial Mariano Arosemena,
Instituto Nacional de Cultura, 1984. 259p. bibliog. (Colección
Ricardo Miró).

This is a mix of poems by Miró and poems commemorating his life and works. Its chief
value lies in an extended biographical note and bibliography. Miró was born in Spain but
spent most of his life and all of his career in Panama. The Miró prizes in the various forms
of literary writing were established in his honour.

654 Poesía selecta. (Selected poetry.)
Ricardo Miró. Panama City: Academia Panameña de la Lengua, 1984. 108p.

The poet Elsie Alvarado de Ricord has selected and introduced poems of Miró (1883-1940), considered to be Panama's most illustrious poet. The national literary competition, established in 1942, is named after him. Miró is essentially a modernist, but in personal tone and seriousness of purpose, he supplies an individuality to his work.

655 El mar de los sargazos. (The Sargasso Sea.)
Manuel Orestes Nieto. Panama City: Editorial Mariano Arosemena, Instituto Nacional de Cultura, 1997. 94p.

Born in 1951, Nieto has won the Miró Poetry Prize several times; this collection garnered the prize for 1996. Other publications are *Dar la cara* (Facing the consequences) (1975), and *Panamá en la memoria de los mares* (Panama in the memory of the seas) (1983).

656 Orquideas; poesías. (Orchids; poems.)
Maria Olimpia de Obaldia. Panama City: Imprenta Nacional, 1926. 112p.

Maria Olimpia de Obaldia (1891-1985) was named National Poetess of Panama and her collected works, *Obras completas* (Complete works), were published in 1976. Separate collections of her lyric work include *Visiones eternas* (1961) (Eternal visions) and *Parnaso infantil* (1948) (Children's Parnassus).

657 A Christmas surprise for Chabelita.
Argentina Palacios, illustrated by Lori Lohstoeter. Mahwah, New Jersey: BridgeWater Books, 1996. 32p.

Chabelita goes to live with her grandparents in a small village when her mother goes to the city to take a better-paying job. Lohstoeter's illustrations reflect the animated quality of life in Panama. It was published in Spanish under the title *Sorpresa de Navidad para Chabelita*.

658 En tu cuerpo cubierto de flores. (On your flower-covered corpse.)
Bertalicia Peralta, sketches by Jorge E. Horna. Panama City: Published by the Author, 1985. 62p.

Bertalicia Peralta (b. 1939) is one of a group of women poets who have been recognized by the award of the Miró Prize, in Panama, and international prizes. She is much published. Representative works include *Dos poemas de Berta Alicia Peralta* (Two poems by Berta Alicia Peralta) (1964); *Libro de fábulas* (Book of fables) (1976) and *Casa flotante* (Floating house) (1979).

659 La muerte va por dentro; drama en tres actos. (Death goes about within; a drama in three acts.)
Mario Riera. Panama City: Imprenta Nacional, 1948. 32p.

Mario Riera (1920-69) won second prize for this drama. He is one of the few Panamanian writers who restrict themselves to one genre, but see also his collection of folktales.

660 Las huellas de mis pasos. (Traces of my passage.)
Pedro Rivera. Panama City: Editorial Mariano Arosemena del
Instituto Nacional de Cultura, 1994. 135p.

Pedro Rivera (b. 1939) writes poetry, short stories and film scripts, often with social
themes. He is a frequent winner of the Miró Prize in one or other of the genres. Among
his other publications, *Los pájaros regresan de la niebla* (The birds return from the fog)
was winner of the 1970 Miró Prize.

661 Peccata minuta. (Small sins.)
Pedro Rivera. Panama City: Editorial Universitaria, 1974. 3rd ed.
110p.

This collection of short stories includes the title story 'Knockout', 'La pequeña guerra de
John (John's little war), and 'Las tarantulas de miel' (Honey tarantulas) by the many-
talented Rivera. The stories are characterized by his terse, highly selective prose style.

**662 An old woman remembers: the recollected history of West
Indians in Panama: a prose-poetry monologue.**
Carlos E. Russell. Brooklyn, New York: Caribbean Diaspora Press,
1995. 50p.

Family recollections have been organized into a literary form. This work is a good
example of preserving the heritage.

663 Libre y cautiva: verso y prosa, obra escogida. (Free and captive:
verse and prose, unpublished works.)
Stella Sierra. Panama City: Printed by Lito Arte Panamex, 1984.
383p.

Sierra (b. 1917) is well represented in this retrospective collection of her writing. A
member of the vanguardist groups of poets that also included Ricardo J. Bermudez and
Esther Maria Osses, she published her first volumes in 1944, one of which, *Sinfonía
jubilosa* (Jubilant symphony), won the first Miró Prize in poetry in 1951. She went on to
win this prize in 1958, 1972, 1974 and 1980. The other volume, *Canciones de mar y luna,
1939-40* (Songs of the sea and moon, 1939-40) also appeared in 1944. A chronology of
her career, a portrait and a collection of family photographs are also included in this
edition.

664 Los pájaros del sueño. (Dream birds.)
Rogelio Sinan (Bernardo Dominguez Alba). Guayaquil, Ecuador:
Casa de la Cultura Ecuatoriana, Nucleo del Guayas, 1978. 185p.

A collection of short stories by Bernardo Dominguez Alba (b. 1904) including 'El sueño
de Serafin del Carmen' (The dream of Serafín del Carmen), 'A la orilla de las estatuas
maduras' (At the edge of the ripe statues), 'La boina roja' (The red beret) and 'Mosquita
muerta' (The dead mosquito). Another collection by Sinan is *El candelabro de los malos
ofidios: y otros cuentos* (1982) (The candelabrum of the bad ophidians, and other tales).

665   El ahogado. (The drowned man.)
Tristán Solarte.   Buenos Aires: Fabril, 1962. 162p.

Tristán Solarte (b. 1924) is the pen-name of Guillermo Sánchez Bourbón. Both a novelist and a poet, his collected poems appeared under the title *Aproximación a la muerte* (Poetic approach to death). *Confesiones de un magistrado* (Confessions of a magistrate) (1969) and *Palo dur* (Hard truncheon) (1986) are characterized by his vigorous social protest.

666   Estudios filosóficos. (Philosophical studies.)
Ricaurte Soler, José de J. Martinez.   Panama City: INCUDE, 1974. 157p.

Soler contributes 'Sobre la dialéctica: Modelo mecanicista y metodo dialéctico' (On dialectics: mechanical model and dialectic method), 'Causalidad en el mecanicismo y causalidad en la dialéctica' (Causality in mechanism and causality in dialectics), and 'Dialéctica de universales e individuales' (Dialectics of universals and individuals). José de J. Martinez (b. 1929) contributes 'Sobre el humanismo en la Edad Media y en el Renacimiento' (Humanism in the Middle Ages and Renaissance) and 'Sobre el problema de la muerte' (On the problem of death).

667   Estudios sobre historia de las ideas en América. (Studies of the history of ideas in America.)
Ricaurte Soler.   Panama City: Imprenta Nacional, 1961. 119p.

This work brings together several essays of Soler, among them 'Criterio historiográfico para una historia del pensamiento americano' (Historiographical criterion for a history of American thought) and 'Presencia del pensamiento de la América Latina en la conciencia europea' (Presence of Latin American thought in the European conscience).

668   Poesía mia que estas en los cielos. (My poetry which is in heaven.)
César Young Núñez.   Panama City: Instituto Nacional de Cultura, Editorial M. Arosemena, 1991. 44p.

We have here *Rosa que te quiero rosa – Sonetos con mucho oficio* (Rose, I love you, Rose – Sonnets of much craft). Earlier works of this poet (b. 1934) are the often-reprinted *Poemas de rutina* (1967) (Routine poems) and *Carta a Blancanieves* (1976) (Letters to Snow White).

Arts

Art, architecture, film and minor arts

669 Arturo Lindsay.
Jenifer P. Borum.   *Artforum*, vol. 32, no. 3 (November 1993),
p. 109.

The work of Arturo Lindsay, an artist-ethnographer, is described in this article. He is especially noted for his Santeria mixed-media shrines.

670 Birdman of Panama: a tenacious entrepreneur and naturalist turns a rusty radar tower into an ornithologist's paradise.
Sara Hart.   *Architecture*, vol. 88, no. 4 (April 1999), p. 136-40.

An ecological project fostered by noted politician and environmentalist Raul Arias de Para is described. The emphasis is on the architectural aspects.

671 Crosscurrents: contemporary painting from Panama, 1968-1998.
Monica E. Kupfer, Edward J. Sullivan, curators.   New York:
Americas Society Art Gallery, 1998. 120p. bibliog.

This is the catalogue of an exhibition held from 15 May to 19 July 1998 at the Americas Society Art Gallery. It was organized by the Americas Society Art Gallery in association with the Museo de Arte Contemporaneo de Panama. The text is in English and Spanish.

672 Desires and disguises: five Latin American photographers.
Edited by Amanda Hopkinson.   London; New York: Serpent's
Tail, 1992. 80p.

Published on the occasion of an exhibition held in 1992 at the Photographers' Gallery, this catalogue includes photographs of Portobelo, Panama by Sandra Eleta, and also biographical data for her.

673 **Historical archaeology in Panama City.**
Richard G. Cooke, Beatriz Elena Rovira. *Archaeology*, vol. 36,
no. 2 (March/April 1983), p. 51-57.
Referencing the excavations at and the artefacts recovered from the Convent of
St Dominic in Panama City, the article surveys historical archaeology in the capital of
Panama.

674 **Ivy, Shreve & Mader presents the Dr. Gilbert N. Plass collection
of United States possessions featuring Canal Zone.**
Dallas, Texas: Ivy, Shreve & Mader Philatelic Auctions, Inc., 1993.
219p.
This auction catalogue of a collection of postage stamps issued by the United States
commemorates, among other territories and possessions, the Panama Canal.

675 **Latin American art.**
New York: Sotheby's, 1986. 1 vol.
A catalogue of an auction held in November 1986 which includes Sale 5517, a collection
of Panamanian art.

676 **The Palace of the Herons.**
Presidents & Prime Ministers, vol. 8, no. 1 (January 1999), p. 34.
This illustrated article describes the official residence of the president of Panama, a part
of which dates to 1673, with additions made in the 1920s.

677 **A Panamanian artist: Guillermo Trujillo: the formative years.**
Monica E. Kupfer. MA thesis, Tulane University, New Orleans,
Louisiana, 1983. 286p. bibliog. (Available from University
Microfilms, Ann Arbor, Michigan).
The author has long been engaged in research in the field of Latin American art. This
comprehensive study of a single artist reflects the vibrancy and experimentation that
characterized art being produced in this period. Kupfer also edited *Crosscurrents* –
described in this bibliography (item no. 671) – and compiled *The bibliography of Latin
American art.*

678 **Ricardo J. Bermudez en la cultura arquitectónica y literaria de
Panamá.** (Ricardo J. Bermudez in the architectural and literary
culture of Panama.)
Ricardo J. Bermudez. Panama City: Editorial La Prensa, 1996.
3 vols.
This compilation is arranged and introduced by Samuel A. Gutierrez and includes
bibliographical references. Ricardo J. Bermudez (b. 1914) was professor of architecture
and a Secretary of Education who wrote surrealist poetry and short stories.

679   The stamps of the Canal Zone.
George L. Toppan.   New York: The Scott Stamp & Coin Co., 1906.
38p.
Reproductions of the postage stamps issued in the Panama Canal (Zone), and commemorative stamps issued around the world. The photographs are in black and white.

680   El teatro en Panamá: Entre problemas, exceptiones y esperanzas. (The theatre in Panama: Among the problems, exceptions and hopes.)
Daniel Domínguez.   *Latin American Theatre Review*, vol. 25, no. 2 (Spring 1992), p. 123-27.
Domínguez provides a ten-year review of theatre in Panama, including material on the general arts climate of the 1980s, a description of theatres available for the mounting of theatrical programmes and some of the more noteworthy productions. Most of the plays listed are international classics. Directors are named and a brief mention is given to Panamanian playwrights.

681   War and the independent filmmaker.
Barbara Trent, Shelton Waldrep.   *The Humanist*, vol. 58, no. 5 (September-October 1998), p. 15-23.
A film about the US invasion of Panama, 'The Panama Deception', is used in this thoughtful and angry article to explore how film distribution and film making is controlled by relatively few persons. 'The Panama Deception' won the Academy Award for best documentary film in 1992.

Music and dance

682   Chicken from Panama.
Dorothea Duryea Ohl.   *Dance Magazine* (November 1958), p. 68-69.
Ohl's descriptive and illustrated note includes directions for the *Chicken Panama* and its figures.

683   La copla en el carnaval tableño. (The *copla* in the carnival of the Tableno region.)
Aristofanes Cedeno E.   Panama City; San José, Costa Rica: Litografia e Imprenta LIL, 1988. 327p. bibliog.
Cedeno describes and details the art form of the *copla*, the improvising of four-line verses, and places it in the carnival culture as experienced in the region.

684 Danzas folklóricas de la villa de Los Santos. (Folk dancing in Los
Santos.)
Julio Arosemena Moreno. Panama City: Editorial M. Arosemena
del Instituto Nacional de Cultura, 1994. 136p. maps. bibliog.

The music and dancing in the town of Los Santos is famous throughout Panama. This
version of the title, an earlier version of which was published in 1977, includes
descriptions for dancing, floor diagrams, and music for such dances as: *La danza de
grandiablos, Danza de la Montezuma Española, El torito, Danza de los diáblicos sucios,*
and *Danza de la Montezuma Cabezona.*

**685 Effects of culture, age, gender, and repeated trials on rote song
learning skills of children 6-9 years old from England, Panama,
Poland, Spain, and the United States.**
Randall S. Moore, Melissa Brotons, Janina Fyk. *Bulletin of the
Council for Research in Music Education,* no. 133 (Summer 1997),
p. 83-88.

Children from England, Panama, Poland, Spain and the United States were tested to see
how accurately they could learn a never-before-heard song. Children from Panama were
second to the fastest and most accurate group, the children from Spain.

686 The lullabies of the San Blas Cuna Indians of Panama.
Sandra Smith McCosker. Göteborg, Sweden: Etnografiska Museet,
1974. 190p. (Ethnological Studies, no. 33/Etnologiska studier,
no. 33).

Cuna lullabies are a significant resource in the acculturation of infants. Those sung to girls
differ from those sung to baby boys. Songs listed in the category 'lullaby' include those
sung while working in the home. This monograph describes the content, the music and
the musical instruments. Some 48 lullabies are analysed and the texts in Cuna and English
of four are given with the scores. This was originally the author's thesis, University of
California at Los Angeles. There is both a bibliography and discography.

687 Mi tesoro de canciones. (My song treasury.)
Compiled by Vilma de Moreno, Maritza de Mendez. Panama City:
Litografia Enan, S.A., 1994. 158p.

The compilers have provided a selection of popular songs without the music.

688 Music and Black ethnicity: the Caribbean and South America.
Edited by Gerard H. Behague. New Brunswick, New Jersey:
Transaction Publishers, 1994. 335p.

These are conference papers from a meeting held at the North-South Center, University
of Miami, 1992. Egberto Bermudez contributes 'Arroz colorado: los congos de Panamá'
(Coloured rice: the congos of Panama).

689 Panama.
Ronald Smith. In: *The Garland encyclopedia of world music.*
v. 2. South America, Mexico, Central America, and the Caribbean.
Edited by Dale A. Olsen, Daniel E. Sheehy. New York: Garland
Publishing, 1998- , p. 163-98.

Written by a noted ethnomusicologist at Indiana University, this article describes in general the state of music in Panama. Topics covered include the historical context, musical instuments and ensembles, dance and dance theatre, such as *congos* and *diábolos,* and vocal music, especially the *décima.* Key festivals are described and musical terms peculiar to Panama are defined. Smith has also published 'Arroz colorado: los congos de Panamá' in *Music and Black ethnicity in the Caribbean and South America,* edited by Gerard Behague (see item no. 688, p. 239-66).

690 Rubén Blades: salsa singer and social activist.
Bárbara Cruz. Springfield, New Jersey: Enslow, 1997. 128p.
(Hispanic Biographies).

All aspects of Blades' career are covered: musician, actor and politician. The discography and filmography add value.

691 Saracunde of Panama: a look at the dance on the street and on the stage.
Elizabeth Rhodes. In: *Proceedings* of the Congress on Research in
Dance. Conference (31st: 1998: Ohio State University), p. 133-40.
bibliog.

Rhodes discusses the *saracunde,* a dance originally performed in Panama as part of Carnival festivities. It has been performed in the town of Los Santos since the 1970s as part of the celebration of Corpus Christi. The dance is also known as *El Cuenecue* or *Danza de los Negros Bozales.*

692 Society of Los Congos of Panama: an ethnomusicological study of the music and dance-theater of an Afro-Panamanian group.
Ronald Richard Smith. PhD thesis, University of Indiana,
Bloomington, Indiana, 1976. 340p. bibliog. (Available from
University Microfilms, Ann Arbor, Michigan).

A detailed description of the activities of an important cultural group in Panama, including a scholarly treatment of Afro-Panamanian dance and Afro-Caribbean dance.

693 Tambor y socavón; un estudio comprensivo de dos temas del folklore panameño, y de sus implicaciones históricas y culturales.
(Drum and *socavón*, a comprehensive study of two Panamanian folklore motifs.)
Manuel F. Zarate, Dora P. de Zarate. Panama City: Ediciones del Ministerio de Educación, Dirección Nacional de Cultura, 1962. 408p. bibliog.

Two folklorists provides a very comprehensive collection of material relating to folk music. The *tambor* and *socavón* represent the two key musical instruments. The drums are hand crafted and three typical varieties are described. The *socavón*, a four-stringed small guitar, is representative of a group that includes the now more prevalent *mejorana*, a 5-stringed guitar. Dances and songs are described in detail, and black-and-white photographs show examples. The words of two *décimas*, a ballad usually sung as a male solo accompanied on the *mejorana*, are reprinted, and the significance explained.

694 Tamborito (Panama).
Let's dance (August-September 1960), p. 14, 18.

These are the directions, description and indication of music to be used for the folk dance known as *tamborito*.

695 They sing with the voice of the drum: Afro-Panamanian musical traditions.
Ronald Smith. In: *More than drumming: essays on African and Afro-Latin music and musicians.* Edited by Irene V. Jackson, prepared under the auspices of the Center for Ethnic Music, Howard University. Westport, Connecticut: Greenwood Press, 1985, p. 163-98. bibliog. (Contributions in Afro-American and African Studies, no. 80).

The African musical presence in Panama is discussed in this essay, with emphasis on the congo tradition. Drums are compared to African drums as well as songs and singing styles. The congo is important, says the author (an ethnomusicologist) because it is the 'most sensational way of expressing non-verbal aspects of the aesthetic'.

696 The violin works of Roque Cordero.
John Edward Brawand. DMA thesis, University of Texas at Austin, 1985. 113p. bibliog. (Available from University Microfilms, Ann Arbor, Michigan).

Brawand's critical discussion of the music of Panamanian composer Roque Cordero (b. 1917) provides information about the composition of serious music in Panama and Central America generally.

Folklore

697 Algunas manifestaciones artísticas del folklore panameño. (Some artistic manifestations of Panamanian folklore.)
Dora Perez Zarate. Panama City: Published by the Author, 1964. 52p.
This illustrated essay is by a folklorist who writes much about Panamanian folk matters.

698 The Ancient Americas: art from sacred landscapes.
Edited by Richard F. Townsend. Chicago, Illinois: Art Institute, 1992. 397p. bibliog.
The work was published in conjunction with the exhibition held at the Art Institute of Chicago, from 10 October 1992 to 3 January 1993.

699 Art, death, and social order: the mortuary arts of pre-Conquest Central Panama.
Peter S. Briggs. Oxford: B.A.R., 1989. 263p. biblog. (BAR International Series, 550).
Briggs discusses the death customs of the Tonosi Region based on the art uncovered at the Conte site.

700 Breviario de folklore; elementos teóricos y observaciones de orden práctico para la orientación de los estudios del folklore.
(Compendium of folklore; theoretical elements and practical observations for the orientation of students of folklore.)
Manuel F. Zarate. Panama City: Ediciones del Ministerio de Educación, Departamento de Bellas Artes y Publicaciones, 1958. 130p.
A manual for students of folklore reflecting the anthropology theories of the time (Kluckhohn, Weber, Boas, Cassier), and applying their theories to specific Panamanian folklore. The introduction by Reina Torres de Iannello, at that time Professor of Anthropology and the University of Panama, notes especially the extensive fieldwork of the author. The text covers briefly such topics as the role of folklore in contemporary culture and the importance of teaching folklore in the schools as a way to integrate traditional and modern values.

701 Creations of the rainbow serpent: polychrome ceramic designs from ancient Panama.
Mary W. Helms. Albuquerque, New Mexico: University of New Mexico Press, 1995. 136p. bibliog.
An explanation of the semiotic characteristics of a collection of ceramics dated about AD 500-1100 by peoples of the Coclé culture. The significance of the colours used, the symbols of the serpents, birds, mammals, body parts and processes, and the tree of life

are illustrated and discussed. A plethora of illustrations, some in colour, accompany the discussion.

702 Cuentos folklóricos de Panamá, recogidos directamente del verbo popular. (Folk tales collected directly from popular language.)
Edited by Mario Riera. Panama City: Departamento de Bellas Artes y Publicaciones del Ministerio de Educación, 1956. 197p.

This collection of folk tales was made by a leading Panamanian playwright, Mario Riera (1920-69).

703 Cuna Indian art; the culture and craft of Panama's San Blas islanders.
Clyde E. Keeler. New York: Exposition Press, 1969. 192p.

An overview of Kuna Indian arts including body and face painting, medicinal aids, the *mola*, cane carving, weaving, beadwork, jewellery and toys. Explanatory drawings accompany some of the text and provide the kind of detail useful for careful study. Emphasis is on the role of the artefacts in the Kuna culture.

704 A fabric collage: contemporary hangings, American quilts, San Blas appliqués.
American Craftsmen's Council. New York: Museum of Contemporary Crafts, 1965. 1 vol.

This is the catalogue of a comparative exhibition of contemporary hangings, quilts and San Blas appliqués. The photographs are in black and white.

705 El folklore panameño en función de las teorías freudianas.
(Panamanian folklore in relation to Freudian theory.)
Luisita Aguilera P. Santiago, Chile: Imprenta 'Los Andes', 1963. 117p.

This extended essay examines selected folklore in terms of Freudian psychology.

706 Icons of power: feline symbolism in the Americas.
Edited by Nicholas J. Saunders. London; New York: Routledge, 1998. 298p.

A collection of papers discussing representation in art of the cat family. The first two chapters discuss the architecture of symbolism of the feline image. Richard Cooks, of the Smithsonian Institution Field Research Station in Panama describes (on pages 77-121) pre-Columbian symbols of jaguar and puma in Panama, and argues that in some instances artists were not working symbolically, but communicating information about the cat through the image they created. He calls for more intensive co-operation with archaeozoologists.

707 **Mitología de los bocatas de Chiriquí.** (Mythology of the *bocatas* of Chriqui.)
Enrique Margery Peña.   Quito, Ecuador: Ediciones Abya-Yala, 1994. 180p. bibliog.

The discussion of the mythology of the people of Boca del Toro (the *bocatas*) is bolstered by the relevant texts in Guaymí and Spanish, and there is an extensive bibliography.

708 *Mola*: **Cuna life stories and art.**
Maricel E. Presilla.   New York: Henry Holt, 1996. 1 vol.

This heavily illustrated volume explains *molas* and how they fit into the clothing styles of Cuna women, suitable for all ages.

709 **The *mola* design book.**
Caren Caraway.   Owings Mills, Maryland: Stemmer House, 1986. 49p. (The International Design Library).

This short work consists chiefly of illustrations and is intended to suggest a kind of needlework that requires craft skills but also allows for unlimited flights of fancy.

710 *Mola* **designs: 45 authentic Indian designs from Panama.**
Frederick W. Shaffer.   New York: Dover Publications, 1985. 48p. (Dover Pictorial Archive Series. Dover Design Library).

Mola designs of the Kuna Indians are known throughout the art world for the quality of their design, their colours and their references to significant events in the designers' world. This collection of 45 black-and-white designs with colour suggestions is designed for makers of reverse appliqué and may be copied for private use. The inside covers show representative *molas* in full colour and a colour guide is included in the short but useful introduction. This is a revised edition of: *Mola design coloring book*, 1982.

711 **Nanas, rimas y juegos infantiles que se practican en Panamá.**
(Lullabies, rhymes and children's games as used in Panama.)
Dora P. de Zárate (Eda Nela), original musical transcriptions of popular songs by Gonzalo Brenes C.   Panama City: Manfer, 1997. 202p.

Children's games and rhymes are discussed by the folklorist Dora Zárate, with music transcribed by Gonzalo Brenes C. This work was originally published in 1958.

712 **La pollera panameña, ensayo monográfico.** (The Panamanian *pollera*, a monographic essay.)
Dora Perez de Zarate, Manuel F. Zarate.   Panama City: University of Panama, 1966. 66p. bibliog.

The *pollera*, a national woman's festive costume, has a long and interesting history, some of which is provided in this monograph by two eminent folklorists. Each region has variations on the style. The dress is long and full skirted with a deep ruffle on the bodice that covers the arms. It can be coloured or white; this publication shows many of the embroidery patterns that are used with white *polleras*.

713 **Profesora Zárate: su vida y su obra.** (Professor Zárate, her life and works.)
Maritza Lowinger. Panama City: ECU Ediciones, 1990. 105p. bibliog.

A biography of Dora Perez de Zárate, a prominent folklorist of Panama, several of whose works are included in this bibliography. A list of her publications is to be found on pages 102-03.

714 **La saga panameña: un tema inquietante.** (The Panamanian saga: a disturbing theme.)
Dora Perez de Zarate. Panama City: Editorial Mariano Arosemena, 1986. 232p. bibliog. (Colección Dabaibe).

Zarate, who has had a long career in literature and folklore, examines the treatment of supernatural creatures and witches and other humans partaking of supernatural powers, usually evil, to be found in Panamanian folklore. Zarate analyses material along the literary-folklore continuum with the elaborated tale, the 'cuento', at one end of the spectrum and direct myth at the other. The method of this study includes long transcriptions of material as told by informants from both city and country and of all ages, from young adult to those of advanced years.

715 **Textiles of the Kuna Indians of Panama.**
Herta Puls. Princes Risborough, England: Shire, 1988. 72p. bibliog. (Shire Ethnography, 6).

The *mola*, a blouse worn by Cuna woman has a specially designed front panel, examples of which can be found in many museums of the world. *Molas* are typically intricate designs, usually invented by the women who work them, and often referencing an unusual event such as bringing in piped water or Panamanian Independence Day. Numerous illustrations accompany the text. One chapter is devoted to the working technique, but most of the short work discusses design. An introductory chapter provides essential information about the Cuna Indians.

716 **Tradiciones y cuentos panameños.** (Panamanian traditions and stories.)
Juana Raquel Oller de Mulford, illustrated by Enrique Mir Verdu. Panama City: Manfer, 1984. 258p.

This charming and well-designed collection of cultural materials has seen several reprintings since it first appeared in 1971. The book is arranged in five sections, dealing respectively with local customs, tales, sayings, legends and traditions. Both indigenous and Catholic materials infuse this popular culture.

Popular culture

717 La cocina al dia. (Everyday cooking.)
Maria Luisa Echeverria, Amparo Moncayo de Pazmino.
Panama City: Imprenta Mercedes, 1960. 178p.

This practical cookery manual provides typical menus using fresh locally obtainable ingredients. With increasing imports of foods from all over the world, Panamanian cuisine has changed extensively in urban areas. This domestic science item is useful in getting a sense of what was local nutritional practice before the globalization of food markets.

718 Los juegos regionales más antiguos. (The oldest regional games.)
Enrique Montesinos, edited by Carolos Uriarte González.   Ponce,
Puerto Rico: Juegos Deportivos Centroamericanos y del Caribe,
1993. 422p. bibliog.

The work comprises a history of sports and games in Central America and the Caribbean.

719 Paint your wagon.
Karen Asis.   *Travel-Holiday*, vol. 165 (February 1986), p. 92.

This article describes the colourful murals on the public buses in Panama.

720 Panama Al Brown: 1902-1951.
Eduardo Arroyo.   Paris: Bernard Grasset, 1998. 301p.

Arroyo provides a biography of a Panamanian sports figure, the boxer Al Brown, 1902-51.

721 Panama's moving murals.
Mary Louise Wilkinson.   *Americas* (English Edition), vol. 39
(March-April 1987), p. 44-47.

As the subtitle has it, 'public buses are automotive piñatas full of surprizes, adorned inside and out with pop art and vibrating with latest rhythms'. Not only is the art of a typical bus described, but also the pleasurable social interaction that relaxes workers on their way to and from work. The illustrations are attractive.

722 Recapturing our heritage: torch bearers to glory, 1925-1955.
Brooklyn, NewYork: Panamanian-West Indian Heritage
Association, 1987. 1 vol.

This volume contains an informal history of black Panamanian athletes.

723 To Culebra: a play in two acts.
Jonathan Bolt.   Salt Lake City, Utah: Peregrine Smith Books, 1989.
81p. (Peregrine Plays).

This short play, suitable for amateur production, develops the grandiloquent character of the older de Lesseps. Taking on the building of the Panama Canal in his seventies, after the international success of the sea-level Suez Canal, de Lesseps comes up against the opposition of his son, daughter-in-law and financiers, as he dismisses out of hand the difficulties posed by this new project. The play dramatically highlights the problems encountered by the first attempt to build a canal across the Isthmus of Panama, centring on the political decisions that override scientific data.

Libraries, Museums, Art Galleries and Archives

724 Archival heritage meets modern records in Panama.
Philip C. Brooks. Chicago, Illinois: Society of American
Archivists, 1960-69, p. 151-59.
Brooks has produced notes about the Panama archives that originally appeared in several
issues of *The American Archivist* during the decade of the 1960s.

**725 Bibliotecas del Caribe; notas de viaje acerca de las bibliotecas
de: República dominicana; Puerto Rico; Curaçao; La Guaira y
Caracas (Venezuela); Barranquilla, (Colombia); Panama
(Panama); San José (Costa Rica); Guatemala (Guatemala); y
San Salvador (El Salvador).** (Caribbean Libraries; travel notes
about the libraries of the Dominican Republic, Puerto Rico, Curaçao,
Venezuela, Columbia, Panama, Costa Rica, Guatemala and San
Salvador.)
Fermin Peraza Sarausa. Havana, Cuba: Anuario bibliográfico
cubano, 1943. 40p.
This interesting historical note of library services in the Caribbean area includes
illustrations.

726 Documentación histórica y nacionalidad. (Historic documents and
nationhood.)
Patricia Pizzurno Gelós. Panama City: Editorial Portobelo, 1996.
26p. (Colección Pequeño formato, 4. Historia-archivología).
This is a history and description of the National Archive of Panama and its holdings.

727   El educador santeño y el Museo Belisario Porras. (The educator
of Los Santos province and the Belisario Porras Museum.)
Oscar A. Velarde B.   Panama City: Instituto Nacional de Cultura,
Dirección Nacional del Patrimonio Histórico, 1990. 14p.
The pamphlet delineates the origin of the museum, with biographical information about
Belisario Porras.

728   Guía de museos de Panamá. (Guide to the museums of Panama.)
Jorge E. Horna.   Panama City: Editorial Mariano Arosemena, 1990.
37p.
Horna's up-to-date guide to the museums is mostly concerned with those in Panama City.

**729   Guide to libraries and archives in Central America and the West
Indies, Panama, Bermuda, and British Guiana, supplemented
with information on private libraries, bookbinding, bookselling
and printing.**
Arthur E. Gropp.   New Orleans: Middle American Research
Institute, Tulane University of Louisiana, 1941. 721p. (Middle
American Research Series. Publication 10).
Of historical value, this work has now been updated by *A bibliography of Latin American
and Caribbean bibliographies, 1985-1989: social sciences and humanities* (see item no.
797).

730   Latin American library resources in London: a guide.
London: Latin American Subject Sub-Committee, Library Resources
Co-ordinating Committee, Institute of Latin American Studies, 1991.
5th ed. 56p.
The guide includes both resources and a directory of Latin Americanists.

**731   Libraries and information in Latin America: a survey based on
published sources.**
Julie Carpenter.   London: British Library Research and
Development Department, 1994. 33p. (British Library R & D report,
6176).
This survey is useful for regional information.

732   El libro en hispanoamérica: origen y desarrollo. (The book in
Latin America: beginnings and development.)
José Luis Martinez.   Madrid: Fundación German Sanchez Ruiperez;
Ediciones Piramide, 1986. 2nd ed. 99p. (Biblioteca del libro. Serie
'Minor').
This is a short, useful history of books and libraries in Latin America with special
reference to the intellectual life.

733 **Museos de Panama.** (Museums of Panama.)
Jorge E. Horna. Panama City: Instituto Nacional de Cultura de
Panamá, Dirección Nacional del Patrimonio Histórico, 1980. 125p.
bibliog.

A more detailed monograph than Horna's later work, *Guía de museos de Panamá* of 1990
(see item no. 728).

734 **Museums of the world. 1997.**
Edited by Bettina Bartz, Bettina Schmidt. Munich, Germany: Saur,
1997. 6th ed. 673p. (Handbook of International Documentation and
Information. Vol. 16, Museums of the World).

In the comprehensive listing of Panama's museums, many small and highly specialized
sites are listed.

735 **Panama.**
In: *The World of Learning.* London: Europa, 1949- . annual. 2 vols.

Comprises a directory of learned societies, libraries, museums, universities and institutes
of higher education.

736 **Situación actual de la información y la documentación educativa
en Panamá.** (Current situation in information and educational
documentation in Panama.)
Elizabeth E. Jaén C. Panama City: Ministerio de Educación;
Madrid: OEI, 1988. 51p. bibliog. (Colección Información,
Documentación, Informática, 14).

Jaén reports on the information services, documentation, and libraries in Panama.

Mass Media

Book trade

737 Agenda de la Comunicación, Panamá. (Communications Notebook, Panama.)
Panama City: Universidad de Panama, Facultad de Comunicación Social, 1991- . annual.

This is a directory of useful organizations, names, newspapers, television, radio and public relations agencies.

738 Jungle stories: North American representations of tropical Panama.
Stephen Frenkel. *The Geographical Review*, vol. 86, no. 3 (July 1996), p. 317-34.

A substantial study of how American public opinion about the American tropics was formed by what was published, whether in non-fiction or fiction. The author, professor of geography at the University of Seattle, Washington, argues that the collective imagination was deliberately formed by government and business to foster acceptance of imperialistic policies. Representative texts from the first half of the twentieth century are examined for the material in them that formulated the images of tropical Panama and the US role.

739   Notas bibliográficas referentes a las primeras producciones de la
      imprenta en algunas ciudades de la América española (Ambata,
      Angostura, Curazao, Guayaquil, Maracaibo, Nueva Orleans,
      Nueva Valencia, Panamá, Popayan, Puerto España, Puerto Rico,
      Queretaro, Santa Marta, Santiago de Cuba, Santo Domingo,
      Tunja y ostros lugares) (1754-1823). (Bibliographical notes
      referring to the first publishing activities of printers in several cities
      of Spanish America [Ambata, Angostura, Curaçao, Guayaquil,
      Maracaibo, New Orleans, New Valencia, Panama, Popayan, Port of
      Spain, Puerto Rico, Queretaro, Santa Marta, Santiago de Cuba,
      Santo Domingo, Tunja and other places] [1754-1823].)
      José Toribio Medina.   Santiago, Chile: Imprenta elzeviriana, 1904.
      Amsterdam: N. Israel, 1964. 116p. facsimiles. (Reprint series of José
      Toribio Medina's bibliographical works, XVI).
      This history of Latin American printing from 1754 to 1823 includes material on printing
      activities in Panama City. Medina lived between 1852 and 1930.

740   Un poco de historia sindical tipográfica panameña. (A little
      history of the Panamanian typographical union.)
      Allan K. Hiram.   Panama City: Published by the Author, 1975. 67p.
      A history of the technical side of printing which gives some sense of governmental
      involvement.

741   A survey of Hispanic health promotion projects using mass
      media: United States, Mexico and Central America.
      Sarah Mason Harding.   Austin, Texas: Center for Research on
      Communication Technology and Society, College of
      Communication, University of Texas at Austin, 1993. 272p.
      In this comparison of methods of presenting information and modes of persuasion in these
      cultures, data for reach, audience, and frequency are given.

742   Teoría y realidad de la comunicación: una visión a la
      comunicación social en Panamá. (Theory and reality of
      communication: a vision of social communication in Panama.)
      Rafael Bolivar Ayala.   Panama City: Impresora de la Nación/INAC,
      1984. 236p. bibliog.
      The author presents a look at mass media in Panama up to and including the 1980s from
      the standpoint of a sociologist.

Newspapers and magazines

743 Crítica libre. (Free Critic.)
Panama City, 1958- . daily.
A Spanish-language newspaper with a readership of 23,000.

744 La Estrella de Panamá. (The Panama Star.)
Panama City, 1853- . daily.
The oldest newspaper in Panama, a daily and Sunday journal with a circulation of 17,000.
For many years it was published in both English and Spanish.

745 El Expresso. (The Express.)
Panama City, 1992- . daily.
A Chinese-language newspaper with a circulation of some 1500.

746 Hoy. (Today.)
Panama City, 1993- . daily.
A Spanish-language daily with a circulation of 12,000.

747 El Panamá América. (Panama America.)
Panama City, 1925- . daily.
A Spanish-language daily with a circulation of 13,000.

748 La Prensa. (The Press.)
Panama City, 1980- . daily.
An independent Spanish-language daily with a circulation of 45,000.

749 *La Prensa* pushes ethics in Panama.
I. Roberto Eisenmann Jr. *Nieman Reports*, vol. 48, no. 1 (Spring
1994), p. 69-70.
Roberto Eisenmann, director of *La Prensa,* a politically independent Panamanian
newspaper, reports that the paper has enjoyed a broad readership and high reputation. He
says that a known code of ethics, broad ownership and good management account for its
success.

**750 Propuesta para la historia de una prensa alternativa en Panamá:
el caso de la revista *Diálogo social*, 1993.** (Proposal for a history of
an alternative press in Panama: the case of the review *Diálogo
social*, 1993.)
James Aparacio. Panama City: Editorial Universitaria, 1997. 150p.
bibliog.
Aparacio provides a history and description of the underground press in Panama.

751 **El Siglo.** (The Century.)
     Panama City, 1985- . daily.
A Spanish-language daily with a circulation of 42,000.

Censorship

752 **Elusive concept.**
     Larry Luxner. *Editor & Publisher*, vol. 125, no. 52 (26 December
     1992), p. 11-12.
In the aftermath of the end of the Noriega control of Panama, there has been much interest
in censorship in Panama, the focus being on the expectation of less control. The article
reports that Roberto Eisenmann Jr, president and director of *La Prensa*, sees that
government control of the press still exists in Panama, and laws have not yet been
modified. Censorship in general has, however, been less stringent.

753 **The media and a changing security environment: from the
     Persian Gulf to Gramm-Rudman-Gorbachev: readings.**
     Newport, Rhode Island: Naval War College, 1990. 1 vol. maps.
These readings include 'A war of words: in Panama, it was the press vs. the military once
again' by P. J. Budahn.

754 **The media and the military: from the Crimea to Desert Strike.**
     Peter R. Young, Peter Jesser. New York: St. Martin's Press, 1997.
     391p.
This study of how media coverage can be managed by armies in the field and in its
capitals takes for its examples the Gulf War, Northern Ireland, the Falklands and Panama.
The contextualizing text discusses the obligations placed on citizens because of the
changed nature of war.

755 **Newsmen & national defense: is conflict inevitable?**
     Lloyd J. Matthews, introduction by Peter Braestrup.   Washington,
     DC: Brassey's (US), 1991. 146p. (AUSA Institute of Land Warfare
     Book).
The general thrust of this work published under the auspices of the US Army War College
Foundation is an attempt to resolve the conflict of interests between the military and the
press. 'The Panama Press Pool Deployment: A Critique' by Fred S. Hoffman (p. 91-109)
includes a response by the Secretary of Defense. The press in general were critical of
official American policy in giving them timely access.

756 Panama.
IPI Report, vol. 41, no. 12 (December 1992), p. 29.
The World Press Freedom Review found, at the time of reporting, that although repressive censorship laws enacted under the presidency of General Noriega were still in force, they were not, in fact, being enforced. Nevertheless, the group found that the presence of the law had a deleterious effect on the quality of journalism in Panama.

757 Panama and the press.
Michael D. Mosettig. *SAIS Review*, vol. 10, no. 2 (Summer-Fall 1990), p. 179-89.
This even-handed discussion of conflict between military and press includes special reference to the US invasion of Panama.

758 Soldiering toward the Information Superhighway: the comparison of old and new communication media use during military operations in the Post-Cold War Era (Internet).
Morten Gaston Ender. PhD thesis, University of Maryland, College Park, 1996. 333p. (Available from University Microfilms, Ann Arbor, Michigan, order no. AAT 9707594).
Communication activities in several military operations are analysed, including Operation Just Cause in Panama.

759 Some lessons from Panama: a strong Latin condemnation.
Carlos Fuentes. *World Press Review*, vol. 37, no. 2 (February 1990), whole issue.
Fuentes' full-spectrum look at early press reaction to the Panama invasion excerpts material from key national newspapers around the world.

Traditional language broadcasting and publishing

760 Media, politics, and artful speech: Kuna radio programs.
Marta Lucia De Gerdes. *Anthropological Linguistics*, vol. 40, no. 4 (Winter 1998), p. 596-616.
The Kuna of San Blas have become dispersed over the past three decades, many to Panama City. One way of keeping in touch has been Kuna-language radio broadcasts aired on local stations, since the Kuna do not have a broadcast facility of their own. The author has produced the first study of the style and content of these broadcasts. Transcripts of a typical broadcast, in Kuna and Spanish, are translated into English and discussed.

761 Periódicos chiricanos de la primera decada del siglo veinte.
(Periodicals of Chiriquí of the first decade of the twentieth century.)
Miguel Espino. Panama City: Ediciones CICS, 1986. 33p. bibliog.
Espino identifies and discusses the Panamanian periodicals published in the Chiriquí province early in the 20th century.

Professional Periodicals

762 Cuadernos de Antropología. (Anthropology Notes.)
Centro de Investigaciones Antropológicas. Panama City:
Universidad de Panamá, 1991- .

These are studies of peoples indigenous to Panama, with details not always to be found in the equivalent international publications. The authors of these studies are usually also to be found in the international journals.

**763 Hombre y Cultura: Revista del Centro de Investigaciones
Antropológicas de la Universidad Nacional.** (Man and Culture,
Review of the Center of Anthropological Research of the National
University.)
Panama City: El Centro, 1962-77; June 1991- . semi-annual.

Suspended from 1977 to 1991, the publication is now providing a means of reporting anthropological research.

**764 Imagen: Revista de Extensión Cultural de la Universidad de
Panamá.** (Image: Review of Cultural Extension of the University of
Panama.)
Panama City: La Universidad, 1982- . irregular.

This general-interest, non-political magazine has an educated readership in mind. Topics vary throughout the spectrum of social sciences and humanities, with popular science also represented. Each issue has a sampling of topics covered.

765 Journal of Afro-Latin American Studies and Literatures.
Washington, DC: Howard University, 1993- . annual.

Sponsored by Howard University in Washington, DC, this refereed journal has as its objective to promote 'the scientific investigation of issues faced by African-Latin

Americans from colonial times to the present'. Articles on African-Latin American contributions to life, culture, literature and arts of the Americas are also published.

766   Littera. (Litter.)
Panama City: Universidad de Panamá, 1995- .
A literary magazine sponsored by the University of Panama.

767   Maga.
Panama City: Editorial Signos, S.A., 1984- .
A quarterly literary publication of the University of Panama.

768   O.P.V.: Otros Puntos de Vista. (Other Points of View.)
Panama City: Instituto Panameño de Estudios Comunitarios, 1994- .
Essays of current issues for Panama in the realms of politics and society.

769   Panama Chronicle = Crónica de Panamá.
Brooklyn, New York: PBT Associates, 1982- . semi-annual.
This chronology and reports on the political situation in Panama is aimed at Panamanians resident in the United States.

770   Panama Update.
Santa Cruz, California: The Task Force, 1992- .
A political quarterly produced by the Fellowship of Reconciliation Task Force on Latin America and the Caribbean.

771   Patrimonio Histórico. Segunda Epoca. (Historic Heritage. Second Series.)
Panama City: INAC, 1992. 1 vol. only.
This short-lived publication continued a publication of the same name that was published by the Historic Heritage Office of the National Institute of Culture between 1971 and 1982 as a vehicle for articles about sites of historical interest and related matters.

772   Revista Cultural *Lotería*. (Cultural Review *Lotería*.)
Panama City: Lotería Nacional de Beneficencia, 1990- . bi-monthly.
Published bi-monthly and continues *Lotería*.

773   Revista de Investigaciones. (Research Journal.)
Universidad de Panamá, Facultad de Administración Pública,
Unidad de Investigaciones del Departamento de Administración
Pública.   Panama City: La Unidad, 1982- .
The journal of the department of public administration of the University of Panama reports results of research.

774 Serie Poesía Panameña Actual. (Modern Panamanian Poetry Series.)
Panama City: Ediciones INAC, 1992- .
Contemporary Panamanian poetry published under the auspices of the Instituto Nacional de Cultura (Panama).

775 Tareas. (Tasks.)
Panama City: Centro de Estudios Latinoamericanos 'Justo Arosemena', 1960- .
Publishes articles in the general area of Panamanian life with emphasis on the social, political, regional and economic issues of interest to an educated readership.

776 Temas de Sociologia: Revista del Colegio Nacional de Sociologos. (Sociological Topics: Review of the National College of Sociologists.)
Panama City: Colegio Nacional de Sociologos; Editorial Portobelo, 1997- .
The combination of researched articles and formal and informal essays in a broad range of social science subject areas is of particular interest to Panamanian readers. The authors are mostly from the University of Panama.

777 Umbral.
Panama City: Asociación Umbral Editores, 1993- .
A little magazine that publishes poetry and literary essays.

Encyclopaedias, Directories and Reference Works

Encyclopaedias and handbooks

778 Encyclopedia of Latin America: dealing with the life, achievement, and national development of the countries of South and Central America, Mexico and Panama, the West Indies, and giving special information on commerce, industry, banking, finance, railways, shipping, transportation, communications, trade, tariff, customs, and all matters of commercial importance.
Edited by Marrion Wilcox, George Edwin Rines.   New York: Encyclopedia Americana, 1917. 887p.

The tone and content of old reference tools can sometimes point today's researcher to an area, the exploring of which will shed new light on the period. This tool belongs in that class.

779 Encyclopedia of the Third World.
New York: Facts on File, 1992. 4th ed. 3 vols. maps.

Volume 3 contains information on Panama based on information gathered for other Facts on File news publications.

780 Central America and the Caribbean.
New York: Marshall Cavendish, 1994. 1994 reference ed., p. 438-576. maps. (Encyclopedia of World Geography, 4).

This reference work is suitable for younger researchers.

781 Manual de organización del gobierno de Panamá. (Organization manual of the government of Panama.)
Panama. Dirección de Planificación y Desarrollo Institucional.
Panama City: El Ministerio, 1992. 10th ed. 606p.

A listing and description of the administrative agencies, executive departments, judicial system and courts with directory information for each part of the government.

782 Manual del inversionista extranjero en Panamá: la Zona Libre de Colón, 'Emporio Comercial del Occidente'. (Foreign investment manual, Panamanian Free Zone of Colón, 'Commercial emporium of the West'.)
Panama City: Revista Puntos Suspensivos, 1992. 67p.

Sponsored by the Chamber of Commerce of Panama's Association of Colón Free Zone users, this handbook has necessary information for foreign investors.

783 Mexico & Central American Handbook.
Bath, England: Trade & Travel Publications; New York: Prentice Hall Press, 1990- . annual.

A yearbook that provides key information and directories. It continues the Mexico and Central America sections of the *South American handbook*.

784 Panama now: portrait of the nation: reference book of the republic = Panama hoy: retrato de la nación: obra de referencia de la república.
Edited by Michele Labrut. El Dorado, Panama: Focus, 1997. 3rd ed. 232p. maps.

An introduction to the Republic of Panama that provides an overall picture of the country in its history, economy, education and other social activities and government. It is particularly useful for a summary of the return of the land occupied by US military bases – a matter of some 3,000 buildings and 65,000 acres – and the government's plans for them. Among its business information is introductory and descriptive information about the Colón Free Zone, ship registry, tourism and other commercial opportunities available, often supplied by the principals. Maps and photographs supply orientation and flavour, and statistical tables provide hard data.

785 **Regents of nations: systematic chronology of states and their political representatives in past and present: a biographical reference book = Regenten der Nationen: systematische Chronologie der Staaten und ihrer politischen Repräsentanten in Vergangenheit und Gegenwart: ein biographisches Nachschlagewerk.**
Peter Truhart.   Munich, Germany; New York: Saur, 1984-88.
3 vols. in 4.

Volume 1 contains the names and brief data of heads of state for Panama up to 1884, with addenda in the final volume. Other volumes included data from the colonial period, and the chronology of key people in the Canal Zone. It is written in both English and German.

786 **U.S.-Latin American policymaking: a reference handbook.**
Westport, Connecticut:Greenwood Press, 1995. 555p. bibliog.

This volume includes materials of use to the Panama researcher, such as several articles on Central American associations, policy-making, and particularly Michael J. Kryzanek's 'Intervention and interventionism', and 'Promoting democracy' by Elizabeth Cohn and Michael J. Nojeim.

Dictionaries

787 **Conceptos de planificación urbana y regional.** (Urban and regional planning concepts.)
Magela Cabrera Arias.   Panama City: Imprenta Universitaria, 1993.
152p. bibliog.

The concepts involved in city and regional planning and their definitions are presented in the form of a dictionary.

788 **Diccionario de la lengua Cuna.** (Dictionary of the Cuna language.)
José Luis de Pando Villarroya.   Toledo, Spain: Pando Ediciones, 1996. 2nd ed. 105p. bibliog. (Colección Diccionarios de Lenguas).

This Cuna-Spanish dictionary was published in Spain.

789 **Diccionario de siglas.** (Dictionary of acronyms.)
Everardo Ernesto Tomlinson Hernández.   Panama City:
E. E. Tomlinson H., 1984. 43p.

The dictionary of acronyms in use in Panama is indispensable in modern communication.

790 **Isthmian ethnobotanical dictionary.**
James A. Duke.   Jodhpur, India: Scientific Publishers, 1986. 3rd ed.
205p. (*Journal of Economic and Taxonomic Botany*. Additional
Series, 3).
This constitutes a reference tool for plant names both scientific and popular.

791 **Lengua de señas panameñas.** (Panamanian sign language.)
Panama City: Asociacicón Nacional de Sordos de Panamá, 1996.
1 vol.
This dictionary of sign language in use in Panama chiefly comprises illustrations of the
signage system used in communication with the deaf.

Directories and biographical directories

792 **Diccionario biográfico ilustrado de Panamá.** (Biographical
dictionary of Panama.)
Jorge Conte Porras.   Panama City: Editorial Diego de Almagro,
1986. 2nd ed. 158p.
The revised edition of *Diccionario biográfico de Panamá* of 1975 includes portraits.

793 **Naturalistas de Istmo de Panamá: un siglo de historia natural
sobre el puente biológico de las Américas.** (Naturalists of the
Isthmus of Panama: a century of natural history about the biological
bridge of the Americas.)
Stanley Heckadon-Moreno.   Balboa, Panama: Instituto Smithsonian
de Investigaciones Tropicales; Fundación Santillana para
Iberoamérica, 1998. 215p. maps. bibliog.
These are biographies of naturalists who have worked in Panama over the years, with
special emphasis on those who are or were allied to the Smithsonian Tropical Research
Institute.

794 **Panama services guide.**
Edgar H. Tejada K.   Panama City: E. H. Tejada and International
Technical Publications, Inc., 1994. 2nd ed. 36p.
This handbook is meant for business entities engaged in shipping, with directories of
related services.

Bibliographies

795 Annotated bibliography of library resources on Central America.
St. Paul, Minnesota: Central America Resource Center, 1990. 251p.
This bibliography of research resources concerns Central America, with special emphasis on US library holdings.

796 The best of the Latino heritage: a guide to the best juvenile books about Latino peoples and cultures.
Isabel Schon.   Metuchen, New Jersey: Scarecrow Press, 1996. 304p.
This is an updated and augmented version of Isabel Schon's *Books in Spanish for children* (see item no. 798).

797 A bibliography of Latin American and Caribbean bibliographies, 1985-1989: social sciences and humanities.
Compiled by Lionel V. Loroña.   Metuchen, New Jersey: Scarecrow Press, 1993. 314p.
The work serves as a 'supplement no. 5 to Arthur E. Gropp's *A Bibliography of Latin American bibliographies*'. Other supplements are published annually, with cumulations, under the auspices of SALALM (Seminar on the Acquisition of Latin American Library Materials).

798 **Books in Spanish for children and young adults: an annotated guide. Series VI = Libros infantiles y juveniles en español: una guía anotada. Serie no. VI.**
Isabel Schon. Metuchen, New Jersey: Scarecrow Press, 1993. 291p.

Books published since 1989 are arranged by country of publication, then grouped by subject. Short annotations suggest grade level and overall quality. An appendix supplies dealer and distributor information.

799 **Compilation of scientific publications, comarca de San Blas, Republic of Panama: Smithsonian Tropical Research Institute, 1972-1986.**
San Blas, Panama: Smithsonian Tropical Research Institute, 1987. 2 vols.

This English and Spanish bibliography covers the ressearch done at the Smithsonain Tropical Research Institute on the ecology of the San Blas area (*comarca*).

800 **An expanded view: panoramic photographs at the National Archives.**
Richard E. Schneider. *Prologue*, vol. 29, no. 3 (1997), p. 244-54.

Among the panoramic photographs at the National Archives, Washington, DC, are historic still photographs of the Panama Canal. Although mined thoroughly by previous researchers, these archival materials may still yield research gold.

801 **A guide to Central American collections in the United States.**
Thomas M. Leonard. Westport, Connecticut: Greenwood Press, 1994. 186p. (Reference Guides to Archival and Manuscript Sources in World History, no. 3).

This guide to US collections of manuscripts, archival resources and directories is of use to researchers.

802 **A guide to crises in Panama and the Dominican Republic: national security files and NSC histories.**
Edited by Paul Kesaris, Robert Lester. Frederick, Maryland: University Publications of America, 1982. 21p.

An index to 6 microfilm reels of relevant presidential documents.

803 **A guide to the microfilm edition of confidential U.S. State Department central files...Panama, 1930- .**
Edited by Blair Hydrick. Bethesda, Maryland: University Publications of America, 1990- . var. pag.

Several series of these guides exist as indexes to the confidential documents relating to Panama as they are declassified and made public. They are useful for researchers.

804 **Historical sketches of Guam, the Virgin Islands and the Panama Canal Zone; appendix to *Bibliographical survey of social, economic, governmental, political, racial and educational factors in the American possessions*. Sponsored by City College of the City University of New York. An unpublished report of project 65-97-239 sub 3, Works Progress administration.**
United States. Work Projects Administration (New York).
New York: WPA, 1935. 45p.

A rare set of bibliographical materials from the Depression Era in the United States that may be fruitful for historical researchers. One copy is available at the New York Public Library Center for Humanities and another at City College of the City University of New York.

805 **Latin America.**
Compiled by Harold W. Turner.   Boston, Massachusetts: G. K. Hall, 1991. 233p. (Bibliography of New Religious Movements in Primal Societies, vol. 5).

This bibliography covers materials published about the religious cults and sects of Central and South America.

806 **Latin American serial publications available by exchange: Mexico, Central America and Panama.**
Edited by Shelley Miller.   Albuquerque, New Mexico: SALALM Secretariat, General Library, University of New Mexico, 1991. 86p. (Bibliography and Reference Series [Seminar on the Acquisition of Latin American Library Materials], 29).

This bibliography is limited to listing publications available for exchange between libraries and complements those serial publications offered for sale. Panama material is listed on pages 83-85. In general the publications are collections of statistical data.

807 **Latin American women artists, Kahlo and look who else: a selective, annotated bibliography.**
Cecilia Puerto.   Westport, Connecticut: Greenwood Press, 1996. 237p. (Art Reference Collection, no. 21).

This bibliography of Latin American women artists working in various media includes film.

808 **Material documental producido por CODEHUCA: período, julio 1989-enero 1991.** (Documentary material produced by CODEHUCA from July 1989 to January 1991.)
Comisión para la Defensa de los Derechos Humanos en Centroamérica.   San José, Costa Rica: CODEHUCA, 1992. 43p.

This is a catalogue of materials in the collection of CODEHUCA's Centro de Documentación Marianella García Villas. The time frame is important for materials covering the US invasion of Panama.

809 Nueva bibliografía sobre los Ngóbe de Panamá. (New
bibliography on the Ngobe of Panama.)
Panama City: Acción Cultural Ngóbe (ACUN), Comarca Ngóbe-
Bugle, 1993. 74p. (Serie 'Aportes', Colección 'Mundo Ngóbe').

ACUN has produced a bibliography of materials about the Guaymí Indians of Panama.

810 The Panama Canal: the African American experience.
Patrice C. Brown. *Prologue*, vol. 29, no. 2 (1997), p. 122-26.

Official records relating to the Panama Canal are described as sources of information for
treatment of African American workers. The series described here include General
Correspondence, 1904-1914; General Records, 1914-1960; and Alpha Files, 1904-1960.

**811 The Third World. A bibliography: Guatemala, Honduras, Belize,
Costa Rica, Panama.**
Compiled by E. Willard Miller.   Monticello, Illinois: Vance
Bibliographies, 1990. 22p. (Public Administration Series –
Bibliography).

Complied by a producer of many information resources in the general area of government
and economics, this geographically selective bibliography offers useful resources for
administrative and government information on Panama and its neighbours.

812 The United States and Latin America: a select bibliography.
Lanham, Maryland: Scarecrow Press; Pasadena, California: Salem
Press, 1997. 277p. (Magill Bibliographies).

In the specialized area of bilateral political and economic relations, this resource is highly
convenient for access to material on key themes. The Panama Canal is treated in Chapter
4 as a key theme: 'The Panama Canal and early United States interventions' (p. 41-46),
and there are six items with long annotations under the rubric of an individual country
(p. 176-79). Panama figures in four video documentaries, in the highly selective array
with which this bibliography ends.

813 Writers of the Caribbean and Central America: a bibliography.
M. J. Fenwick.   New York: Garland, 1992. 2 vols. (Garland
Reference Library of the Humanities, vol. 1244).

Panamanian authors are treated in volume 2, on pages 1095-1141. Especially useful in
identifying Panamanian authors represented in anthologies, the brief information given
includes birth date, genres in which the writer works and anthologies that provide access
to his or her work. Some authors are under-represented and others, for instance Armando
Fortune, are omitted, but for some authors it is an invaluable finding resource.

Indexes

There follow three separate indexes: authors (personal or corporate); titles; and subjects. Title entries are italicized and refer either to the main titles, or to other works cited in the annotations. The numbers refer to bibliographical entry rather than page number. Individual index entries are arranged in alphabetical sequence.

Index of Authors

192

194

Index of Titles

Index of Subjects

215

221

223

224

Map of Panama

This map shows the more important features.

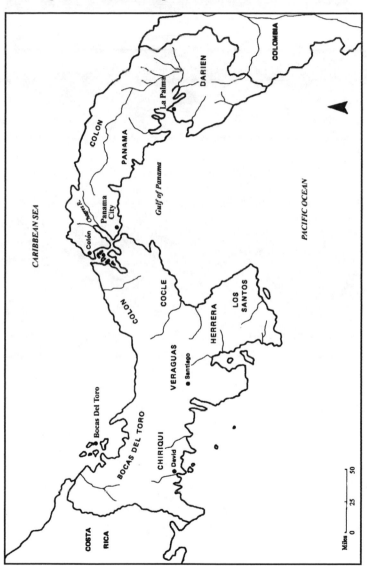

ALSO FROM CLIO PRESS

INTERNATIONAL ORGANIZATIONS SERIES

Each volume in the International Organizations Series is either devoted to one specific organization, or to a number of different organizations operating in a particular region, or engaged in a specific field of activity. The scope of the series is wide ranging and includes intergovernmental organizations, international non-governmental organizations, and national bodies dealing with international issues. The series is aimed mainly at the English-speaker and each volume provides a selective, annotated, critical bibliography of the organization, or organizations, concerned. The bibliographies cover books, articles, pamphlets, directories, databases and theses and, wherever possible, attention is focused on material about the organizations rather than on the organizations' own publications. Notwithstanding this, the most important official publications, and guides to those publications, will be included. The views expressed in individual volumes, however, are not necessarily those of the publishers.

VOLUMES IN THE SERIES

DATE DUE